C-4637

CAREER EXAMINATION SERIES

THIS IS YOUR **PASSBOOK**® FOR ...

BUILDING MAINTENANCE MECHANIC

NATIONAL LEARNING CORPORATION®
passbooks.com

COPYRIGHT NOTICE

212 Michael Drive, Syosset, NY 11791
(516) 921-8888 • www.passbooks.com
E-mail: info@passbooks.com

PUBLISHED IN THE UNITED STATES OF AMERICA

PASSBOOK® SERIES

THE *PASSBOOK® SERIES* has been created to prepare applicants and candidates for the ultimate academic battlefield – the examination room.

At some time in our lives, each and every one of us may be required to take an examination – for validation, matriculation, admission, qualification, registration, certification, or licensure.

Based on the assumption that every applicant or candidate has met the basic formal educational standards, has taken the required number of courses, and read the necessary texts, the *PASSBOOK® SERIES* furnishes the one special preparation which may assure passing with confidence, instead of failing with insecurity. Examination questions – together with answers – are furnished as the basic vehicle for study so that the mysteries of the examination and its compounding difficulties may be eliminated or diminished by a sure method.

This book is meant to help you pass your examination provided that you qualify and are serious in your objective.

The entire field is reviewed through the huge store of content information which is succinctly presented through a provocative and challenging approach – the question-and-answer method.

A climate of success is established by furnishing the correct answers at the end of each test.

You soon learn to recognize types of questions, forms of questions, and patterns of questioning. You may even begin to anticipate expected outcomes.

You perceive that many questions are repeated or adapted so that you can gain acute insights, which may enable you to score many sure points.

You learn how to confront new questions, or types of questions, and to attack them confidently and work out the correct answers.

You note objectives and emphases, and recognize pitfalls and dangers, so that you may make positive educational adjustments.

Moreover, you are kept fully informed in relation to new concepts, methods, practices, and directions in the field.

You discover that you arre actually taking the examination all the time: you are preparing for the examination by "taking" an examination, not by reading extraneous and/or supererogatory textbooks.

In short, this PASSBOOK®, used directedly, should be an important factor in helping you to pass your test.

BUILDING MAINTENANCE MECHANIC

DUTIES

This class involves a variety of building maintenance and repair tasks of a skilled nature. Although employees in this class, by reason of personal training and experience, generally devote most of their time to work of a single specialized field, they are required to work along various mechanical lines as the occasion demands. In this respect the class differs from such classes as Painter, Carpenter, Plumber, etc. which limit incumbents to a single trade. The duties of this class differ from Building Maintenance Worker by reason of the more skilled nature of the work involved. Incumbents perform their duties with some latitude for independent planning or laying out of the working details. In those cases where supervisory responsibilities are involved, the Building Maintenance Mechanic supervises a number of workers who perform maintenance and repair jobs of a semi-skilled nature. Does related work as required.

SUBJECTS OF EXAMINATION

The written test designed to evaluate knowledge, skills and/or abilities in the following areas:

1. **Building maintenance and repair** - These questions test for knowledge of the basic principles, practices and techniques essential to the proper maintenance and repair of various types of buildings, including such areas as building maintenance, preventive maintenance, and minor repair of building structures, electrical, and plumbing systems. This may include maintenance and repair of roofs, windows, walls, floors, millwork, insulation, masonry, pipes and valves, electrical wiring and switches, and painting. Questions may also include topics such as the proper tools and materials used in building maintenance and repair work as well as proper and safe practices and techniques when using these tools and materials.
2. **Building trades, including mechanical and electrical** - These questions test for knowledge of the principles and practices involved in overseeing physical plant facilities and may include such areas as maintenance and repair activities involving carpentry, electrical systems, plumbing and sanitary systems, heating and ventilating systems, painting, masonry work, roofing, and similar types of physical plant maintenance and upkeep.
3. **Tools and their uses** - These questions test for knowledge of the various types of tools used in building maintenance and repair work, including the proper use of these tools.
4. **Operation and maintenance of heating, ventilating and air conditioning systems** - These questions test for knowledge of basic principles, practices and techniques essential to the correct operation and maintenance of heating, ventilating and air conditioning systems, including such areas as air supply and exhaust systems, circulating fan capacities, building ventilation requirements, steam, hot water, and hot air heating systems; boiler operation; the refrigeration cycle, types and characteristics of refrigerants, troubleshooting air conditioning system problems, and proper maintenance of air conditioning systems.

HOW TO TAKE A TEST

I. YOU MUST PASS AN EXAMINATION

A. WHAT EVERY CANDIDATE SHOULD KNOW

Examination applicants often ask us for help in preparing for the written test. What can I study in advance? What kinds of questions will be asked? How will the test be given? How will the papers be graded?

As an applicant for a civil service examination, you may be wondering about some of these things. Our purpose here is to suggest effective methods of advance study and to describe civil service examinations.

Your chances for success on this examination can be increased if you know how to prepare. Those "pre-examination jitters" can be reduced if you know what to expect. You can even experience an adventure in good citizenship if you know why civil service exams are given.

B. WHY ARE CIVIL SERVICE EXAMINATIONS GIVEN?

Civil service examinations are important to you in two ways. As a citizen, you want public jobs filled by employees who know how to do their work. As a job seeker, you want a fair chance to compete for that job on an equal footing with other candidates. The best-known means of accomplishing this two-fold goal is the competitive examination.

Exams are widely publicized throughout the nation. They may be administered for jobs in federal, state, city, municipal, town or village governments or agencies.

Any citizen may apply, with some limitations, such as the age or residence of applicants. Your experience and education may be reviewed to see whether you meet the requirements for the particular examination. When these requirements exist, they are reasonable and applied consistently to all applicants. Thus, a competitive examination may cause you some uneasiness now, but it is your privilege and safeguard.

C. HOW ARE CIVIL SERVICE EXAMS DEVELOPED?

Examinations are carefully written by trained technicians who are specialists in the field known as "psychological measurement," in consultation with recognized authorities in the field of work that the test will cover. These experts recommend the subject matter areas or skills to be tested; only those knowledges or skills important to your success on the job are included. The most reliable books and source materials available are used as references. Together, the experts and technicians judge the difficulty level of the questions.

Test technicians know how to phrase questions so that the problem is clearly stated. Their ethics do not permit "trick" or "catch" questions. Questions may have been tried out on sample groups, or subjected to statistical analysis, to determine their usefulness.

Written tests are often used in combination with performance tests, ratings of training and experience, and oral interviews. All of these measures combine to form the best-known means of finding the right person for the right job.

II. HOW TO PASS THE WRITTEN TEST

A. NATURE OF THE EXAMINATION

To prepare intelligently for civil service examinations, you should know how they differ from school examinations you have taken. In school you were assigned certain definite pages to read or subjects to cover. The examination questions were quite detailed and usually emphasized memory. Civil service exams, on the other hand, try to discover your present ability to perform the duties of a position, plus your potentiality to learn these duties. In other words, a civil service exam attempts to predict how successful you will be. Questions cover such a broad area that they cannot be as minute and detailed as school exam questions.

In the public service similar kinds of work, or positions, are grouped together in one "class." This process is known as *position-classification*. All the positions in a class are paid according to the salary range for that class. One class title covers all of these positions, and they are all tested by the same examination.

B. FOUR BASIC STEPS

1) Study the announcement

How, then, can you know what subjects to study? Our best answer is: "Learn as much as possible about the class of positions for which you've applied." The exam will test the knowledge, skills and abilities needed to do the work.

Your most valuable source of information about the position you want is the official exam announcement. This announcement lists the training and experience qualifications. Check these standards and apply only if you come reasonably close to meeting them.

The brief description of the position in the examination announcement offers some clues to the subjects which will be tested. Think about the job itself. Review the duties in your mind. Can you perform them, or are there some in which you are rusty? Fill in the blank spots in your preparation.

Many jurisdictions preview the written test in the exam announcement by including a section called "Knowledge and Abilities Required," "Scope of the Examination," or some similar heading. Here you will find out specifically what fields will be tested.

2) Review your own background

Once you learn in general what the position is all about, and what you need to know to do the work, ask yourself which subjects you already know fairly well and which need improvement. You may wonder whether to concentrate on improving your strong areas or on building some background in your fields of weakness. When the announcement has specified "some knowledge" or "considerable knowledge," or has used adjectives like "beginning principles of..." or "advanced ... methods," you can get a clue as to the number and difficulty of questions to be asked in any given field. More questions, and hence broader coverage, would be included for those subjects which are more important in the work. Now weigh your strengths and weaknesses against the job requirements and prepare accordingly.

3) Determine the level of the position

Another way to tell how intensively you should prepare is to understand the level of the job for which you are applying. Is it the entering level? In other words, is this the position in which beginners in a field of work are hired? Or is it an intermediate or advanced level? Sometimes this is indicated by such words as "Junior" or "Senior" in the class title. Other jurisdictions use Roman numerals to designate the level – Clerk I, Clerk II, for example. The word "Supervisor" sometimes appears in the title. If the level is not indicated by the title, check the description of duties. Will you be working under very close supervision, or will you have responsibility for independent decisions in this work?

4) Choose appropriate study materials

Now that you know the subjects to be examined and the relative amount of each subject to be covered, you can choose suitable study materials. For beginning level jobs, or even advanced ones, if you have a pronounced weakness in some aspect of your training, read a modern, standard textbook in that field. Be sure it is up to date and has general coverage. Such books are normally available at your library, and the librarian will be glad to help you locate one. For entry-level positions, questions of appropriate difficulty are chosen – neither highly advanced questions, nor those too simple. Such questions require careful thought but not advanced training.

If the position for which you are applying is technical or advanced, you will read more advanced, specialized material. If you are already familiar with the basic principles of your field, elementary textbooks would waste your time. Concentrate on advanced textbooks and technical periodicals. Think through the concepts and review difficult problems in your field.

These are all general sources. You can get more ideas on your own initiative, following these leads. For example, training manuals and publications of the government agency which employs workers in your field can be useful, particularly for technical and professional positions. A letter or visit to the government department involved may result in more specific study suggestions, and certainly will provide you with a more definite idea of the exact nature of the position you are seeking.

III. KINDS OF TESTS

Tests are used for purposes other than measuring knowledge and ability to perform specified duties. For some positions, it is equally important to test ability to make adjustments to new situations or to profit from training. In others, basic mental abilities not dependent on information are essential. Questions which test these things may not appear as pertinent to the duties of the position as those which test for knowledge and information. Yet they are often highly important parts of a fair examination. For very general questions, it is almost impossible to help you direct your study efforts. What we can do is to point out some of the more common of these general abilities needed in public service positions and describe some typical questions.

1) General information

Broad, general information has been found useful for predicting job success in some kinds of work. This is tested in a variety of ways, from vocabulary lists to questions about current events. Basic background in some field of work, such as sociology or economics, may be sampled in a group of questions. Often these are principles which have become familiar to most persons through exposure rather than through formal training. It is difficult to advise you how to study for these questions; being alert to the world around you is our best suggestion.

2) Verbal ability

An example of an ability needed in many positions is verbal or language ability. Verbal ability is, in brief, the ability to use and understand words. Vocabulary and grammar tests are typical measures of this ability. Reading comprehension or paragraph interpretation questions are common in many kinds of civil service tests. You are given a paragraph of written material and asked to find its central meaning.

3) Numerical ability

Number skills can be tested by the familiar arithmetic problem, by checking paired lists of numbers to see which are alike and which are different, or by interpreting charts and graphs. In the latter test, a graph may be printed in the test booklet which you are asked to use as the basis for answering questions.

4) Observation

A popular test for law-enforcement positions is the observation test. A picture is shown to you for several minutes, then taken away. Questions about the picture test your ability to observe both details and larger elements.

5) Following directions

In many positions in the public service, the employee must be able to carry out written instructions dependably and accurately. You may be given a chart with several columns, each column listing a variety of information. The questions require you to carry out directions involving the information given in the chart.

6) Skills and aptitudes

Performance tests effectively measure some manual skills and aptitudes. When the skill is one in which you are trained, such as typing or shorthand, you can practice. These tests are often very much like those given in business school or high school courses. For many of the other skills and aptitudes, however, no short-time preparation can be made. Skills and abilities natural to you or that you have developed throughout your lifetime are being tested.

Many of the general questions just described provide all the data needed to answer the questions and ask you to use your reasoning ability to find the answers. Your best preparation for these tests, as well as for tests of facts and ideas, is to be at your physical and mental best. You, no doubt, have your own methods of getting into an exam-taking mood and keeping "in shape." The next section lists some ideas on this subject.

IV. KINDS OF QUESTIONS

Only rarely is the "essay" question, which you answer in narrative form, used in civil service tests. Civil service tests are usually of the short-answer type. Full instructions for answering these questions will be given to you at the examination. But in case this is your first experience with short-answer questions and separate answer sheets, here is what you need to know:

1) Multiple-choice Questions

Most popular of the short-answer questions is the "multiple choice" or "best answer" question. It can be used, for example, to test for factual knowledge, ability to solve problems or judgment in meeting situations found at work.

A multiple-choice question is normally one of three types—

- It can begin with an incomplete statement followed by several possible endings. You are to find the one ending which *best* completes the statement, although some of the others may not be entirely wrong.
- It can also be a complete statement in the form of a question which is answered by choosing one of the statements listed.
- It can be in the form of a problem – again you select the best answer.

Here is an example of a multiple-choice question with a discussion which should give you some clues as to the method for choosing the right answer:

When an employee has a complaint about his assignment, the action which will *best* help him overcome his difficulty is to

A. discuss his difficulty with his coworkers
B. take the problem to the head of the organization
C. take the problem to the person who gave him the assignment
D. say nothing to anyone about his complaint

In answering this question, you should study each of the choices to find which is best. Consider choice "A" – Certainly an employee may discuss his complaint with fellow employees, but no change or improvement can result, and the complaint remains unresolved. Choice "B" is a poor choice since the head of the organization probably does not know what assignment you have been given, and taking your problem to him is known as "going over the head" of the supervisor. The supervisor, or person who made the assignment, is the person who can clarify it or correct any injustice. Choice "C" is, therefore, correct. To say nothing, as in choice "D," is unwise. Supervisors have and interest in knowing the problems employees are facing, and the employee is seeking a solution to his problem.

2) True/False Questions

The "true/false" or "right/wrong" form of question is sometimes used. Here a complete statement is given. Your job is to decide whether the statement is right or wrong.

SAMPLE: A roaming cell-phone call to a nearby city costs less than a non-roaming call to a distant city.

This statement is wrong, or false, since roaming calls are more expensive.

This is not a complete list of all possible question forms, although most of the others are variations of these common types. You will always get complete directions for answering questions. Be sure you understand *how* to mark your answers – ask questions until you do.

V. RECORDING YOUR ANSWERS

Computer terminals are used more and more today for many different kinds of exams.

For an examination with very few applicants, you may be told to record your answers in the test booklet itself. Separate answer sheets are much more common. If this separate answer sheet is to be scored by machine – and this is often the case – it is highly important that you mark your answers correctly in order to get credit.

An electronic scoring machine is often used in civil service offices because of the speed with which papers can be scored. Machine-scored answer sheets must be marked with a pencil, which will be given to you. This pencil has a high graphite content which responds to the electronic scoring machine. As a matter of fact, stray dots may register as answers, so do not let your pencil rest on the answer sheet while you are pondering the correct answer. Also, if your pencil lead breaks or is otherwise defective, ask for another.

Since the answer sheet will be dropped in a slot in the scoring machine, be careful not to bend the corners or get the paper crumpled.

The answer sheet normally has five vertical columns of numbers, with 30 numbers to a column. These numbers correspond to the question numbers in your test booklet. After each number, going across the page are four or five pairs of dotted lines. These short dotted lines have small letters or numbers above them. The first two pairs may also have a "T" or "F" above the letters. This indicates that the first two pairs only are to be used if the questions are of the true-false type. If the questions are multiple choice, disregard the "T" and "F" and pay attention only to the small letters or numbers.

Answer your questions in the manner of the sample that follows:

32. The largest city in the United States is
    A. Washington, D.C.
    B. New York City
    C. Chicago
    D. Detroit
    E. San Francisco

1) Choose the answer you think is best. (New York City is the largest, so "B" is correct.)
2) Find the row of dotted lines numbered the same as the question you are answering. (Find row number 32)
3) Find the pair of dotted lines corresponding to the answer. (Find the pair of lines under the mark "B.")
4) Make a solid black mark between the dotted lines.

VI. BEFORE THE TEST

Common sense will help you find procedures to follow to get ready for an examination. Too many of us, however, overlook these sensible measures. Indeed, nervousness and fatigue have been found to be the most serious reasons why applicants fail to do their best on civil service tests. Here is a list of reminders:

- Begin your preparation early – Don't wait until the last minute to go scurrying around for books and materials or to find out what the position is all about.
- Prepare continuously – An hour a night for a week is better than an all-night cram session. This has been definitely established. What is more, a night a week for a month will return better dividends than crowding your study into a shorter period of time.
- Locate the place of the exam – You have been sent a notice telling you when and where to report for the examination. If the location is in a different town or otherwise unfamiliar to you, it would be well to inquire the best route and learn something about the building.
- Relax the night before the test – Allow your mind to rest. Do not study at all that night. Plan some mild recreation or diversion; then go to bed early and get a good night's sleep.
- Get up early enough to make a leisurely trip to the place for the test – This way unforeseen events, traffic snarls, unfamiliar buildings, etc. will not upset you.
- Dress comfortably – A written test is not a fashion show. You will be known by number and not by name, so wear something comfortable.
- Leave excess paraphernalia at home – Shopping bags and odd bundles will get in your way. You need bring only the items mentioned in the official notice you received; usually everything you need is provided. Do not bring reference books to the exam. They will only confuse those last minutes and be taken away from you when in the test room.
- Arrive somewhat ahead of time – If because of transportation schedules you must get there very early, bring a newspaper or magazine to take your mind off yourself while waiting.
- Locate the examination room – When you have found the proper room, you will be directed to the seat or part of the room where you will sit. Sometimes you are given a sheet of instructions to read while you are waiting. Do not fill out any forms until you are told to do so; just read them and be prepared.
- Relax and prepare to listen to the instructions
- If you have any physical problem that may keep you from doing your best, be sure to tell the test administrator. If you are sick or in poor health, you really cannot do your best on the exam. You can come back and take the test some other time.

VII. AT THE TEST

The day of the test is here and you have the test booklet in your hand. The temptation to get going is very strong. Caution! There is more to success than knowing the right answers. You must know how to identify your papers and understand variations in the type of short-answer question used in this particular examination. Follow these suggestions for maximum results from your efforts:

1) Cooperate with the monitor

The test administrator has a duty to create a situation in which you can be as much at ease as possible. He will give instructions, tell you when to begin, check to see that you are marking your answer sheet correctly, and so on. He is not there to guard you, although he will see that your competitors do not take unfair advantage. He wants to help you do your best.

2) Listen to all instructions

Don't jump the gun! Wait until you understand all directions. In most civil service tests you get more time than you need to answer the questions. So don't be in a hurry. Read each word of instructions until you clearly understand the meaning. Study the examples, listen to all announcements and follow directions. Ask questions if you do not understand what to do.

3) Identify your papers

Civil service exams are usually identified by number only. You will be assigned a number; you must not put your name on your test papers. Be sure to copy your number correctly. Since more than one exam may be given, copy your exact examination title.

4) Plan your time

Unless you are told that a test is a "speed" or "rate of work" test, speed itself is usually not important. Time enough to answer all the questions will be provided, but this does not mean that you have all day. An overall time limit has been set. Divide the total time (in minutes) by the number of questions to determine the approximate time you have for each question.

5) Do not linger over difficult questions

If you come across a difficult question, mark it with a paper clip (useful to have along) and come back to it when you have been through the booklet. One caution if you do this – be sure to skip a number on your answer sheet as well. Check often to be sure that you have not lost your place and that you are marking in the row numbered the same as the question you are answering.

6) Read the questions

Be sure you know what the question asks! Many capable people are unsuccessful because they failed to *read* the questions correctly.

7) Answer all questions

Unless you have been instructed that a penalty will be deducted for incorrect answers, it is better to guess than to omit a question.

8) Speed tests

It is often better NOT to guess on speed tests. It has been found that on timed tests people are tempted to spend the last few seconds before time is called in marking answers at random – without even reading them – in the hope of picking up a few extra points. To discourage this practice, the instructions may warn you that your score will be "corrected" for guessing. That is, a penalty will be applied. The incorrect answers will be deducted from the correct ones, or some other penalty formula will be used.

9) Review your answers

If you finish before time is called, go back to the questions you guessed or omitted to give them further thought. Review other answers if you have time.

10) Return your test materials

If you are ready to leave before others have finished or time is called, take ALL your materials to the monitor and leave quietly. Never take any test material with you. The monitor can discover whose papers are not complete, and taking a test booklet may be grounds for disqualification.

VIII. EXAMINATION TECHNIQUES

1) Read the general instructions carefully. These are usually printed on the first page of the exam booklet. As a rule, these instructions refer to the timing of the examination; the fact that you should not start work until the signal and must stop work at a signal, etc. If there are any *special* instructions, such as a choice of questions to be answered, make sure that you note this instruction carefully.

2) When you are ready to start work on the examination, that is as soon as the signal has been given, read the instructions to each question booklet, underline any key words or phrases, such as *least, best, outline, describe* and the like. In this way you will tend to answer as requested rather than discover on reviewing your paper that you *listed without describing*, that you selected the *worst* choice rather than the *best* choice, etc.

3) If the examination is of the objective or multiple-choice type – that is, each question will also give a series of possible answers: A, B, C or D, and you are called upon to select the best answer and write the letter next to that answer on your answer paper – it is advisable to start answering each question in turn. There may be anywhere from 50 to 100 such questions in the three or four hours allotted and you can see how much time would be taken if you read through all the questions before beginning to answer any. Furthermore, if you come across a question or group of questions which you know would be difficult to answer, it would undoubtedly affect your handling of all the other questions.

4) If the examination is of the essay type and contains but a few questions, it is a moot point as to whether you should read all the questions before starting to answer any one. Of course, if you are given a choice – say five out of seven and the like – then it is essential to read all the questions so you can eliminate the two that are most difficult. If, however, you are asked to answer all the questions, there may be danger in trying to answer the easiest one first because you may find that you will spend too much time on it. The best technique is to answer the first question, then proceed to the second, etc.

5) Time your answers. Before the exam begins, write down the time it started, then add the time allowed for the examination and write down the time it must be completed, then divide the time available somewhat as follows:

- If 3-1/2 hours are allowed, that would be 210 minutes. If you have 80 objective-type questions, that would be an average of 2-1/2 minutes per question. Allow yourself no more than 2 minutes per question, or a total of 160 minutes, which will permit about 50 minutes to review.
- If for the time allotment of 210 minutes there are 7 essay questions to answer, that would average about 30 minutes a question. Give yourself only 25 minutes per question so that you have about 35 minutes to review.

6) The most important instruction is to *read each question* and make sure you know what is wanted. The second most important instruction is to *time yourself properly* so that you answer every question. The third most important instruction is to *answer every question*. Guess if you have to but include something for each question. Remember that you will receive no credit for a blank and will probably receive some credit if you write something in answer to an essay question. If you guess a letter – say "B" for a multiple-choice question – you may have guessed right. If you leave a blank as an answer to a multiple-choice question, the examiners may respect your feelings but it will not add a point to your score. Some exams may penalize you for wrong answers, so in such cases *only*, you may not want to guess unless you have some basis for your answer.

7) Suggestions
   a. Objective-type questions
      1. Examine the question booklet for proper sequence of pages and questions
      2. Read all instructions carefully
      3. Skip any question which seems too difficult; return to it after all other questions have been answered
      4. Apportion your time properly; do not spend too much time on any single question or group of questions
      5. Note and underline key words – *all, most, fewest, least, best, worst, same, opposite,* etc.
      6. Pay particular attention to negatives
      7. Note unusual option, e.g., unduly long, short, complex, different or similar in content to the body of the question
      8. Observe the use of "hedging" words – *probably, may, most likely,* etc.
      9. Make sure that your answer is put next to the same number as the question
      10. Do not second-guess unless you have good reason to believe the second answer is definitely more correct
      11. Cross out original answer if you decide another answer is more accurate; do not erase until you are ready to hand your paper in
      12. Answer all questions; guess unless instructed otherwise
      13. Leave time for review

   b. Essay questions
      1. Read each question carefully
      2. Determine exactly what is wanted. Underline key words or phrases.
      3. Decide on outline or paragraph answer

4. Include many different points and elements unless asked to develop any one or two points or elements
5. Show impartiality by giving pros and cons unless directed to select one side only
6. Make and write down any assumptions you find necessary to answer the questions
7. Watch your English, grammar, punctuation and choice of words
8. Time your answers; don't crowd material

8) Answering the essay question

Most essay questions can be answered by framing the specific response around several key words or ideas. Here are a few such key words or ideas:

M's: manpower, materials, methods, money, management
P's: purpose, program, policy, plan, procedure, practice, problems, pitfalls, personnel, public relations

a. Six basic steps in handling problems:
    1. Preliminary plan and background development
    2. Collect information, data and facts
    3. Analyze and interpret information, data and facts
    4. Analyze and develop solutions as well as make recommendations
    5. Prepare report and sell recommendations
    6. Install recommendations and follow up effectiveness

b. Pitfalls to avoid
    1. *Taking things for granted* – A statement of the situation does not necessarily imply that each of the elements is necessarily true; for example, a complaint may be invalid and biased so that all that can be taken for granted is that a complaint has been registered
    2. *Considering only one side of a situation* – Wherever possible, indicate several alternatives and then point out the reasons you selected the best one
    3. *Failing to indicate follow up* – Whenever your answer indicates action on your part, make certain that you will take proper follow-up action to see how successful your recommendations, procedures or actions turn out to be
    4. *Taking too long in answering any single question* – Remember to time your answers properly

IX. AFTER THE TEST

Scoring procedures differ in detail among civil service jurisdictions although the general principles are the same. Whether the papers are hand-scored or graded by machine we have described, they are nearly always graded by number. That is, the person who marks the paper knows only the number – never the name – of the applicant. Not until all the papers have been graded will they be matched with names. If other tests, such as training and experience or oral interview ratings have been given, scores will be combined. Different parts of the examination usually have different weights. For example, the written test might count 60 percent of the final grade, and a rating of training and experience 40 percent. In many jurisdictions, veterans will have a certain number of points added to their grades.

After the final grade has been determined, the names are placed in grade order and an eligible list is established. There are various methods for resolving ties between those who get the same final grade – probably the most common is to place first the name of the person whose application was received first. Job offers are made from the eligible list in the order the names appear on it. You will be notified of your grade and your rank as soon as all these computations have been made. This will be done as rapidly as possible.

People who are found to meet the requirements in the announcement are called "eligibles." Their names are put on a list of eligible candidates. An eligible's chances of getting a job depend on how high he stands on this list and how fast agencies are filling jobs from the list.

When a job is to be filled from a list of eligibles, the agency asks for the names of people on the list of eligibles for that job. When the civil service commission receives this request, it sends to the agency the names of the three people highest on this list. Or, if the job to be filled has specialized requirements, the office sends the agency the names of the top three persons who meet these requirements from the general list.

The appointing officer makes a choice from among the three people whose names were sent to him. If the selected person accepts the appointment, the names of the others are put back on the list to be considered for future openings.

That is the rule in hiring from all kinds of eligible lists, whether they are for typist, carpenter, chemist, or something else. For every vacancy, the appointing officer has his choice of any one of the top three eligibles on the list. This explains why the person whose name is on top of the list sometimes does not get an appointment when some of the persons lower on the list do. If the appointing officer chooses the second or third eligible, the No. 1 eligible does not get a job at once, but stays on the list until he is appointed or the list is terminated.

X. HOW TO PASS THE INTERVIEW TEST

The examination for which you applied requires an oral interview test. You have already taken the written test and you are now being called for the interview test – the final part of the formal examination.

You may think that it is not possible to prepare for an interview test and that there are no procedures to follow during an interview. Our purpose is to point out some things you can do in advance that will help you and some good rules to follow and pitfalls to avoid while you are being interviewed.

What is an interview supposed to test?

The written examination is designed to test the technical knowledge and competence of the candidate; the oral is designed to evaluate intangible qualities, not readily measured otherwise, and to establish a list showing the relative fitness of each candidate – as measured against his competitors – for the position sought. Scoring is not on the basis of "right" and "wrong," but on a sliding scale of values ranging from "not passable" to "outstanding." As a matter of fact, it is possible to achieve a relatively low score without a single "incorrect" answer because of evident weakness in the qualities being measured.

Occasionally, an examination may consist entirely of an oral test – either an individual or a group oral. In such cases, information is sought concerning the technical knowledges and abilities of the candidate, since there has been no written examination for this purpose. More commonly, however, an oral test is used to supplement a written examination.

Who conducts interviews?

The composition of oral boards varies among different jurisdictions. In nearly all, a representative of the personnel department serves as chairman. One of the members of the board may be a representative of the department in which the candidate would work. In some cases, "outside experts" are used, and, frequently, a businessman or some other representative of the general public is asked to serve. Labor and management or other special groups may be represented. The aim is to secure the services of experts in the appropriate field.

However the board is composed, it is a good idea (and not at all improper or unethical) to ascertain in advance of the interview who the members are and what groups they represent. When you are introduced to them, you will have some idea of their backgrounds and interests, and at least you will not stutter and stammer over their names.

What should be done before the interview?

While knowledge about the board members is useful and takes some of the surprise element out of the interview, there is other preparation which is more substantive. It *is* possible to prepare for an oral interview – in several ways:

1) Keep a copy of your application and review it carefully before the interview

This may be the only document before the oral board, and the starting point of the interview. Know what education and experience you have listed there, and the sequence and dates of all of it. Sometimes the board will ask you to review the highlights of your experience for them; you should not have to hem and haw doing it.

2) Study the class specification and the examination announcement

Usually, the oral board has one or both of these to guide them. The qualities, characteristics or knowledges required by the position sought are stated in these documents. They offer valuable clues as to the nature of the oral interview. For example, if the job involves supervisory responsibilities, the announcement will usually indicate that knowledge of modern supervisory methods and the qualifications of the candidate as a supervisor will be tested. If so, you can expect such questions, frequently in the form of a hypothetical situation which you are expected to solve. NEVER go into an oral without knowledge of the duties and responsibilities of the job you seek.

3) Think through each qualification required

Try to visualize the kind of questions you would ask if you were a board member. How well could you answer them? Try especially to appraise your own knowledge and background in each area, *measured against the job sought*, and identify any areas in which you are weak. Be critical and realistic – do not flatter yourself.

4) Do some general reading in areas in which you feel you may be weak

For example, if the job involves supervision and your past experience has NOT, some general reading in supervisory methods and practices, particularly in the field of human relations, might be useful. Do NOT study agency procedures or detailed manuals. The oral board will be testing your understanding and capacity, not your memory.

5) Get a good night's sleep and watch your general health and mental attitude

You will want a clear head at the interview. Take care of a cold or any other minor ailment, and of course, no hangovers.

What should be done on the day of the interview?

Now comes the day of the interview itself. Give yourself plenty of time to get there. Plan to arrive somewhat ahead of the scheduled time, particularly if your appointment is in the fore part of the day. If a previous candidate fails to appear, the board might be ready for you a bit early. By early afternoon an oral board is almost invariably behind schedule if there are many candidates, and you may have to wait. Take along a book or magazine to read, or your application to review, but leave any extraneous material in the waiting room when you go in for your interview. In any event, relax and compose yourself.

The matter of dress is important. The board is forming impressions about you – from your experience, your manners, your attitude, and your appearance. Give your personal appearance careful attention. Dress your best, but not your flashiest. Choose conservative, appropriate clothing, and be sure it is immaculate. This is a business interview, and your appearance should indicate that you regard it as such. Besides, being well groomed and properly dressed will help boost your confidence.

Sooner or later, someone will call your name and escort you into the interview room. *This is it.* From here on you are on your own. It is too late for any more preparation. But remember, you asked for this opportunity to prove your fitness, and you are here because your request was granted.

What happens when you go in?

The usual sequence of events will be as follows: The clerk (who is often the board stenographer) will introduce you to the chairman of the oral board, who will introduce you to the other members of the board. Acknowledge the introductions before you sit down. Do not be surprised if you find a microphone facing you or a stenotypist sitting by. Oral interviews are usually recorded in the event of an appeal or other review.

Usually the chairman of the board will open the interview by reviewing the highlights of your education and work experience from your application – primarily for the benefit of the other members of the board, as well as to get the material into the record. Do not interrupt or comment unless there is an error or significant misinterpretation; if that is the case, do not hesitate. But do not quibble about insignificant matters. Also, he will usually ask you some question about your education, experience or your present job – partly to get you to start talking and to establish the interviewing "rapport." He may start the actual questioning, or turn it over to one of the other members. Frequently, each member undertakes the questioning on a particular area, one in which he is perhaps most competent, so you can expect each member to participate in the examination. Because time is limited, you may also expect some rather abrupt switches in the direction the questioning takes, so do not be upset by it. Normally, a board member will not pursue a single line of questioning unless he discovers a particular strength or weakness.

After each member has participated, the chairman will usually ask whether any member has any further questions, then will ask you if you have anything you wish to add. Unless you are expecting this question, it may floor you. Worse, it may start you off on an extended, extemporaneous speech. The board is not usually seeking more information. The question is principally to offer you a last opportunity to present further qualifications or to indicate that you have nothing to add. So, if you feel that a significant qualification or characteristic has been overlooked, it is proper to point it out in a sentence or so. Do not compliment the board on the thoroughness of their examination – they have been sketchy, and you know it. If you wish, merely say, "No thank you, I have nothing further to add." This is a point where you can "talk yourself out" of a good impression or fail to present an important bit of information. Remember, *you close the interview yourself.*

The chairman will then say, "That is all, Mr. ______, thank you." Do not be startled; the interview is over, and quicker than you think. Thank him, gather your belongings and take your leave. Save your sigh of relief for the other side of the door.

How to put your best foot forward

Throughout this entire process, you may feel that the board individually and collectively is trying to pierce your defenses, seek out your hidden weaknesses and embarrass and confuse you. Actually, this is not true. They are obliged to make an appraisal of your qualifications for the job you are seeking, and they want to see you in your best light. Remember, they must interview all candidates and a non-cooperative candidate may become a failure in spite of their best efforts to bring out his qualifications. Here are 15 suggestions that will help you:

1) Be natural – Keep your attitude confident, not cocky

If you are not confident that you can do the job, do not expect the board to be. Do not apologize for your weaknesses, try to bring out your strong points. The board is interested in a positive, not negative, presentation. Cockiness will antagonize any board member and make him wonder if you are covering up a weakness by a false show of strength.

2) Get comfortable, but don't lounge or sprawl

Sit erectly but not stiffly. A careless posture may lead the board to conclude that you are careless in other things, or at least that you are not impressed by the importance of the occasion. Either conclusion is natural, even if incorrect. Do not fuss with your clothing, a pencil or an ashtray. Your hands may occasionally be useful to emphasize a point; do not let them become a point of distraction.

3) Do not wisecrack or make small talk

This is a serious situation, and your attitude should show that you consider it as such. Further, the time of the board is limited – they do not want to waste it, and neither should you.

4) Do not exaggerate your experience or abilities

In the first place, from information in the application or other interviews and sources, the board may know more about you than you think. Secondly, you probably will not get away with it. An experienced board is rather adept at spotting such a situation, so do not take the chance.

5) If you know a board member, do not make a point of it, yet do not hide it

Certainly you are not fooling him, and probably not the other members of the board. Do not try to take advantage of your acquaintanceship – it will probably do you little good.

6) Do not dominate the interview

Let the board do that. They will give you the clues – do not assume that you have to do all the talking. Realize that the board has a number of questions to ask you, and do not try to take up all the interview time by showing off your extensive knowledge of the answer to the first one.

7) Be attentive

You only have 20 minutes or so, and you should keep your attention at its sharpest throughout. When a member is addressing a problem or question to you, give him your undivided attention. Address your reply principally to him, but do not exclude the other board members.

8) Do not interrupt

A board member may be stating a problem for you to analyze. He will ask you a question when the time comes. Let him state the problem, and wait for the question.

9) Make sure you understand the question

Do not try to answer until you are sure what the question is. If it is not clear, restate it in your own words or ask the board member to clarify it for you. However, do not haggle about minor elements.

10) Reply promptly but not hastily

A common entry on oral board rating sheets is "candidate responded readily," or "candidate hesitated in replies." Respond as promptly and quickly as you can, but do not jump to a hasty, ill-considered answer.

11) Do not be peremptory in your answers

A brief answer is proper – but do not fire your answer back. That is a losing game from your point of view. The board member can probably ask questions much faster than you can answer them.

12) Do not try to create the answer you think the board member wants

He is interested in what kind of mind you have and how it works – not in playing games. Furthermore, he can usually spot this practice and will actually grade you down on it.

13) Do not switch sides in your reply merely to agree with a board member

Frequently, a member will take a contrary position merely to draw you out and to see if you are willing and able to defend your point of view. Do not start a debate, yet do not surrender a good position. If a position is worth taking, it is worth defending.

14) Do not be afraid to admit an error in judgment if you are shown to be wrong

The board knows that you are forced to reply without any opportunity for careful consideration. Your answer may be demonstrably wrong. If so, admit it and get on with the interview.

15) Do not dwell at length on your present job

The opening question may relate to your present assignment. Answer the question but do not go into an extended discussion. You are being examined for a *new* job, not your present one. As a matter of fact, try to phrase ALL your answers in terms of the job for which you are being examined.

Basis of Rating

Probably you will forget most of these "do's" and "don'ts" when you walk into the oral interview room. Even remembering them all will not ensure you a passing grade. Perhaps you did not have the qualifications in the first place. But remembering them will help you to put your best foot forward, without treading on the toes of the board members.

Rumor and popular opinion to the contrary notwithstanding, an oral board wants you to make the best appearance possible. They know you are under pressure – but they also want to see how you respond to it as a guide to what your reaction would be under the pressures of the job you seek. They will be influenced by the degree of poise you display, the personal traits you show and the manner in which you respond.

ABOUT THIS BOOK

This book contains tests divided into Examination Sections. Go through each test, answering every question in the margin. At the end of each test look at the answer key and check your answers. On the ones you got wrong, look at the right answer choice and learn. Do not fill in the answers first. Do not memorize the questions and answers, but understand the answer and principles involved. On your test, the questions will likely be different from the samples. Questions are changed and new ones added. If you understand these past questions you should have success with any changes that arise. Tests may consist of several types of questions. We have additional books on each subject should more study be advisable or necessary for you. Finally, the more you study, the better prepared you will be. This book is intended to be the last thing you study before you walk into the examination room. Prior study of relevant texts is also recommended. NLC publishes some of these in our Fundamental Series. Knowledge and good sense are important factors in passing your exam. Good luck also helps. So now study this Passbook, absorb the material contained within and take that knowledge into the examination. Then do your best to pass that exam.

EXAMINATION SECTION

EXAMINATION SECTION
TEST 1

DIRECTIONS: Each question or incomplete statement is followed by several suggested answers or completions. Select the one that BEST answers the question or completes the statement. *PRINT THE LETTER OF THE CORRECT ANSWER IN THE SPACE AT THE RIGHT.*

Questions 1-3.

DIRECTIONS: Questions 1 through 3, inclusive, are to be answered in accordance with the American Standard Graphical Symbols for Pipe Fittings, Valves, and Piping and American Standard Graphical Symbols for Heating, Ventilating and Air Conditioning.

1. The symbol ⊙+—— shown on a piping drawing represents a ______ elbow. 1.____

   A. turned down
   B. reducing
   C. long radius
   D. turned up

2. The symbol ——+▭+—— shown on a heating drawing represents a(n) 2.____

   A. expansion joint
   B. hanger or support
   C. heat exchanger
   D. air eliminator

3. The symbol —+⋈+— shown on a piping drawing represents a ______ gate valve. 3.____

   A. welded
   B. flanged
   C. screwed
   D. bell and spigot

4. The MAIN purpose for the inspection of plant equipment, buildings, and facilities is to 4.____

   A. determine the quality of maintenance work of all the trades
   B. prevent the overstocking of equipment and materials used in maintenance work
   C. forecast normal maintenance jobs for existing equipment, buildings, and facilities
   D. prevent unscheduled interruptions of operating equipment and excessive deterioration of buildings and facilities

5. Of the following devices, the one that is used to determine the rating, in cubic feet per minute, of a unit ventilator is a(n) 5.____

   A. psychrometer
   B. pyrometer
   C. anemometer
   D. manometer

6. A number of 4' x 6' skids loaded with material are to be stored. Assume that the total weight of each loaded skid is 1200 pounds and that the maximum allowable floor load is 280 lbs. per sq. ft.
   The MAXIMUM number of skids that can be stacked vertically without exceeding the MAXIMUM allowable floor load is 6.____

   A. 4
   B. 5
   C. 6
   D. 7

7. Specifications which contain the term *slump test* would MOST likely refer to 7.____

A. lumber B. paint C. concrete D. water

8. Of the following sizes of copper conductors, the one which has the LEAST current-carrying capacity is ______ AWG. 8.____

A. 000 B. 0 C. 8 D. 12

9. The size of a steel beam is shown on a steel drawing as W 8 x 15. 9.____
In accordance with the latest edition of the Steel Construction Manual of the American Institute of Steel Construction, the number 8 in W 8 x 15 represents the beam's *approximate*

A. depth
B. flange thickness
C. width
D. web thickness

10. For expediting control functions such as work methods, planning, scheduling, and work measurement, EQUIPMENT RECORDS must contain specific data. 10.____
Of the following, the data which is NOT usually indicated on an EQUIPMENT RECORD card is

A. machinery and parts specifications numbers
B. a breakdown history
C. a preventive maintenance history
D. salvage value on the open market

11. Refrigeration piping, valves, fittings, and related parts used in the construction and installation of refrigeration systems shall conform to the 11.____

A. American Society of Mechanical Engineers Boiler and Pressure Vessel Code
B. American Standards Association Code for Pressure Piping
C. Pipe Fabrication Institute Standards
D. Underwriters Laboratory Standards

12. The maintenance term *downtime* means MOST NEARLY the 12.____

A. period of time in which a machine is out of service
B. routine replacement of parts or materials to a piece of equipment
C. labor required for clean-up of equipment to insure its proper operation
D. maintenance work which is confined to checking, adjusting, and lubrication of equipment

13. A supplier quotes a list price of $172.00 less 15 and 10 percent for twelve tools. 13.____
The ACTUAL cost for these twelve tools is MOST NEARLY

A. $146 B. $132 C. $129 D. $112

14. Of the following colors of electrical conductor coverings, the one which indicates a conductor used SOLELY for grounding portable or fixed electrical equipment is 14.____

A. blue B. green C. red D. black

15. A *medium duty* type of scaffold is one on which the working load on the platform surface must NOT exceed ______ pounds per square foot. 15.____

A. 50 B. 70 C. 90 D. 110

16. Assume that a mechanic is using a powder-actuated tool and the cartridge misfires. According to recommended safe practices regarding a misfired cartridge, the FIRST course of action the mechanic should take is to 16.____

A. place the misfired cartridge carefully into a metal container filled with water
B. carefully reload the tool with the misfired cartridge and try it again
C. immediately bury the misfired cartridge at least two feet in the ground
D. remove the wadding from the misfired cartridge and empty the powder into a pail of sand

17. The ratings used in classifying fire resistant building construction materials are MOST frequently expressed in 17.____

A. Btu's B. hours C. temperatures D. pounds

18. The only legible portion of the nameplate on a piece of equipment reads: *208 volts, 3 phase, 10 H.P.* 18.____
This data would MOST NEARLY indicate that the piece of equipment is a(n)

A. amplifier
B. fixture ballast
C. motor
D. rectifier

19. Of the following items relating to the maintenance of roofs, the one which is of the LEAST value in a preventive maintenance program for roofs is knowledge of the 19.____

A. roofing specifications
B. application procedures
C. process of deterioration
D. frequency of rainstorms

20. In an oxyacetylene cutting outfit, the color of the hose that is connected to the oxygen cylinder is USUALLY 20.____

A. white B. yellow C. red D. green

21. Assume that a welding generator is to be used to weld partitions made of 18 gauge steel. Of the following settings, the BEST one to use would be a ______ setting of voltage and a ______ setting of amperage. 21.____

A. high; high B. high; low C. low; high D. low; low

22. According to the administrative code, when color marking is used, potable water lines shall be painted 22.____

A. yellow B. blue C. red D. green

23. A set of mechanical plan drawings is drawn to a scale of 1/8" = 1 foot. 23.____
If a length of pipe measures 15 7/16" on the drawing, the ACTUAL length of the pipe is ______ feet.

A. 121.5 B. 122.5 C. 123.5 D. 124.5

24. A portion of a specification states: *Concrete, other than that placed under water, should be compacted and worked into place by spading or puddling.* 24.____
The MAIN reason why *spading and puddling* is required is to

A. insure that all water in the concrete mix is brought to the surface
B. eliminate stone pockets and large bubbles of air

C. provide a means to obtain a spade full of concrete for test purposes
D. make allowances for *bleeding and segregation* of the concrete

25. Assume that the following statement appears in a construction contract: *Payment will be made for the number of pounds of bar reinforcement incorporated in the work as shown on the plans.* 25.____
This type of contract is MOST likely

A. cost plus B. lump sum C. subcontract D. unit price

26. Partial payments to outside contractors are USUALLY based on the 26.____

A. breakdown estimate submitted after the contract was signed
B. actual cost of labor and material plus overhead and profit
C. estimate of work completed which is generally submitted periodically
D. estimate of material delivered to the job

27. Building contracts usually require that estimates for changes made in the field be submitted for approval before the work can start. 27.____
The MAIN reason for this requirement is to

A. make sure that the contractor understands the change
B. discourage such changes
C. keep the contractor honest
D. enable the department to control its expenses

28. An *addendum* to contract specifications means MOST NEARLY 28.____

A. a substantial completion payment to the contractor for work almost completed
B. final acceptance of the work by authorities of all contract work still to be done
C. additional contract provisions issued in writing by authorities prior to receipt of bids
D. work other than that required by the contract at the time of its execution

29. Of the following terms, the one which is usually NOT used to describe the types of payments to outside contractors for work done is the ______ payment. 29.____

A. partial payment B. substantial completion
C. final D. surety

30. Of the following metals, the one which is a ferrous metal is 30.____

A. cast iron B. brass C. bronze D. babbit

31. Assume that you have assigned six mechanics to do a job that must be finished in four days. At the end of three days, your men have completed only two-thirds of the job. In order to complete the job on time and because the job is such that it cannot be speeded up, you should assign a MINIMUM of ______ extra men. 31.____

A. 3 B. 4 C. 5 D. 6

32. Of the following traps, the one which is NORMALLY used to retain steam in a heating unit or piping is the ______ trap. 32.____

A. P B. running C. float D. bell

33. Of the following materials, the one which is a convenient and powerful adhesive for cementing tears in canvas jackets that are wrapped around warm pipe insulation is 33.____

A. cylinder oil B. wheat paste
C. water glass D. latex paint

34. Pipe chases should be provided with an access door PRIMARILY to provide means to 34.____

A. replace piping lines
B. either inspect or manipulate valves
C. prevent condensate from forming on the pipes
D. check the chase for possible structural defects

35. Electric power is measured in 35.____

A. volts B. amperes C. watts D. ohms

KEY (CORRECT ANSWERS)

1.	D	16.	A
2.	A	17.	B
3.	B	18.	C
4.	D	19.	D
5.	C	20.	D
6.	B	21.	B
7.	C	22.	D
8.	D	23.	C
9.	A	24.	B
10.	D	25.	D
11.	B	26.	C
12.	A	27.	D
13.	B	28.	C
14.	B	29.	D
15.	A	30.	A

31. A
32. C
33. C
34. B
35. C

TEST 2

DIRECTIONS: Each question or incomplete statement is followed by several suggested answers or completions. Select the one that BEST answers the question or completes the statement. *PRINT THE LETTER OF THE CORRECT ANSWER IN THE SPACE AT THE RIGHT.*

1. The HIGHEST quality tools should 1.____

   A. always be bought
   B. never be bought
   C. be bought when they offer an overall advantage
   D. be bought only for foreman

2. Master keys should have no markings that will identify them as such. 2.____
   This statement is

   A. *false;* it would be impossible to keep records about them without such markings
   B. *true;* markings are subject to alteration and vandalization
   C. *false;* without such markings, they would be too lightly regarded by those to whom issued
   D. *true;* markings would only highlight their value to a potential wrongdoer

3. For a foreman to usually delay for a few weeks handling grievances his men make is a 3.____

   A. *poor* practice; it can affect the morale of the men
   B. *good* practice; it will discourage grievances
   C. *poor* practice; the causes of grievances usually disappear if action is delayed
   D. *good* practice; most employee grievances are not justified

4. Whenever an important change in procedure is contemplated, some foremen make a point of discussing the matter with their subordinates in order to get their viewpoint on the proposed change. 4.____
   In general, this practice is advisable MAINLY for the reason that

   A. subordinates can often see the effects of procedural changes more clearly than foremen
   B. the foreman has an opportunity to explain the advantages of the new procedure
   C. future changes will be welcomed if subordinates are kept informed
   D. participation in work planning helps to build a spirit of cooperation among employees

5. An estimate of employee morale could LEAST effectively be appraised by 5.____

   A. checking accident and absenteeism records
   B. determining the attitudes of employees toward their job
   C. examining the number of requests for emergency leaves of absence
   D. reviewing the number and nature of employee suggestions

6. Assume that you are a foreman and that a visitor at the job site asks you what your crew is doing. 6.____
   You should

A. respectfully decline to answer since all questions must be answered by the proper authority
B. answer as concisely as possible but discourage undue conversation
C. refer the man to your superiors
D. give the person complete details of the job

7. Cooperation can BEST be obtained from the general public by 7.____

A. siding with them whenever they have a complaint
B. sticking carefully to your work and ignoring everything else
C. explaining the department's objectives and why the public must occasionally be temporarily inconvenienced
D. listening politely to their complaints and telling them that the complaints will be forwarded to the main office

8. While you are working for the city, a man says to you that one of the rules of your job doesn't make sense and he gets mad. 8.____
You should say to him

A. Leave me alone so I can get my work done
B. Everyone must follow the rules
C. Let me tell you the reason for the rule
D. I'm only doing my job so don't get mad at me

9. One approach to preparing written reports to superiors is to present first the conclusions and recommendations and then the data on which the conclusions and recommendations are based. 9.____
The use of this approach is BEST justified when the

A. data completely support the conclusions and recommendations
B. superiors lack the specific training and experience required to understand and interpret the data
C. data contain more information than is required for making the conclusions and recommendations
D. superiors are more interested in the conclusions and recommendations than in the data

10. The MOST important reason why separate paragraphs might be used in writing a report is that this 10.____

A. makes it easier to understand the report
B. permits the report to be condensed
C. gives a better appearance to the report
D. prevents accidental elimination of important facts

11. On a drawing, the following standard cross-section represents MOST NEARLY 11.____

A. sand B. concrete C. earth D. rock

12. On a drawing, the following standard cross-section represents MOST NEARLY 12.____

A. malleable iron
B. steel
C. bronze
D. lead

13. On a piping plan drawing, the symbol represents a 90° ______ elbow. 13.____

A. flanged
B. screwed
C. bell and spigot
D. welded

14. On a drawing, the symbol represents 14.____

A. stone B. steel C. glass D. wood

15. On a heating piping drawing, the symbol represents piping. 15.____

A. high-pressure steam
B. medium-pressure steam
C. low-pressure
D. hot water supply

16. Of the following devices, the one that is LEAST frequently used to attach a piece of equipment to concrete or masonry walls is a(n) 16.____

A. carriage bolt
B. through bolt
C. lag screw
D. expansion bolt

17. A vapor barrier is usually installed in conjunction with 17.____

A. drainage piping
B. roof flashing
C. building insulation
D. wood sheathing

Questions 18-20.

DIRECTIONS: Questions 18 through 20 are to be answered in accordance with the following table

	Man Days Borough 1 Oct.	Nov.	Man Days Borough 2 Oct.	Nov.	Man Days Borough 3 Oct.	Nov.	Man Days Borough 4 Oct.	Nov.
Carpenter	70	100	35	180	145	205	120	85
Plumber	95	135	195	100	70	130	135	80
House Painter	90	90	120	80	85	85	95	195
Electrician	120	110	135	155	120	95	70	205
Blacksmith	125	145	60	180	205	145	80	125

18. In accordance with the above table, if the average daily pay of the five trades listed above is $47.50, the approximate labor cost of work done by the five trades during the month of October for Borough 1 is MOST NEARLY 18.____

A. $22,800 B. $23,450 C. $23,750 D. $26,125

19. In accordance with the above table, the Borough which MOST NEARLY made up 22.4% of the total plumbing work force for the month of November is Borough 19.____

A. 1 B. 2 C. 3 D. 4

20. In accordance with the above table, the average man days per month per Borough spent on electrical work for all Boroughs combined is MOST NEARLY 20.____

A. 120 B. 126 C. 130 D. 136

21. Of the following percentages of carbon, the one that would indicate a medium carbon steel is 21.____

A. 0.2% B. 0.4% C. 0.8% D. 1.2%

22. A *screw pitch gage* measures only the 22.____

A. looseness of threads
B. tightness of threads
C. number of threads per inch
D. gage number

23. Assume that you are to make an inspection of a building to determine the need for painting. 23.____
Of the following tools, the one which is LEAST needed to aid you in your inspection is a

A. sharp penknife
B. putty knife
C. lightweight tack hammer
D. six-foot rule

24. A *slump test* for concrete is used MAINLY to measure the concrete's 24.____

A. strength B. consistency C. flexibility D. porosity

25. Specifications which contain the term *kiln dried* would MOST likely refer to 25.____

A. asphalt shingles
B. brick veneer
C. paint lacquer
D. lumber

26. In accordance with established jurisdictional work procedures among the trades, the person you would assign to replace a malfunctioning fire sprinkler head would be a 26.____

A. plumber B. laborer C. housesmith D. steamfitter

27. Of the following types of union shops, the one which is illegal under the Taft-Hartley Law is the ______ shop. 27.____

A. closed
B. open
C. union
D. union representative

28. Of the following types of contracts, the one that in city work would MOST likely be limited to emergency work *only* is 28.____

A. lump-sum
B. unit-price
C. cost-plus
D. partial cost-plus and lump-sum

29. Of the following qualifications of outside work contractors, the one which is the LEAST important requirement for determining eligible contractors is 29.____

A. availability
B. size of work force
C. experience
D. location of business

30. Of the following piping materials, the one that combines the physical strength of mild steel with the corrosion resistance of gray iron is 30.____

A. grade A steel
B. grey cast iron
C. welded wrought iron
D. ductile iron

31. Assume that a can of red lead paint needs to be thinned slightly. Of the following, the one that should be used is 31.____

A. turpentine
B. lacquer thinner
C. water
D. alcohol

32. Assume that a trench is 42" wide, 5' deep, and 100' long. If the unit price of excavating the trench is $35 per cubic yard, the cost of excavating the trench is MOST NEARLY 32.____

A. $2,275 B. $5,110 C. $7,000 D. $21,000

33. Of the following uses, the one for which a bituminous compound would usually be used is to 33.____

A. prevent corrosion of buried steel tanks
B. increase the strength of concrete
C. caulk water pipes
D. paint inside wood columns

34. An electrical drawing is drawn to a scale of 1/4" = 1'. If a length of conduit on the drawing measures 7 3/8", the actual length of the conduit, in feet, is MOST NEARLY 34.____

A. 7.5' B. 15.5' C. 22.5' D. 29.5'

35. Of the following steam heating systems, the one that operates under both vacuum and low pressure conditions, without using a vacuum pump, is generally known as a ______ system. 35.____

A. one pipe low pressure
B. vacuum
C. vapor
D. high pressure

36. Of the following valve trim symbols, the one which designates a valve trim made of monel material is 36.____

A. 8-18 B. NI-CU C. SM D. MI

37. A replacement part for a piece of equipment is to be made of S.A.E. 4047 steel. This material is MOST likely a ______ steel. 37.____

A. wrought
B. nickel
C. chrome-vanadium
D. molybdenum

38. A metallic underground water piping system is to be used as a means of grounding. Of the following statements concerning use of this system, the one that is MOST NEARLY CORRECT is that this use is 38.____

A. not permitted
B. permitted where available
C. absolutely required
D. permitted only in certain cases

39. For pipe sizes up to 8", schedule 40 pipe is identical to ______ pipe. 39.____

A. standard
B. extra strong
C. double extra strong
D. type M copper

40. Assume that a shop is undergoing a general housecleaning, and all excess unused materials have been removed. *Clean-up work,* as pertains to painting in this case, means MOST NEARLY 40.____

A. a thorough two-coat paint job
B. only that surface which was marred to be painted
C. a one-coat job to *freshen things up*
D. only that iron work is to be painted

41. The *United States Standard Gage* is used to measure sheet metal thicknesses of 41.____

A. iron and steel
B. aluminum
C. copper
D. tin

42. Headers and stretchers are used in the construction of 42.____

A. floors B. walls C. ceilings D. roofs

Questions 43-44.

DIRECTIONS: Questions 43 and 44, inclusive, are to be answered in accordance with the following paragraph.

For cast iron pipe lines, the middle ring or sleeve shall have <u>*beveled*</u> *ends and shall be high quality cast iron. The middle ring shall have a minimum wall thickness of 3/8" for pipe up to 8", 7/16" for pipe 10" to 30", and 1/2" for pipe over 30", nominal diameter. Minimum length of middle ring shall be 5" for pipe up to 10", 6" for pipe 10" to 30", and 10" for pipe 30" nominal diameter and larger. The middle ring shall not have a center pipe stop, unless otherwise specified.*

43. As used in the above paragraph, the word *beveled* means MOST NEARLY 43.____

A. straight B. slanted C. curved D. rounded

44. In accordance with the above paragraph, the middle ring of a 24" nominal diameter pipe would have a minimum wall thickness and length of ______ thick and ______ long. 44.____

A. 3/8"; 5" B. 3/8"; 6" C. 7/16"; 6" D. 1/2"; 6"

45. A work order is NOT usually issued for which one of the following jobs: 45.____

A. Repairing wood door frames
B. Taking daily inventory
C. Installing electric switches in maintenance shop
D. Repairing a number of valves in boiler room

46. Of the following statements, the one which usually does NOT pertain to preventative maintenance programs is 46.____

A. periodic inspection of facilities
B. lubrication of equipment
C. minor repair of equipment
D. complete replacement of deteriorated equipment

Questions 47-50.

DIRECTIONS: Questions 47 through 50, inclusive, are based on the sketch of metal sheet shown below. (Sketch not to scale.)

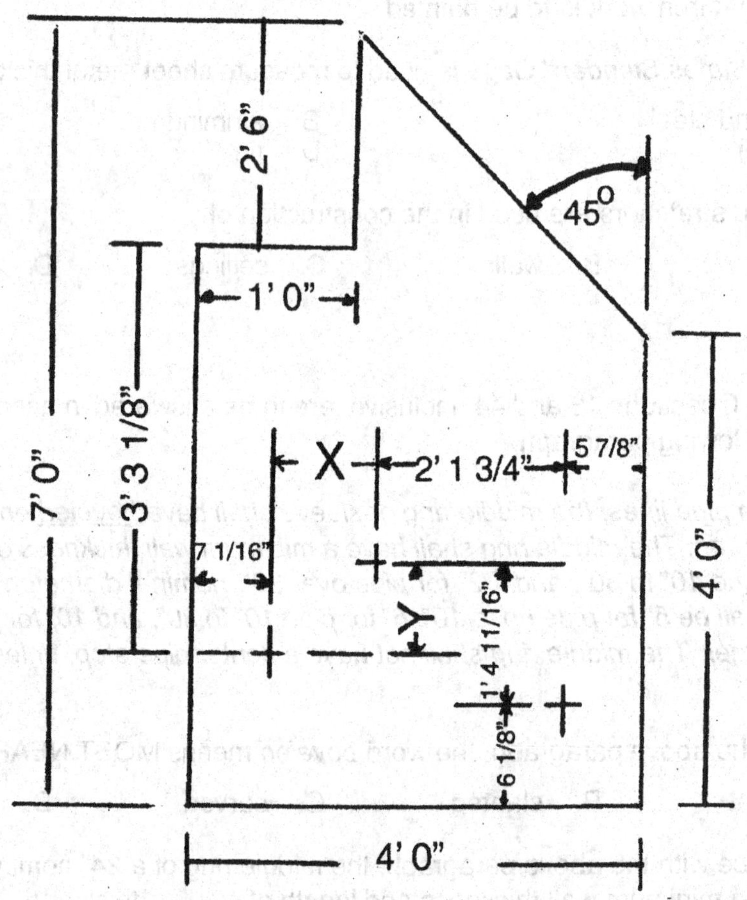

47. From the above sketch, the distance marked **X** is MOST NEARLY 47.____

A. 5 1/4" B. 6 5/16" C. 7 1/8" D. 9 5/16"

48. From the above sketch, the distance marked **Y** is MOST NEARLY 48.____

A. 5 11/16" B. 6 3/16" C. 7 5/16" D. 8 11/16"

49. In reference to the above sketch, if each piece is made from a rectangular piece of metal measuring 4' x 7', the percent of waste material is MOST NEARLY 49.____

A. 10% B. 15% C. 25% D. 30%

50. In reference to the above sketch, if the metal is 1/4" thick and weighs 144 pounds per cubic foot, the net weight of one piece would be MOST NEARLY ______ pounds. 50.____

A. 51 B. 63 C. 75 D. 749

KEY (CORRECT ANSWERS)

1.	C	11.	A	21.	B	31.	A	41.	A
2.	D	12.	C	22.	C	32.	A	42.	B
3.	A	13.	A	23.	D	33.	A	43.	B
4.	D	14.	D	24.	B	34.	D	44.	C
5.	C	15.	B	25.	D	35.	C	45.	B
6.	B	16.	A	26.	D	36.	B	46.	D
7.	C	17.	C	27.	A	37.	D	47.	D
8.	C	18.	C	28.	C	38.	B	48.	D
9.	D	19.	B	29.	D	39.	A	49.	C
10.	A	20.	B	30.	D	40.	C	50.	B

EXAMINATION SECTION
TEST 1

DIRECTIONS: Each question or incomplete statement is followed by several suggested answers or completions. Select the one that BEST answers the question or completes the statement. *PRINT THE LETTER OF THE CORRECT ANSWER IN THE SPACE AT THE RIGHT.*

1. Linseed oil putty would MOST likely be used to secure glass in ______ windows. 1.____

   A. steel casement
   B. aluminum jalousie
   C. wood double hung
   D. aluminum storm

2. Of the following, the one type of glass that should NOT be cut with the ordinary type glass cutter is ______ glass. 2.____

   A. safety
   B. plate
   C. wire
   D. herculite

3. Thermopane is made of two sheets of glass separated by 3.____

   A. a sheet of celluloid
   B. wire mesh
   C. an air space
   D. mica

4. Glass is NEVER cut so that it fits snugly inside the frame of a steel casement window. Of the following, the MAIN reason for allowing this space between the glass and the side of the frame is to 4.____

   A. prevent cracking of the glass in cold weather
   B. permit the glass to be lined up properly
   C. allow space for the putty
   D. eliminate the necessity of polishing the edges of the glass

5. Glass is held in steel sash by means of 5.____

   A. points
   B. clips
   C. plates
   D. blocks

6. When nailing felt to a roof, the nails should be driven through a 6.____

   A. tinned disc
   B. steel washer
   C. brass plate
   D. plastic bushing

7. An opening in a parapet wall for draining water from a roof is MOST often called a 7.____

   A. leader
   B. gutter
   C. downspout
   D. scupper

8. Roofing nails are usually 8.____

   A. brass
   B. cement coated
   C. galvanized
   D. nickel plated

9. A *street ell* is a fitting having 9.____

   A. male threads at both ends
   B. male threads at one end and female threads at the other end
   C. female threads at both ends
   D. male threads at one end and a solder connection at the other end

10. Of the following pieces of equipment, the one on which you would MOST likely find a safety (pop-off) valve is a(n) 10.____

A. hot air furnace
B. air conditioning compressor
C. hot water heater
D. dehumidifier

11. Compression fittings are MOST often used with 11.____

A. cast iron bell and spigot pipe
B. steel flange pipe
C. copper tubing
D. transite

12. Water hammer is BEST eliminated by 12.____

A. increasing the size of all the piping
B. installing an air chamber
C. replacing the valve seats with neoprene gaskets
D. flushing the system to remove corrosion

13. The BEST type of pipe to use in a gas line in a domestic installation is 13.____

A. black iron
B. galvanized iron
C. cast iron
D. wrought steel

14. If there is a pinhole in the float of a toilet tank, the 14.____

A. water will flush continually
B. toilet cannot flush
C. tank cannot be filled with water
D. valve will not shut off so water will overflow into the overflow tube

15. Condensation of moisture in humid weather occurs MOST often on ______ pipe(s). 15.____

A. sewage
B. gas
C. hot water
D. cold water

16. A gas appliance should be connected to a gas line by means of a(n) 16.____

A. union
B. right and left coupling
C. elbow
D. close nipple

17. A PRINCIPAL difference between a pipe thread and a machine thread is that the pipe thread is 17.____

A. tapered
B. finer
C. flat
D. longer

18. When joining galvanized iron pipe, pipe joint compound is placed on 18.____

A. the female threads only
B. the male threads only
C. both the male and female threads
D. either the male or the female threads depending on the type of fitting

19. If moisture is trapped between the layers of a 3-ply roof, the heat of a summer day will 19.____

A. dry the roof out
B. cause blisters to be formed in the roofing
C. rot the felt material
D. have no effect on the roofing

20. Of the following, the metal MOST often used for leaders and gutters is 20.____

A. monel
B. brass
C. steel
D. galvanized iron

21. When drilling a small hole in sheet copper, the BEST practice is to 21.____

A. make a dent with a center punch first
B. put some cutting oil at the point you intend to drill
C. use a slow speed drill to prevent overheating
D. use an auger type bit

22. The reason for annealing sheet copper is to make it 22.____

A. soft and easier to work
B. more resistant to weather
C. easier to solder
D. harder and more resistant to blows

23. In draw filing, 23.____

A. only the edge of the file is used
B. a triangle file is generally used
C. the file is pulled toward the mechanic's body in filing
D. the file must have a safe edge

24. The type of paint that uses water as a thinner is 24.____

A. enamel B. latex C. shellac D. lacquer

25. The reason for placing a 6" sub-base of cinders under a concrete sidewalk is to 25.____

A. provide flexibility in the surface
B. permit drainage of water
C. prevent chemicals in the soil from damaging the sidewalk
D. allow room for the concrete to expand

26. The BEST material to use to lubricate a door lock is 26.____

A. penetrating oil
B. pike oil
C. graphite
D. light grease

27. Assume that the color of the flame from a gas stove is bright yellow.
To correct this, you should 27.____

A. close the air flap
B. open the air flap
C. increase the gas pressure
D. increase the size of the gas opening

28. In a 110-220 volt three-wire circuit, the neutral wire is usually 28.____

A. black B. red C. white D. green

29. Brushes on fractional horsepower universal motors are MOST often made of 29.____

A. flexible copper strands
B. rigid carbon blocks
C. thin wire strips
D. collector rings

30. Leaks from the stem of a faucet can generally be stopped by replacing the 30.____

A. bibb washer B. seat C. packing D. gasket

31. Of the following, the BEST procedure to follow with a frozen water pipe is to 31.____

A. allow the pipe to thaw out by itself as the weather gets warmer
B. put anti-freeze into the pipe above the section that is frozen
C. turn on the hot water heater
D. open the faucet closest to the frozen pipe and warm the pipe with a blow torch, starting at this point

32. The one of the following that is NOT usually changed by a central air conditioning system is the 32.____

A. volume of air in the system
B. humidity of the air
C. dust in the air
D. air pressure of the system

33. The temperature of a domestic hot water system is MOST often controlled by a(n) 33.____

A. relief valve B. aquastat C. barometer D. thermostat

34. Draft in a chimney is MOST often controlled by a(n) 34.____

A. damper
B. gate
C. orifice
D. cross connection

35. Assume that a refrigerator motor operates continuously for excessively long periods of time. 35.____
The FIRST item you should check to locate the defect is the

A. plug in the outlet
B. door gasket
C. direction of rotation of the motor
D. motor switch

36. Assume that after replacing a defective motor for a large electric fan, you find that the fan is rotating in the wrong direction. 36.____
If the motor is a split phase motor, with the shaft at one end only, the trouble could be CORRECTED by

A. reversing the fan on its shaft
B. turning the motor end for end
C. interchanging the connections on the field terminals of the motor
D. reversing the plug in the electric outlet

37. In order to properly hang a door, shims are frequently inserted under the hinges. These shims are MOST often made of 37.____

A. cardboard
B. sheet steel
C. bakelite
D. the same materials as the hinges

38. Flooring nails are usually _______ nails. 38.____

A. casing B. common C. cut D. clinch

39. Over a doorway, to support brick, you will usually find 39.____

A. steel angles B. hanger bolts
C. wooden headers D. stirrups

40. Insulation of steam pipes is MOST often done with 40.____

A. asbestos B. celotex C. alundum D. sheathing

41. Assume that only the first few coils of a hot water convector used for heating a room are hot. 41.____
To correct this, you should FIRST

A. increase the water pressure
B. increase the water temperature
C. bleed the air out of the convector
D. clean the convector pipes

42. The MAIN reason for grounding the outer sheel of an electric fixture is to 42.____

A. provide additional support for the fixture
B. reduce the cost of installation of the fixture
C. provide a terminal to which the wires can be attached
D. reduce the chance of electric shock

43. In woodwork, countersinking is MOST often done for 43.____

A. lag screws B. carriage bolts
C. hanger bolts D. flat head screws

44. Bridging is MOST often used in connection with 44.____

A. door frames B. window openings
C. floor joists D. stud walls

45. A saddle is part of a 45.____

A. doorway B. window
C. stair well D. bulkhead

46. To make it easier to drive screws into hard wood, it is BEST to 46.____

A. use a screwdriver that is longer than that used for soft wood
B. rub the threads of the screw on a bar of soap
C. oil the screw threads
D. use a square shank screwdriver assisted by a wrench

47. In using a doweled joint to make a repair of a wooden door, it is important to remember that the dowel 47.____

A. hole must be smaller in diameter than the dowel so that there is a tight fit
B. hole must be longer than the dowel to provide a room for excess glue
C. must be of the same type of wood as the door frame
D. must be held in place by a small screw while waiting for the glue to set

48. The edges of MOST finished wood flooring are 48.____

A. tongue and groove
B. mortise and tenon
C. bevel and miter
D. lap and scarf

49. For the SMOOTHEST finish, sanding of wood should be done 49.____

A. in a circular direction
B. diagonally against the grain
C. across the grain
D. parallel with the grain

50. To prevent splintering of wood when boring a hole through it, the BEST practice is to 50.____

A. drill at a slow speed
B. use a scrap piece to back up the work
C. use an auger bit
D. ease up the pressure on the drill when the drill is almost through the wood

---

KEY (CORRECT ANSWERS)

1. C	11. C	21. A	31. D	41. C
2. D	12. B	22. A	32. D	42. D
3. C	13. A	23. C	33. B	43. D
4. A	14. D	24. B	34. A	44. C
5. B	15. D	25. B	35. B	45. A
6. A	16. B	26. C	36. C	46. B
7. D	17. A	27. B	37. A	47. B
8. C	18. B	28. C	38. C	48. A
9. B	19. B	29. B	39. A	49. D
10. C	20. D	30. C	40. A	50. B

TEST 2

DIRECTIONS: Each question or incomplete statement is followed by several suggested answers or completions. Select the one that BEST answers the question or completes the statement. *PRINT THE LETTER OF THE CORRECT ANSWER IN THE SPACE AT THE RIGHT.*

1. A *speed nut* has 1.____

   A. no threads
   B. threads that are coarser than a standard nut
   C. threads that are finer than s standard nut
   D. fewer threads than a standard nut

2. The BEST tool to use to remove the burr and sharp edge resulting from cutting tubing with a tube cutter is a 2.____

   A. file B. scraper C. reamer D. knife

3. A router is used PRINCIPALLY to 3.____

   A. clean pipe B. cut grooves in wood
   C. bend electric conduit D. sharpen tools

4. The principle of operation of a sabre saw is MOST similar to that of a ______ saw. 4.____

   A. circular B. radial C. swing D. jig

5. A full thread cutting set would have both taps and 5.____

   A. cutters B. bushings C. dies D. plugs

6. The proper flux to use for soldering electric wire connections is 6.____

   A. rosin B. killed acid
   C. borax D. zinc chloride

7. A fusestat differs from an ordinary plug fuse in that a fusestat has 7.____

   A. less current carrying capacity
   B. different size threads
   C. an aluminum shell instead of a copper shell
   D. no threads

8. A grounding type 120-volt receptacle differs from an ordinary electric receptacle MAINLY in that a grounding receptacle 8.____

   A. is larger than the ordinary receptacle
   B. has openings for a three prong plug
   C. can be used for larger machinery
   D. has a built-in circuit breaker

9. A carbide tip is MOST often found on a bit used for drilling 9.____

   A. concrete B. wood C. steel D. brass

10. The MAIN reason for using oil on an oilstone is to 10.____

    A. make the surface of the stone smoother
    B. prevent clogging of the pores of the stone
    C. reduce the number of times the stone has to be *dressed*
    D. prevent gouging of the stone's surface

11. The sum of the following numbers, 1 3/4, 3 1/6, 5 1/2, 6 5/8, and 9 1/4, is 11.____

    A. 26 1/8 B. 26 1/4 C. 26 1/2 D. 26 3/4

12. If a piece of plywood measures 5' 1 1/4" x 3' 2 1/2", the number of square feet in this board is MOST NEARLY 12.____

    A. 15.8 B. 16.1 C. 16.4 D. 16.7

13. Assume that in quantity purchases the city receives a discount of 33 1/3%. If a one gallon can of paint retails at $5.33 per gallon, the cost of 375 gallons of this paint is MOST NEARLY 13.____

    A. $1,332.50 B. $1,332.75 C. $1,333.00 D. $1,333.25

14. Assume that eight barrels of cement together weigh a total of 3004 lbs. and 12 oz. If there are four bags of cement per barrel, then the weight of one bag of cement is MOST NEARLY ______ lbs. 14.____

    A. 93.1 B. 93.5 C. 93.9 D. 94.3

15. Assume that one man cuts 50 nameplates per hour, whereas his co-worker cuts 55 nameplates per hour. At the end of 7 hours, the first man will have cut fewer nameplates than the second man by 15.____

    A. 9.3% B. 9.5% C. 9.7% D. 9.9%

16. Under the same conditions, the one of the following that dries the FASTEST is 16.____

    A. shellac B. varnish C. enamel D. lacquer

17. Interior wood trim in a building is MOST often made of 17.____

    A. hemlock B. pine C. cedar D. oak

18. Gaskets are seldom made of 18.____

    A. rubber B. lead C. asbestos D. vinyl

19. Toggle bolts are MOST frequently used to 19.____

    A. fasten shelf supports to a hollow block wall
    B. fasten furniture legs to table tops
    C. anchor machinery to a concrete floor
    D. join two pieces of sheet metal

20. Rubber will deteriorate FASTEST when it is constantly in contact with 20.____

    A. air B. water C. oil D. soapsuds

21. Stoppage of water flow is often caused by dirt <u>accumulating</u> in an elbow. 21.____
As used in the above sentence, the word <u>accumulating</u> means MOST NEARLY

A. clogging B. collecting C. rusting D. confined

22. The surface of the metal was <u>embossed</u>. 22.____
As used in the above sentence, the word <u>embossed</u> means MOST NEARLY

A. polished B. rough C. raised D. painted

Questions 23-24.

DIRECTIONS: Questions 23 and 24 are to be answered in accordance with the following paragraph.

When fixing an upper sash cord, you must also remove the lower sash. To do this, the parting strip between the sash must be removed. Now remove the cover from the weight box channel, cut off the cord as before, and pull it over the pulleys. Pull your new cord over the pulleys and down into the channel, where it may be fastened to the weight. The cord for an upper sash is cut off 1" or 2" below the pulley with the weight resting on the floor of the pocket and the cord held taut. These measurements allow for slight stretching of the cord. When the cord is cut to length, it can be pulled up over the pulley and tied with a single common knot in the end to fit into the socket in the sash groove. If the knot protrudes beyond the face of the sash, tap it gently to flatten. In this way, it will not become frayed from constant rubbing against the groove.

23. When repairing the upper sash cord, the FIRST thing to do is to 23.____

A. remove the lower sash
B. cut the existing sash cord
C. remove the parting strip
D. measure the length of new cord necessary

24. According to the above paragraph, the rope may become frayed if the 24.____

A. pulley is too small B. knot sticks out
C. cord is too long D. weight is too heavy

25. In the repair of the sash cord mentioned in the paragraph for Questions 23 and 24, the MAIN reason for cutting off the sash cord below the bottom of the pulley is to 25.____

A. prevent the cord from tangling
B. save on amount of cord used
C. prevent the sash weight from hitting the bottom of the frame in use
D. provide room for tying the knot

26. Of the following drawings, the one that would be considered an *elevation* of a building is the 26.____

A. floor plan B. front view C. cross section D. site plan

27. On a plan, the symbol shown at the right USUALLY represents a(n) 27.____

A. duplex receptacle B. electric switch
C. ceiling outlet D. pull box

28. On a plan, the symbol _____ - _____ - USUALLY represents a 28.____

A. center line
B. hidden outline
C. long break
D. dimension line

29. Assume that on a plan you see the following: 1/4" - 20 NC-2. This refers to the 29.____

A. diameter of a hole
B. size and type of screw thread
C. taper of a pin
D. scale at which the plan is drawn

30. 30.____

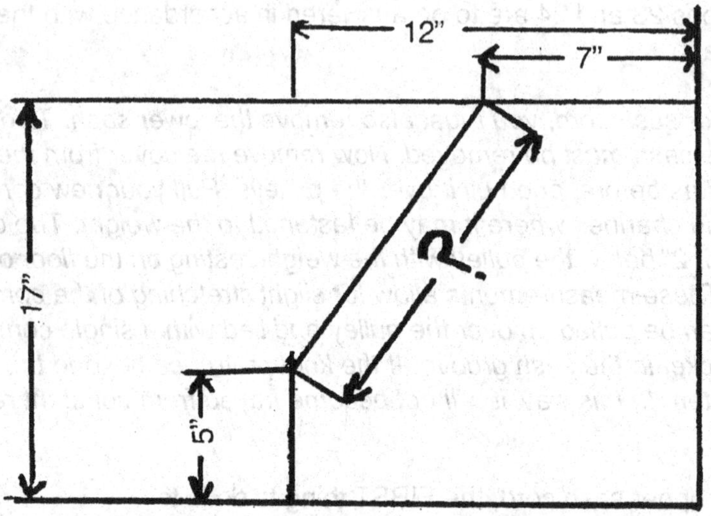

12"
7"
17"
5"
?

In reference to the above sketch, the length of the diagonal part of the plate indicated by the question mark is MOST NEARLY

A. 13"
B. 14"
C. 15"
D. 16"

31. To increase the workability of concrete without changing its strength, the BEST procedure to follow is to increase the percentage of 31.____

A. water
B. cement and sand
C. cement and water
D. water and sand

32. The MAIN reason for covering freshly poured concrete with tar paper is to 32.____

A. prevent evaporation of water
B. stop people from walking on the concrete
C. protect the concrete from rain
D. keep back any earth that may fall on the concrete

33. The MAIN reason for using air-entrained cement in sidewalks is to 33.____

A. protect the concrete from the effects of freezing
B. color the concrete
C. speed up the setting time of the concrete
D. make the concrete more workable

34. Assume that a reinforcing bar used for concrete is badly rusted. Before using this bar, 34.____

A. it is not necessary to remove any rust
B. only loose rust need be removed
C. all rust should be removed
D. all rust should be removed and a coat of red lead paint is applied

35. Assume that freshly poured concrete has been exposed to freezing temperatures for 6 hours. In all likelihood, this concrete 35.____

A. has been permanently damaged
B. will harden properly as soon as the air temperature warms up
C. will harden properly even though the temperature remains below freezing
D. will eventually harden properly, but it will take much longer than usual

36. Assume that concrete for a floor in a play yard is to be placed directly on the earth. On checking, you find that, because of a recent rain, the earth is damp. You should 36.____

A. wait till the sun dries the earth before placing the concrete
B. use a waterproofing material between the concrete slab and the earth
C. use less water in the concrete mix
D. ignore the damp earth and place the concrete as you normally would

37. The MAJOR disadvantage of *floating* the surface of concrete too much is that the 37.____

A. surface will become too rough
B. surface will become weak and will wear rapidly
C. initial set will be disturbed
D. concrete cannot be cured properly

38. In addition to water and sand, mortar mix for a cinder block wall is usually made of 38.____

A. gravel and lime
B. plaster and cement
C. gravel and cement
D. lime and cement

39. The *nominal* size of a standard cinder block is 39.____

A. 8" x 6" x 16"
B. 8" x 8" x 16"
C. 8" x 12" x 12"
D. 6" x 8" x 12"

40. The *bond* of a brick wall refers to the 40.____

A. arrangement of headers and stretchers
B. time it takes for the mortar to set
C. way a brick wall is tied in to an intersecting wall
D. type of mortar used in the wall

41. The purpose of *tooling* when erecting a brick wall is to 41.____

A. cut the brick to fit into a small space
B. insure that the brick is laid level
C. compact the mortar at the joints
D. hold the brick in place till the mortar sets

42. Mortar is BEST cleaned off the face of a brick wall by using 42.____

A. muriatic acid
B. lye
C. oxalic acid
D. sodium hypochlorite

43. A brick wall is *pointed* to 43.____

A. make sure it is the correct height
B. repair the mortar joints
C. set the brick in place
D. arrange the mortar bed before setting the brick

44. The second coat in a three-coat plaster job is the _____ coat. 44.____

A. scratch
B. brown
C. putty
D. lime

45. To repair fine cracks in a plastered wall, the PROPER material to use is 45.____

A. lime
B. cement wash
C. perlite
D. spackle

46. Gypsum lath for plastering is purchased in 46.____

A. strips 5/16" x 1 1/2" x 4'
B. rolls 3/8" x 48" x 96"
C. boards 1/2" x 16" x 48"
D. sheets 5/16" x 27" x 96"

47. The PRINCIPAL reason for using acoustic tile instead of ordinary tile is that the acoustic tile 47.____

A. deadens sound
B. is easier to apply
C. is longer lasting
D. costs less

48. The MAXIMUM thickness of the finish coat of white plaster is MOST NEARLY 48.____

A. 1/8"
B. 1/4"
C. 3/8"
D. 1/2"

49. When using tape to conceal joints in dry wall construction, the FIRST operation is 49.____

A. channelling the grooves between boards
B. applying cement to the joints
C. sanding the edges of the joints
D. packing the tape into the joints

50. For the FIRST coat of plaster on wire lath, plaster of paris is mixed with 50.____

A. cement
B. sand
C. lime
D. mortar

KEY (CORRECT ANSWERS)

1. A
2. C
3. B
4. D
5. C

6. A
7. B
8. B
9. A
10. B

11. B
12. C
13. A
14. C
15. D

16. D
17. B
18. D
19. A
20. C

21. B
22. C
23. C
24. B
25. C

26. B
27. C
28. A
29. B
30. A

31. C
32. A
33. A
34. B
35. A

36. D
37. B
38. D
39. B
40. A

41. C
42. A
43. B
44. B
45. D

46. C
47. A
48. A
49. B
50. B

EXAMINATION SECTION
TEST 1

DIRECTIONS: Each question or incomplete statement is followed by several suggested answers or completions. Select the one that BEST answers the question or completes the statement. *PRINT THE LETTER OF THE CORRECT ANSWER IN THE SPACE AT THE RIGHT.*

1. 1.____

1 2 3

4

The saw that is used PRINCIPALLY where curved cuts are to be made is numbered

A. 1 B. 2 C. 3 D. 4

2. 2.____

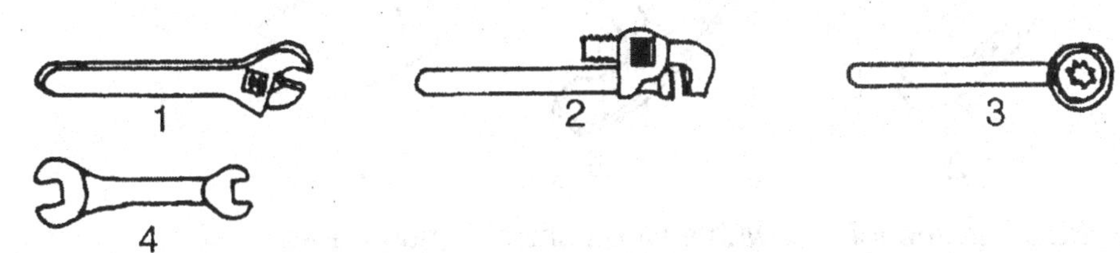

The wrench that is used PRINCIPALLY for pipe work is numbered

A. 1 B. 2 C. 3 D. 4

3. 3.____

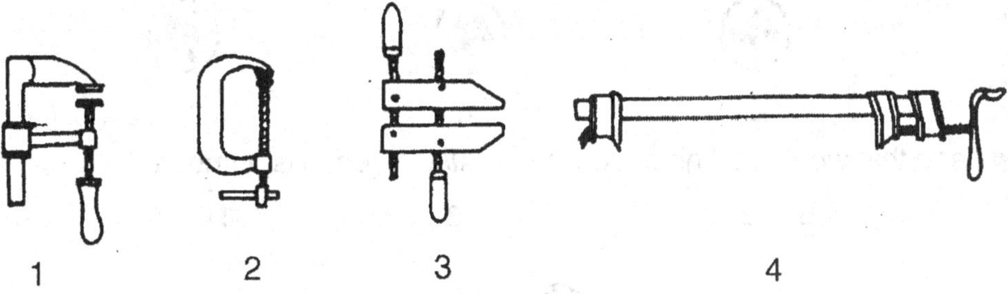

The carpenter's *hand screw* is numbered

A. 1 B. 2 C. 3 D. 4

4. 4.____

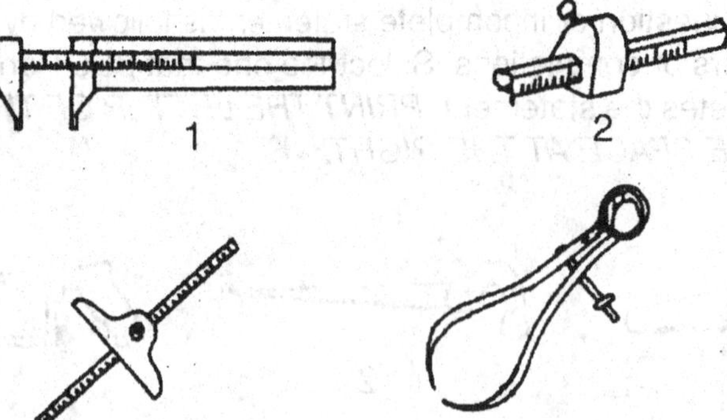

3 4

The tool used to measure the depth of a hole is numbered

A. 1 B. 2 C. 3 D. 4

5. 5.____

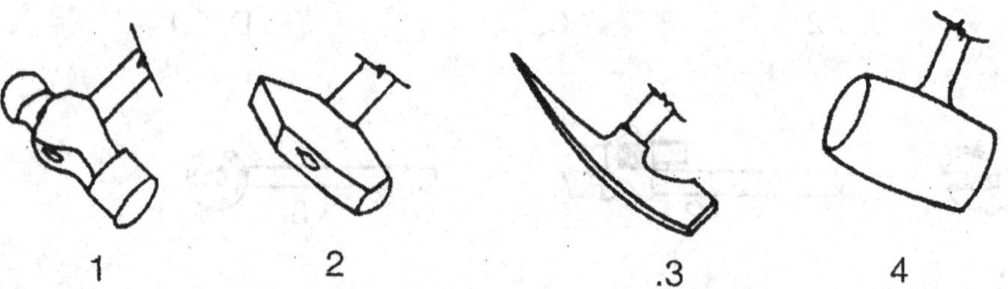

1 2 .3 4

The tool that is BEST suited for use with a wood chisel is numbered

A. 1 B. 2 C. 3 D. 4

6. 6.____

1 2 3 4

The screw head that would be tightened with an *Allen* wrench is numbered

A. 1 B. 2 C. 3 D. 4

7. 7.____

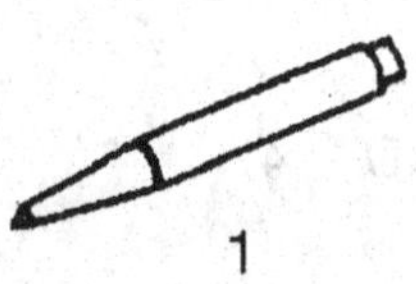

1 2

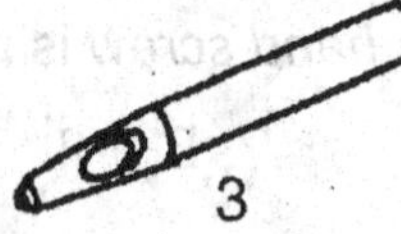

3

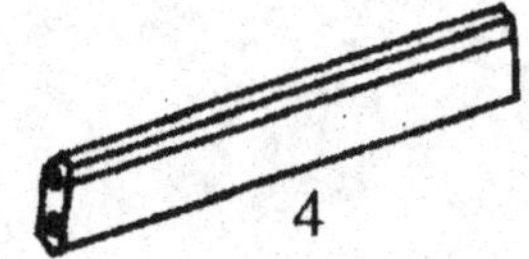

4

The center punch is numbered

A. 1 B. 2 C. 3 D. 4

8. 8.____

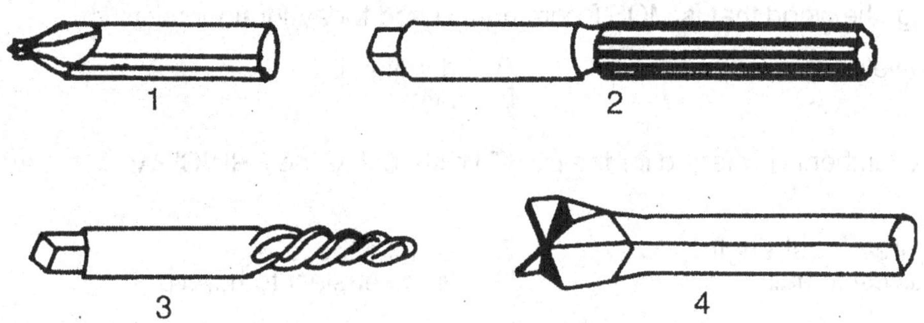

1 2

3 4

The tool used to drill a hole in concrete is numbered

A. 1 B. 2 C. 3 D. 4

9. 9.____

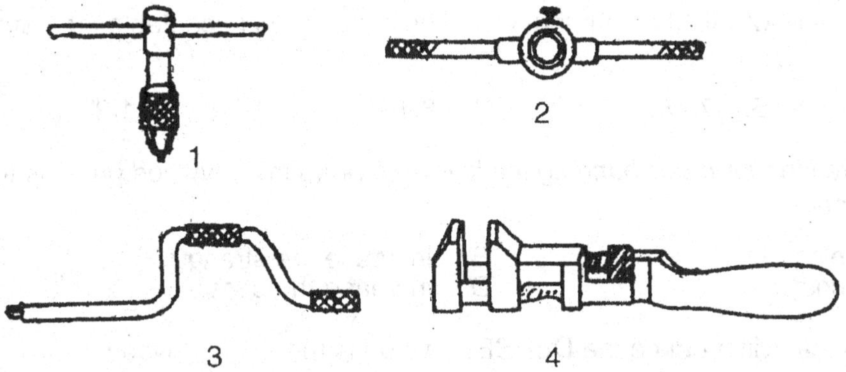

1 2

3 4

The wrench whose PRINCIPAL purpose to to hold taps for threading is numbered

A. 1 B. 2 C. 3 D. 4

10. 10.____

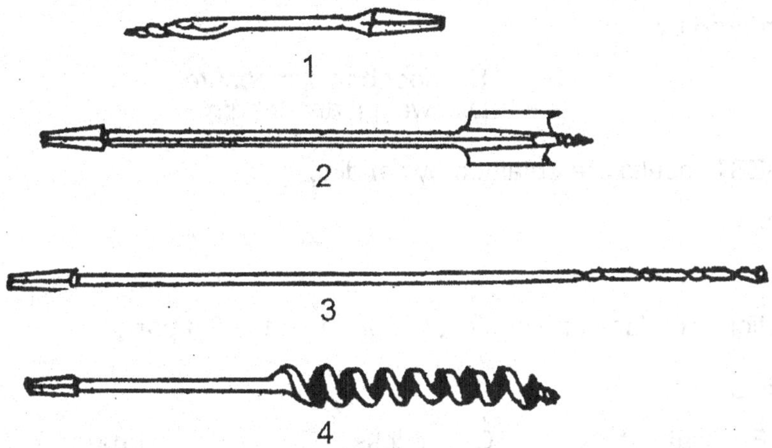

1

2

3

4

The electrician's bit is indicated by the number

A. 1 B. 2 C. 3 D. 4

11. The ends of a joist in a brick building are cut to a bevel. This is done PRINCIPALLY to prevent damage to 11.____

A. joist B. floor C. sill D. wall

12. Of the following, the wood that is MOST commonly used today for floor joists is 12.____

A. long leaf yellow pine
B. douglas fir
C. oak
D. birch

13. Quarter-sawed lumber is preferred for the BEST finished flooring PRINCIPALLY because it 13.____

A. has the greatest strength
B. shrinks the least
C. is the easiest to nail
D. is the easiest to handle

14. A tool used in hanging doors is a 14.____

A. miter gauge
B. line level
C. try square
D. butt gauge

15. Of the following, the MAXIMUM height that would be considered acceptable for a stair riser is 15.____

A. 6 1/2"
B. 7 1/2"
C. 8 1/2"
D. 9 1/2"

16. The PRINCIPAL reason for *cross banding* the layers of wood in a plywood panel is to ______ of the panel. 16.____

A. reduce warping
B. increase the strength
C. reduce the cost
D. increase the beauty

17. The part of a tree that will produce the DENSEST wood is the ______ wood. 17.____

A. spring
B. summer
C. sap
D. heart

18. Casing nails MOST NEARLY resemble ______ nails. 18.____

A. common
B. roofing
C. form
D. finishing

19. Lumber in quantity is ordered by 19.____

A. cubic feet
B. foot board measure
C. lineal feet
D. weight and length

20. For finishing of wood, BEST results are obtained by sanding 20.____

A. with a circular motion
B. against the grain
C. with the grain
D. with a circular motion on edges and against the grain on the flat parts

21. A *chase* in a brick wall is a 21.____

A. pilaster
B. waterstop
C. recess
D. corbel

22. Parging refers to 22.____

A. increasing the thickness of a brick wall
B. plastering the back of face brickwork
C. bonding face brick to backing blocks
D. leveling each course of brick

23. The PRINCIPAL reason for requiring brick to be wetted before laying is that 23._____

    A. less water is required in the mortar
    B. efflorescence is prevented
    C. the brick will not absorb as much water from the mortar
    D. cool brick is easier to handle

24. In brickwork, muriatic acid is commonly used to 24._____

    A. increase the strength of the mortar
    B. etch the brick
    C. waterproof the wall
    D. clean the wall

25. Cement mortar can be made easier to work by the addition of a small quantity of 25._____

    A. lime B. soda C. litharge D. plaster

26. Headers in brickwork are used to ______ the wall. 26._____

    A. strengthen B. reduce the cost of
    C. speed the erection of D. align

27. Joints in brick walls are tooled 27._____

    A. immediately after each brick is laid
    B. after the mortar has had its initial set
    C. after the entire wall is completed
    D. 28 days after the wall has been built

28. If cement mortar has begun to set before it can be used in a wall, the BEST thing to do is to 28._____

    A. use the mortar immediately as is
    B. add a small quantity of lime
    C. add some water and mix thoroughly
    D. discard the mortar

29. A *bat* in brickwork is a 29._____

    A. brace to hold a wall temporarily in place
    B. stick used to aid in mixing of mortar
    C. broken piece of brick used to fill short spaces
    D. curved brick used in ornamental work

30. The proportions by volume of cement, lime, and sand in a cement-lime mortar should be, according to the Building Code, 30._____

    A. 1:1:3 B. 2:1:6 C. 1:1:6 D. 1:2:6

31. The BEST flux to use when soldering galvanized iron is 31._____

    A. killed acid B. sal-ammoniac
    C. muriatic acid D. resin

32. When soldering a vertical joint, the soldering iron should be tinned on ______ side(s). 32.____

A. 1 B. 2 C. 3 D. 4

33. The difference between *right hand* and *left hand* tin snips is the 33.____

A. relative position of the cutting jaws
B. shape of the cutting jaws
C. shape of the handles
D. relative position of the handles

34. A machine used to bend sheet metal is called a 34.____

A. router B. planer C. brake D. swage

35. The type of solder that would be used in *hard soldering* would be ______ solder. 35.____

A. bismuth B. wiping C. 50-50 D. silver

36. Roll roofing material is usually felt which has been impregnated with 36.____

A. cement B. mastic C. tar D. latex

37. The purpose of flashing on roofs is to 37.____

A. secure roofing materials to the roof
B. make it easier to lay the roofing
C. prevent leaks through the roof
D. insulate the roof from excessive heat

38. The tool used to spread hot pitch on a three-ply roofing job is a 38.____

A. mop B. spreader C. pusher D. broom

39. The cutting of glass can be facilitated by dipping the cutting wheel in 39.____

A. *3-in-1* oil B. water C. lard D. kerosene

40. The strips of metal used to hold glass to the window frame while it is being puttied are called 40.____

A. hold-downs B. points C. wedges D. triangles

41. The type of chain used with sash weights is ______ link. 41.____

A. flat B. round
C. figure-eight D. basket-weave

42. The material that would be used to seal around a window frame is 42.____

A. oakum B. litharge C. grout D. calking

43. The function of a window sill is MOST NEARLY the same as that of a 43.____

A. jamb B. coping C. lintel D. brick

44. Lightweight plaster would be made with 44.____

A. sand B. cinders C. potash D. vermiculite

45. The FIRST coat of plaster to be applied on a three-coat plaster job is the ______ coat. 45.____

A. brown B. scratch C. white D. keene

46. Screeds in plaster work are used to 46.____

A. remove larger sizes of sand
B. hold the batch of plaster before it is applied
C. apply the plaster to the wall
D. guide the plasterer in making, an even wall

47. The FIRST coat of plaster over rock lath should be a ______ plaster. 47.____

A. gypsum B. lime
C. portland cement D. puzzolan cement

48. In plastering, a *hawk* is used to ______ plaster. 48.____

A. apply B. hold C. scratch D. smooth

49. When mixing concrete by hand, the order in which the ingredients should be mixed is: 49.____

A. water, cement, sand, stone
B. sand, cement, water, stone
C. stone, water, sand, cement
D. stone, sand, cement, water

50. The PRINCIPAL reason for covering a concrete sidewalk with straw or paper after the concrete has been poured is to 50.____

A. prevent people from walking on the concrete while it is still wet
B. impart a rough non-slip surface to the concrete
C. prevent excessive evaporation of water in the concrete
D. shorten the length of time it would take for the concrete to harden

---

KEY (CORRECT ANSWERS)

1. B	11. D	21. C	31. C	41. A
2. B	12. B	22. B	32. A	42. D
3. C	13. B	23. C	33. A	43. B
4. C	14. D	24. D	34. C	44. D
5. D	15. B	25. A	35. D	45. B
6. C	16. A	26. A	36. C	46. D
7. A	17. D	27. B	37. C	47. A
8. D	18. D	28. D	38. A	48. B
9. A	19. B	29. C	39. D	49. D
10. C	20. C	30. C	40. B	50. C

TEST 2

DIRECTIONS: Each question or incomplete statement is followed by several suggested answers or completions. Select the one that BEST answers the question or completes the statement. *PRINT THE LETTER OF THE CORRECT ANSWER IN THE SPACE AT THE RIGHT.*

1. When colored concrete is required, the colors used should be 1.____

   A. colors in oil
   B. mineral pigments
   C. tempera colors
   D. water colors

2. Concrete is *rubbed* with a(n) 2.____

   A. emery wheel
   B. carborundum brick
   C. sandstone
   D. alundum stick

3. To prevent concrete from sticking to forms, the forms should be painted with 3.____

   A. oil
   B. kerosene
   C. water
   D. lime

4. The reinforcement in a concrete floor slab is referred to as 6"-6" x #6-#6. The type of reinforcing that is being used is 4.____

   A. steel bars
   B. wire mesh
   C. angle irons
   D. grating plate

5. One method of measuring the consistency of a concrete mix is by means of a ______ test. 5.____

   A. penetration
   B. flow
   C. slump
   D. weight

6. A chemical that is sometimes used to prevent the freezing of concrete in cold weather is 6.____

   A. alum
   B. glycerine
   C. calcium chloride
   D. sodium nitrate

7. The one of the following that is LEAST commonly used for columns is 7.____

   A. wide flange beams
   B. angles
   C. concrete-filled pipe
   D. *I* beams

8. Fire protection of steel floor beams is MOST frequently accomplished by the use of 8.____

   A. gypsum block
   B. brick
   C. rock wool fill
   D. vermiculite gypsum plaster

9. A *Pittsburgh lock* is a(n) 9.____

   A. emergency door lock
   B. sheet metal joint
   C. elevator safety
   D. boiler valve

10. In order to drill a hole at right angle to the horizontal axis of a round bar, the bar should be held in a 10.____

    A. step block
    B. C-block
    C. hand pliers
    D. V-block

11. The procedure to follow in the lubrication of maintenance shop equipment is to lubricate 11.____

 A. when you can spare the time
 B. only when necessary
 C. at regular intervals
 D. when the equipment is in operation

12. Of the following items, the one which is NOT used in making fastenings to masonry or plaster walls is a(n) 12.____

 A. lead shield B. expansion bolt
 C. rawl plug D. steel bushing

13. When a common straight ladder is used to paint a wall, the safe distance that the foot of the ladder should be set away from the wall is MOST NEARLY ______ the length of the ladder. 13.____

 A. one-eighth B. one-quarter
 C. one-half D. five-eighths

14. The term *bell and spigot* usually refers to 14.____

 A. refrigerator motors B. cast iron pipes
 C. steam radiator outlets D. electrical receptacles

15. In plumbing work, a valve which allows water to flow in one direction only is commonly known as a ______ valve. 15.____

 A. check B. globe C. gate D. stop

16. A pipe coupling is BEST used to connect two pieces of pipe of 16.____

 A. the same diameter in a straight line
 B. the same diameter at right angles to each other
 C. different diameters at a 45° angle
 D. different diameters at an 1/8th bend

17. A fitting or pipe with many outlets relatively close together is commonly called a 17.____

 A. manifold B. gooseneck
 C. flange union D. return bend

18. To locate the center in the end of a sound shaft, the BEST tool to use is a(n) 18.____

 A. ruler B. divider
 C. hermaphrodite caliper D. micrometer

19. When cutting a piece of 1 1/4" O.D. 20 gauge brass tubing with a hand hacksaw, it is BEST to use a blade having ______ teeth per inch. 19.____

 A. 14 B. 18 C. 22 D. 32

20. When cutting a piece of 1" O.D. extra-heavy pipe with a pipe cutter, a burr usually forms on the inside and the outside of the pipe. These burrs are BEST removed by means of a pipe 20.____

 A. tap and a file B. wrench and rough stone
 C. reamer and a file D. drill and a chisel

21. Artificial respiration should be started immediately on a man who has suffered an electric shock if he is 21.____

A. *unconscious* and breathing
B. *unconscious* and not breathing
C. *conscious* and in a daze
D. *conscious* and badly burned

22. The fuse of a certain circuit has blown and is replaced with a fuse of the same rating which also blows when the switch is closed. 22.____
In this case,

A. a fuse of higher current rating should be used
B. a fuse of higher voltage rating should be used
C. the fuse should be temporarily replaced by a heavy piece of wire
D. the circuit should be checked

23. Operating an incandescent electric light bulb at less than its rated voltage will result in 23.____

A. shorter life and brighter light
B. longer life and dimmer light
C. brighter light and longer life
D. dimmer light and shorter life

24. In order to control a lamp from two different positions, it is necessary to use 24.____

A. two single pole switches
B. one single pole switch and one four-way switch
C. two three-way switches
D. one single pole switch and one four-way switch

25. 25.____

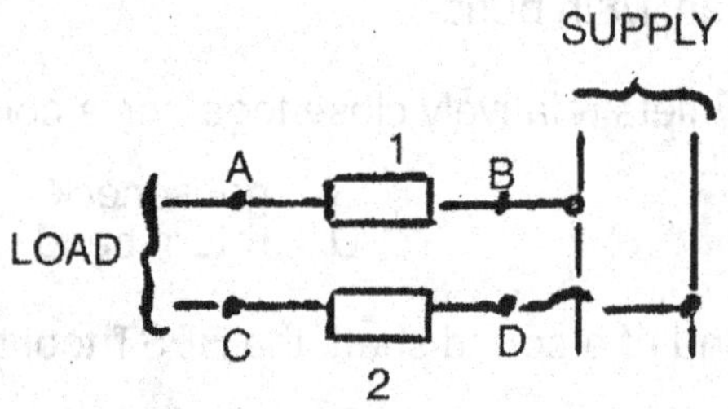

One method of testing fuses is to connect a pair of test lamps in the circuit in such a manner that the test lamp will light up if the fuse is good and will remain dark if the fuse is bad. In the above illustration 1 and 2 are fuses.
In order to test if fuse 1 is bad, test lamps should be connected between

A. A and B B. B and D C. A and D D. C and B

26. The PRINCIPAL reason for the grounding of electrical equipment and circuits is to 26.____

A. prevent short circuits
B. insure safety from shock
C. save power
D. increase voltage

27. The ordinary single-pole flush wall type switch must be connected 27.____

A. across the line
B. in the *hot* conductor
C. in the grounded conductor
D. in the white conductor

28. A D.C. shunt motor runs in the wrong direction. This fault can be CORRECTED by 28.____

A. reversing the connections of both the field and the armature
B. interchanging the connections of either main or auxiliar windings
C. interchanging the connections to either the field or the armature windings
D. interchanging the connections to the line of the power leads

29. The MOST common type of motor that can be used with both A.C. and D.C. sources is the ______ motor. 29.____

A. compound
B. repulsion
C. series
D. shunt

30. A fluorescent fixture in a new building has been in use for several months without trouble. Recently, the ends of the fluorscent lamp have remained lighted when the light was switched off. 30.____
The BEST way to clear up this trouble is to replace the

A. lamp
B. ballast
C. starter
D. sockets

31. The BEST wood to use for handles of tools such as axes and hammers is 31.____

A. hemlock
B. pine
C. oak
D. hickory

32. A *hanger bolt* 32.____

A. has a square head
B. is bent in a *U* shape
C. has a different type of thread at each end
D. is threaded the entire length from point to head

33. A stone frequently used to sharpen tools is 33.____

A. carborundum
B. bauxite
C. resin
D. slate

34. A strike plate is MOST closely associated with a 34.____

A. lock
B. sash
C. butt
D. tie rod

35. The material that distinguishes a terrazzo floor from an ordinary concrete floor is 35.____

A. cinders
B. marble chip
C. cut stone
D. non-slip aggregate

36. A room is 7'6" wide by 9'0" long with a ceiling height of 8'0". One gallon of flat paint will cover approximately 400 square feet of wall. 36.____
The number of gallons of this paint required to paint the walls of this room, making no deductions for windows or doors, is MOST NEARLY ______ gallon.

A. 1/4
B. 1/2
C. 3/4
D. 1

37. The cost of a certain job is broken down as follows: 37.____

Materials	$375
Rental of equipment	120
Labor	315

The percentage of the total cost of the job that can be charged to materials is MOST NEARLY

A. 40% B. 42% C. 44% D. 46%

38. By trial, it is found that by using two cubic feet of sand, a five cubic foot batch of concrete is produced. 38.____
Using the same proportions, the amount of sand required to produce 2 cubic yards of concrete is MOST NEARLY ______ cu.ft.

A. 20 B. 22 C. 24 D. 26

39. It takes 4 men 6 days to do a certain job. 39.____
Working at the same speed, the number of days it will take 3 men to do this job is

A. 7 B. 8 C. 9 D. 10

40. The cost of rawl plugs is $2.75 per gross. The cost of 2,448 rawl plugs is 40.____

A. $46.75 B. $47.25 C. $47.75 D. $48.25

41. *Rigidity of the hammer handle enables the operator to control and direct the force of the blow.* 41.____
As used above, *rigidity* means MOST NEARLY

A. straightness
B. strength
C. shape
D. stiffness

42. *For precision work, center punches are ground to a fine tapered point.* As used above, *tapered* means MOST NEARLY 42.____

A. conical B. straight C. accurate D. smooth

43. *There are limitations to the drilling of metals by hand power.* 43.____
As used above, *limitations* means MOST NEARLY

A. advantages
B. restrictions
C. difficulties
D. benefits

Questions 44-45.

DIRECTIONS: Questions 44 and 45 are based on the following paragraph.

Because electric drills run at high speed, the cutting edges of a twist drill are heated quickly. If the metal is thick, the drill point must be withdrawn from the hole frequently to cool it and clear out chips. Forcing the drill continuously into a deep hole will heat it, thereby spoiling its temper and cutting edges. A portable electric drill has the advantage that it can be taken to the work and used to drill holes in material too large to handle in a drill press.

44. According to the above paragraph, overheating of a twist drill will 44.____

A. slow down the work
B. cause excessive drill breakage
C. dull the drill
D. spoil the accuracy of the work

45. According to the above paragraph, one method of preventing overheating of a twist drill is to 45.____

A. use cooling oil
B. drill a smaller pilot hole first
C. use a drill press
D. remove the drill from the work frequently

Questions 46-50.

DIRECTIONS: Questions 46 to 50 are to be answered in accordance with the sketch shown below.

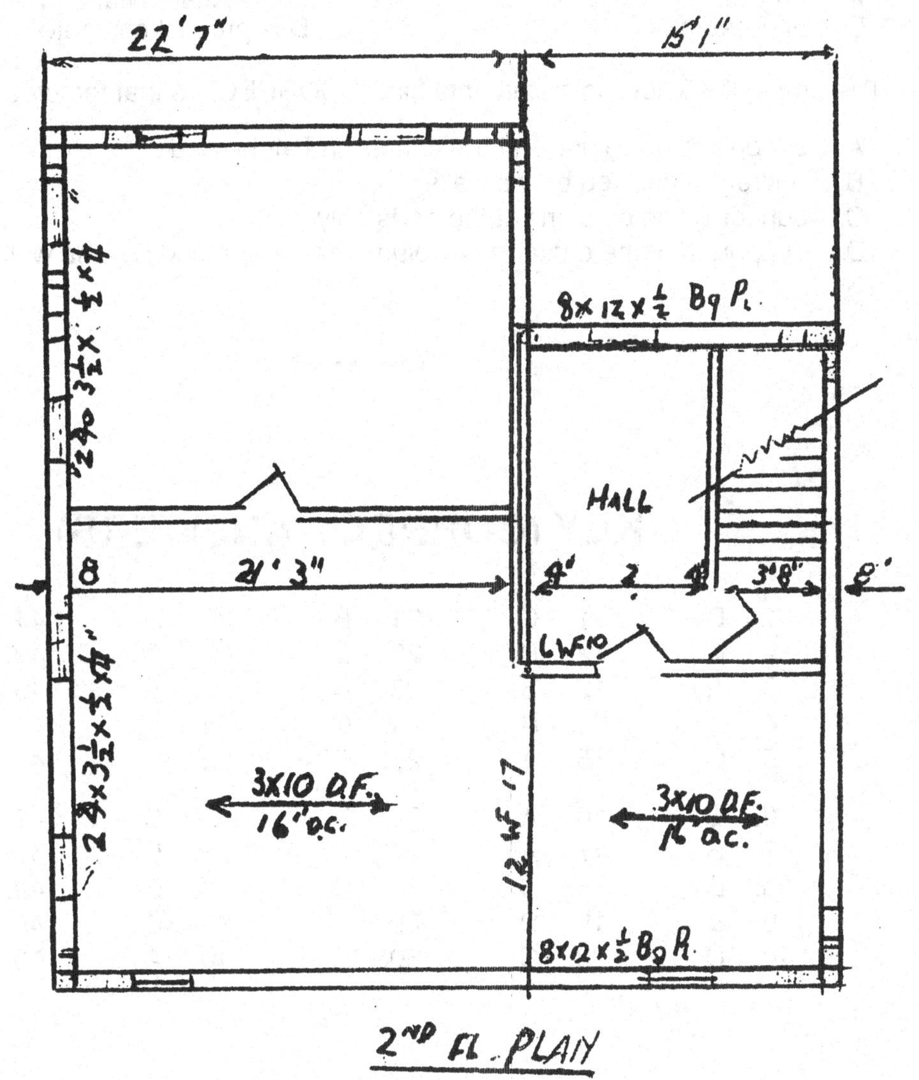

46. The one of the following statements that is CORRECT is the building 46.____

A. is of fireproof construction
B. has masonry walls with wood joists
C. is of wood frame construction
D. has timber joists and girders

47. The one of the following statements that is CORRECT is 47.____

A. the stairway from the ground continues through the roof
B. there are two means of egress from the second floor of this building
C. the door on the second floor stair landing opens in the direction of egress
D. the entire stair is shown on this plan

48. The width of the hall is 48.____

A. 10'3" B. 10'5" C. 10'7" D. 10'9"

49. The lintels shown are 49.____

A. angles B. a channel and an angle
C. an I-beam D. precast concrete

50. The one of the following statements that is CORRECT is that the steel beam is 50.____

A. supported by columns at the center and at the ends
B. entirely supported by the walls
C. supported on columns at the ends only
D. supported at the center by a column and at the ends by the walls

---

KEY (CORRECT ANSWERS)

1. B	11. C	21. B	31. D	41. D
2. B	12. D	22. D	32. C	42. A
3. A	13. B	23. B	33. A	43. B
4. B	14. B	24. C	34. A	44. C
5. C	15. A	25. C	35. B	45. D
6. C	16. A	26. B	36. C	46. B
7. B	17. A	27. B	37. D	47. C
8. D	18. C	28. C	38. B	48. D
9. B	19. D	29. C	39. B	49. A
10. D	20. C	30. C	40. A	50. D

EXAMINATION SECTION
TEST 1

DIRECTIONS: Each question or incomplete statement is followed by several suggested answers or completions. Select the one that BEST answers the question or completes the statement. *PRINT THE LETTER OF THE CORRECT ANSWER IN THE SPACE AT THE RIGHT.*

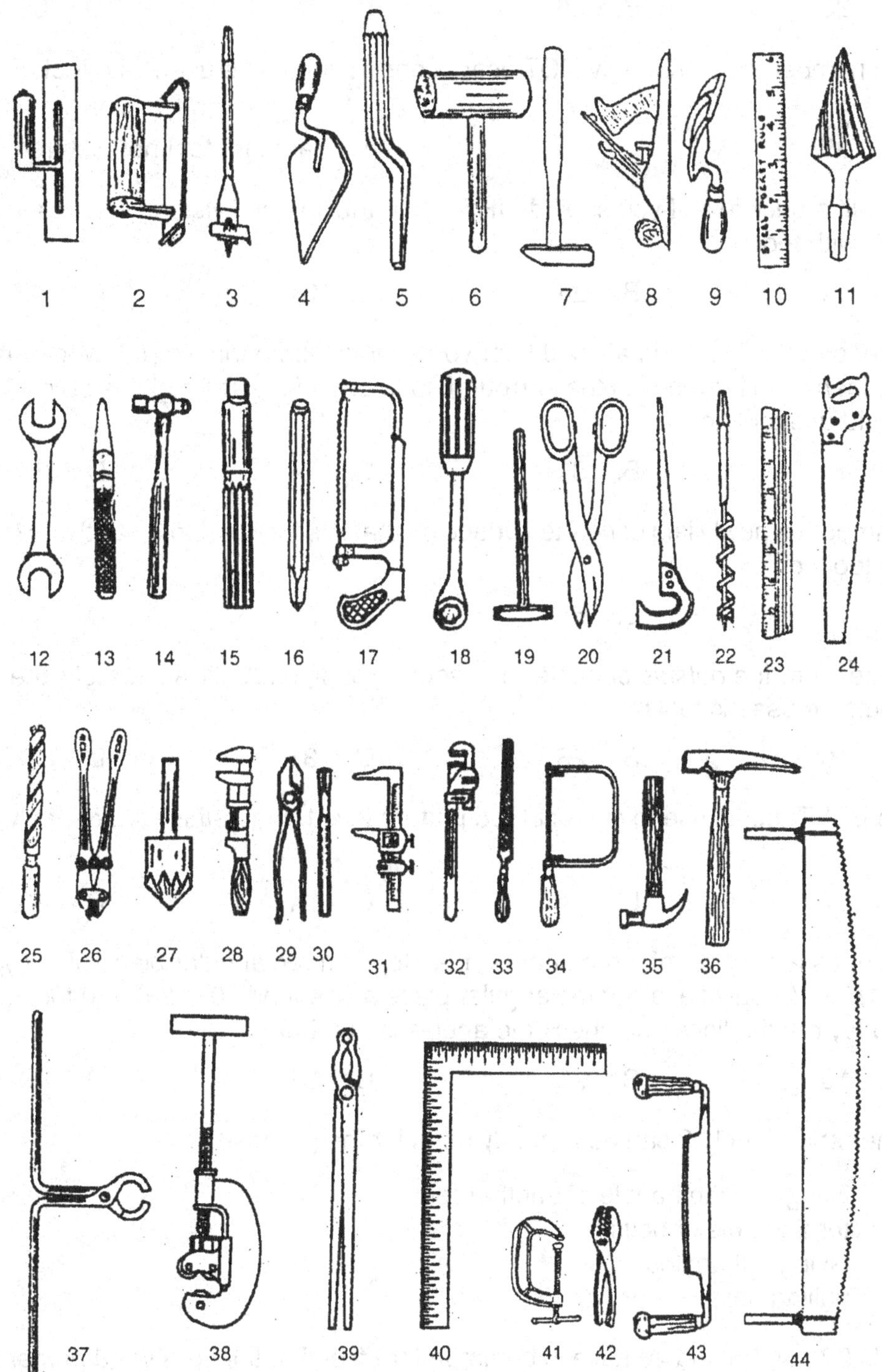

1. Of the following, which group of three tools is used *most nearly* in the same way? 1.____

   A. Tools 4, 21, 39
   B. Tools 11, 16, 42
   C. Tools 14, 35, 36
   D. Tools 5, 6, 13

2. If you want to cut a disc out of sheet metal, you should use tool no. 2.____

   A. 20 B. 26 C. 29 D. 38

3. Tool number 25 is ordinarily NOT used alone; it should be used with tool no. 3.____

   A. 28
   B. 35
   C. 39
   D. another tool not pictured

4. To split a brick in half you should FIRST chip the line of division all the way around the brick with tool no. 4.____

   A. 14 B. 24 C. 34 D. 36

5. To repair wide cracks in a wood floor you should glue a thin strip of wood into the crack and then level it even with the surrounding floor surface.To level this strip of wood you should use tool no. 5.____

   A. 1 B. 8 C. 24 D. 33

6. To smooth a newly laid concrete surface so that it is free of ripples and marks, you should use tool no. 6.____

   A. 1 B. 6 C. 8 D. 9

7. To measure the *outside* diameter of a section of pipe MOST accurately, the tool that should be used is tool no. 7.____

   A. 10 B. 23 C. 31 D. 40

8. The BEST tool to use to cut a curved pattern in a 1/4 inch-thick sheet of plywood is tool no. 8.____

   A. 17 B. 24 C. 34 D. 43

9. If you, as a member of a repair crew, plan to cut a rectangular piece of plywood measuring 18" x 12" out of a larger rectangular piece measuring 30" x 24", the tool that will BEST help lay out the lines and check the angles is number 9.____

   A. 10 B. 23 C. 31 D. 40

10. Either end of tool 12 can be *properly* used for the purpose of 10.____

    A. fitting into the handle of another tool
    B. turning nuts or bolts
    C. laying out angles
    D. pulling nails

11. Tools 22, 24, 35 and 40 have in common that fact that they are used *primarily* in 11.____

    A. masonry
    B. plumbing
    C. sheet metal work
    D. woodworking

12. Which tool requires the use of BOTH hands on the tool to operate it properly? 12.____

A. Tool 8 B. Tool 12 C. Tool 20 D. Tool 24

13. Of the following, the tool designed to be used for turning nuts of various sizes is tool no. 13.____

A. 19 B. 28 C. 29 D. 31

14. To cut a section of pipe to the required length, the MOST appropriate tool is number 14.____

A. 20 B. 29 C. 31 D. 38

15. In the picture below of a roof, which one of the numbered arrows points to the "flashing"? 15.____

A. 1 B. 2 C. 3 D. 4

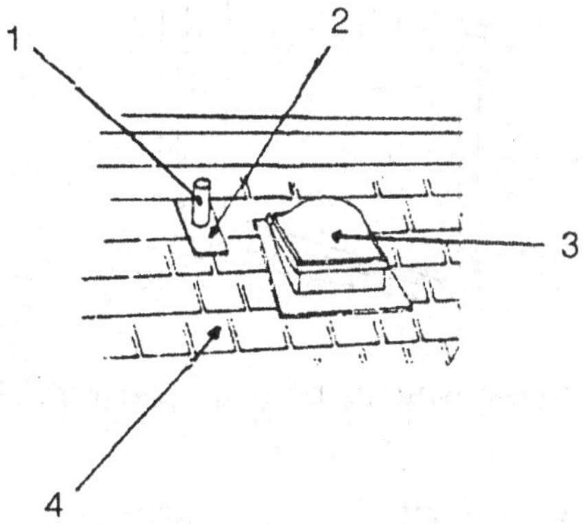

1
2
3
4

16. The function of glazier's points is to 16.____

A. keep the putty from dirtying the glass
B. make it easy to cut glass in a straight line
C. hold a pane of glass in place
D. aid in applying putty evenly around the glass

17. It is *desirable* for a putty knife used for patching plaster cracks to be flexible because a flexible putty knife 17.____

A. makes it difficult for the user to cut his hands while applying the plaster
B. is easier to keep clean than one made of rigid material
C. can press the patching materials into the crack, filling it completely
D. makes it possible to pick up the exact amount of plaster required

18. Using a fuse with a *larger* rated capacity than that of the circuit is 18.____

A. *advisable;* such use prevents the fuse from blowing
B. *advisable;* larger capacity fuses last longer than smaller capacity fuses
C. *inadvisable;* larger capacity fuses are more expensive than smaller capacity fuses
D. *inadvisable;* such use may cause a fire

19. You can MOST easily tell when a screw-in type fuse has blown because the center of the strip of metal in the fuse is 19.____

A. broken B. visible
C. nicked D. cool to the touch

20. In the picture below, which of the numbered arrows points to the door "jamb"? 20.____

A. 1 B. 2 C. 3 D. 4

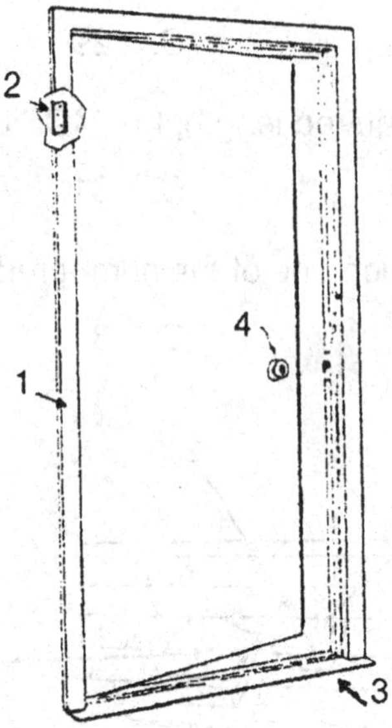

21. Of the following, the MAIN reason why flashing is used in the building trade is to make an area 21.____

A. decorative B. watertight C. level D. heat-resistant

22. To prepare a ready-mixed concrete material for use, you FIRST add 22.____

A. gravel B. salt C. sand D. water

23. When working on wet floors with an electrically powered tool, additional safety against electric shock can BEST be provided by 23.____

A. a longer electric cord
B. an AC-DC converter
C. rubber gloves
D. loose clothing

24. Which one of the wrenches pictured below is designed to grip round pipes in making plumbing repairs? 24.____

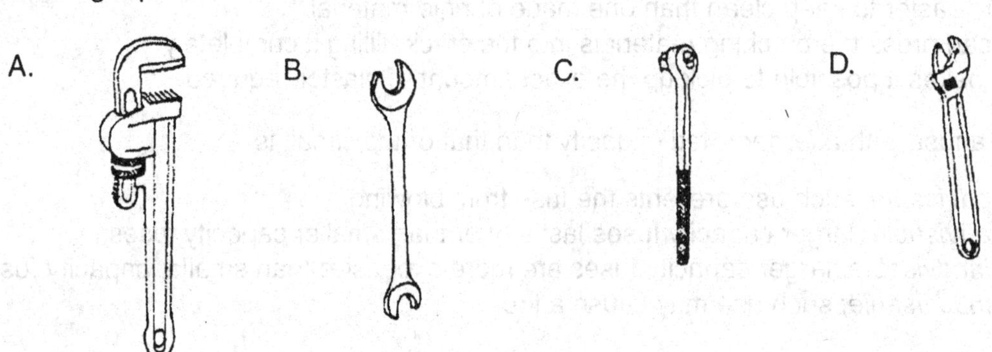

25. Which one of the saws pictured below would be BEST to use to cut steel bar stock? 25.____

A. 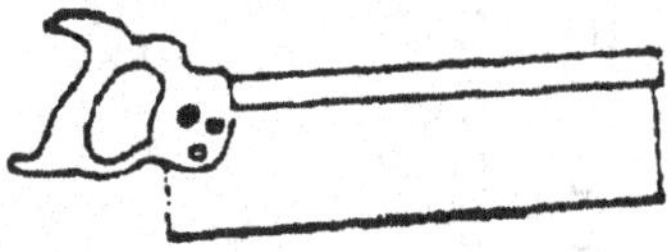 B.

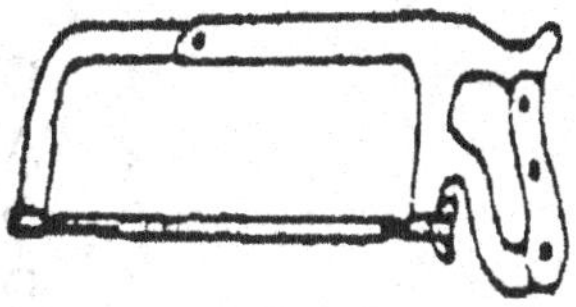

C. 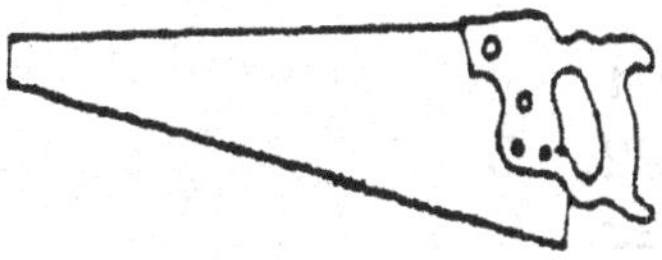 D.

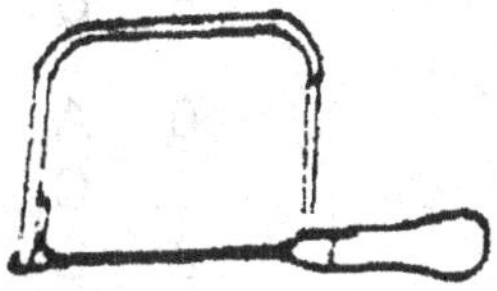

26. Which one of the hammers pictured below is a claw hammer? 26.____

A. 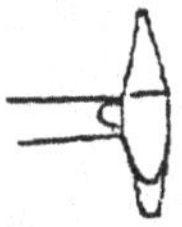 B.  C.  D.

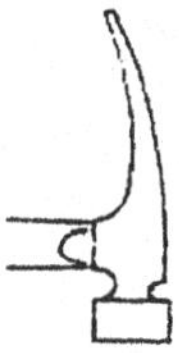

27. The terms "dovetail" and "dowel" are used to describe types of 27.____

A. glues B. joints C. clamps D. tile

28. A three-prong plug on a power tool used on a 120-volt line indicates that the tool 28.____

A. may be grounded against electric shock
B. is provided with additional power through the third prong
C. has a defect and should be returned
D. is adaptable for use with AC or DC current

29. A bit and brace should be used to 29.____

A. saw wood
B. glue wood
C. drill holes
D. support or hold work

30. Which of the following would ordinarily occur FIRST in a toilet tank after the handle is pushed down to flush the toilet? 30.____

A. Float ball drops with water level, opening the ballcock assembly through which fresh water flows into the tank
B. Tank ball sinks slowly into place
C. Rising water pushes the float ball up until it closes the ballcock assembly, shutting off the supply of fresh water when the tank is full
D. The tank ball lifts, opening the outlet so water can flow from tank to bowl

KEY (CORRECT ANSWERS)

1. C
2. A
3. D
4. D
5. B

6. A
7. C
8. C
9. D
10. B

11. D
12. A
13. B
14. D
15. B

16. C
17. C
18. D
19. A
20. A

21. B
22. D
23. C
24. A
25. B

26. C
27. B
28. A
29. C
30. D

TEST 2

DIRECTIONS: Each question or incomplete statement is followed by several suggested answers or completions. Select the one that BEST answers the question or completes the statement. *PRINT THE LETTER OF THE CORRECT ANSWER IN THE SPACE AT THE RIGHT.*

1. Of the following, the MAIN reason for clear glass doors to have a painted design about four and one-half feet above the floor is to 1.____

   A. look attractive
   B. prevent glare
   C. improve safety
   D. make damage, if any, less noticeable

2. When using a wrench to make a repair on a faucet, it is a good idea to cover the wrench with rags in order to 2.____

   A. protect the finish on the faucet
   B. get a closer fit over the faucet
   C. get a better grip on the wrench
   D. get a better grip on the faucet

3. The length of the screw in the sketch below is *most nearly* 3.____

   A. 1 7/8" B. 2" C. 2 1/4" D. 2 5/16"

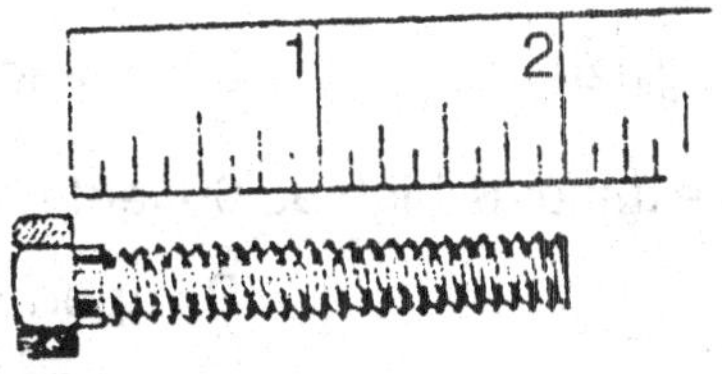

4. Panel doors may have horns which must be cut off before the door is hung. In the sketch below, the arrow which indicates a horn is labeled number 4.____

   A. 1 B. 2 C. 3 D. 4

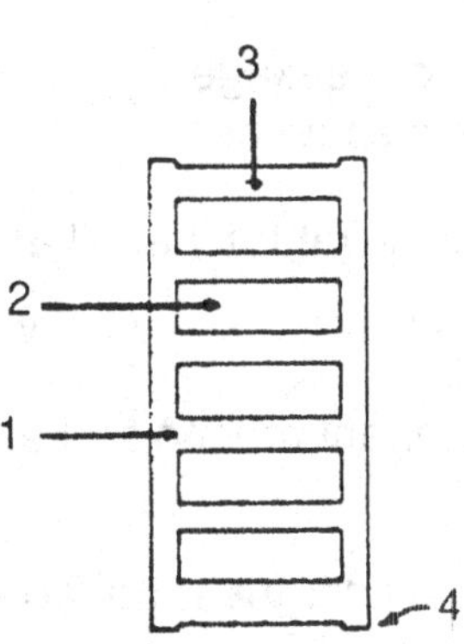

5. To "shim a hinge" means to 5.____
   A. swing the hinge from side to side
   B. paint the hinge
   C. polish the hinge
   D. raise up the hinge

6. To hold work that is being planed, sawed, drilled, shaped, sharpened or riveted, you should use a 6.____

   A. punch B. rasp C. reamer D. vise

7. A good deal of the trouble caused by faulty and worn locks and hinges can be avoided by proper lubrication. 7.____
   The tool you would use to lubricate locks and hinges is

   A. 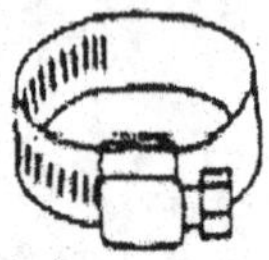 B.  C.  D.

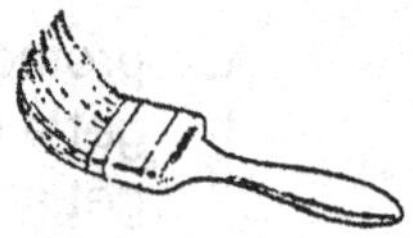

8. The terms ALLIGATORING, BLISTERING, and PEELING refer to 8.____
   A. carpentry B. masonry C. painting D. plumbing

9. The terms BAT and STRETCHER refer to 9.____
   A. carpentry B. glazing C. masonry D. painting

10. Ladders which are used to extend as high as 60 feet are called 10.____
    A. extension ladders B. portable ladders
    C. single-section ladders D. stepladders

11. Of the following, the MOST important advantage that Plexiglass has over regular glass, when used in windows, is that it 11.____

    A. is available in a wide range of thicknesses
    B. is easier to clean
    C. offers greater resistance to breakage
    D. offers greater resistance to scratches

12. Clutch-head, offset, Phillips and spiral-ratchet all are different types of 12.____
    A. drills B. files C. wrenches D. screwdrivers

13. Of the following, the MOST important reason for keeping tools in perfect working order is to make sure 13.____

    A. the proper tool is being used for the required work
    B. the tools can be operated safely
    C. each employee can repair a variety of building defects
    D. no employee uses a tool for his private use

14. When repairing a hole in a leaking pipe which of the following should be done FIRST? 14.____

    A. Wrap tape around the hole
    B. Turn off the water supply
    C. Tighten a clamp around the hole
    D. Seal the hole with epoxy

15. Freshly cut threads on pipe should be handled with caution *mainly* because the threads 15.____

    A. are the weakest section of the pipe and break easily
    B. do not give a firm handhold for carrying
    C. make a tight seal around a joint
    D. are always sharp

16. When a repair worker must enter a confined space through a small opening, it is a GOOD idea to attach a rope to his body *mainly* because the 16.____

    A. rope reduces unnecessary strain on the body
    B. rope may provide a way to reach the worker in an emergency
    C. worker will be able to get to areas that are not easily reached
    D. worker may be able to use the rope to remove debris from the work space

17. Hitting the handle of a screw driver with a hammer to remove an imbedded screw is a 17.____

    A. *good* practice, since it supplies the necessary force to get the screw started
    B. *poor* practice, since the shank part of the screw driver can be bent and the tool made useless
    C. *good* practice, since hammers and screw drivers are available in every tool kit just for this purpose
    D. *poor* practice, since the blade tip of the screw driver cannot be guided into the screw slot when both hands are holding the tools

18. Of the following, the reason why a tank, such as that pictured below, that is otherwise working correctly might fail to fill up sufficiently to deliver enough water to the toilet bowl at the time it is needed is that the 18.____

    A. ball may not drop back over the valve seat
    B. excess water may be flowing into the drain
    C. float rod may be bent up
    D. valve seat may be worn or nicked

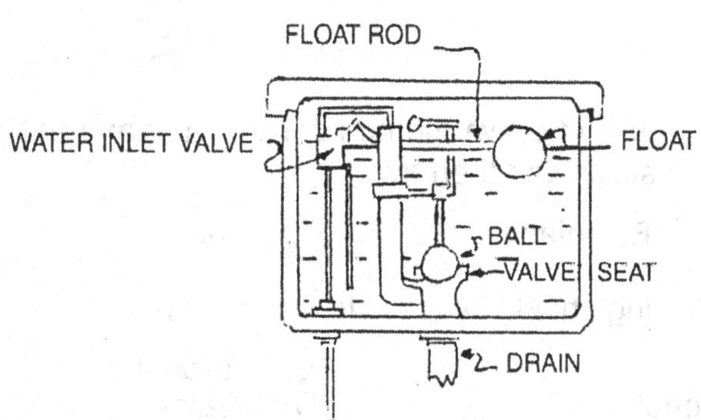

19. In the sketch below, the measurement of the inside diameter is *most nearly* ______ inches. 19.____

A. 24 B. 3 C. 3 1/2 D. 4

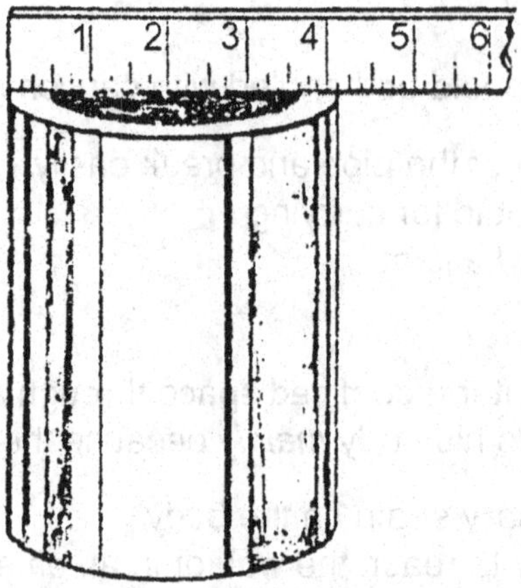

1 2 3 4 5 6

20. In a two-wire electrical system, the color of the wire which is grounded is *usually* 20.____

A. white B. red C. black D. green

21. It is generally recommended that wooden ladders be kept coated with a suitable protective coating. 21.____
The one of the following which is NOT a suitable protective coating is

A. clear lacquer
B. clear varnish
C. linseed oil
D. paint

22. The tool you should use to mend metal by soldering is 22.____

A. B. 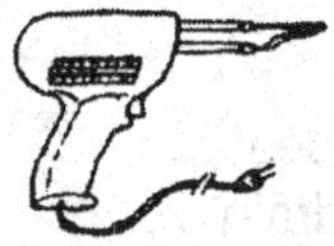 C. 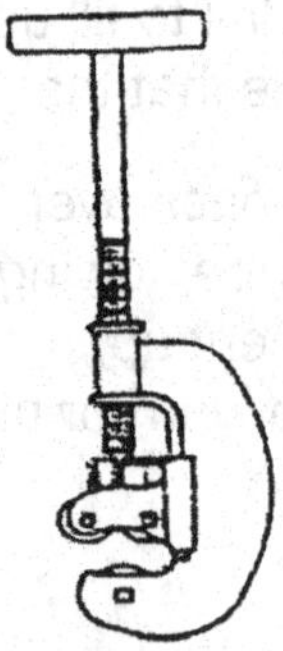 D.

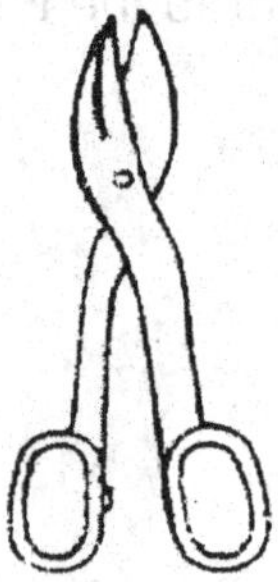

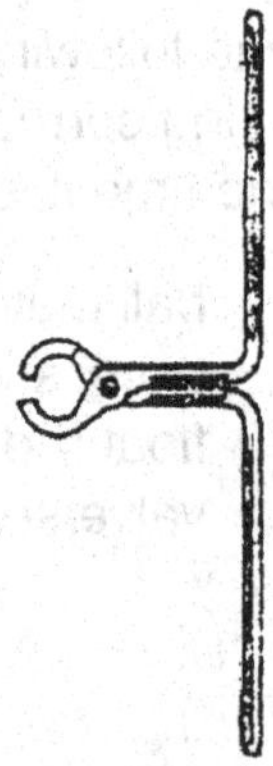

23. Of the following, the MOST effective method of fixing a door that sticks is to locate the area of the door which sticks and then to ______ it. 23.____

A. lacquer B. plane C. tape D. varnish

24. Which one of the following should be used to thin latex paint? 24.____

A. Mineral spirits
B. Turpentine
C. Denatured alcohol
D. Water

25. Of the following, the MAIN reason you should NOT place a ladder directly in front of a door that opens toward the ladder is that 25.____

    A. there is not enough space to support the weight of the ladder
    B. you would have to step down off the ladder each time someone wants to use the door
    C. this would prove to be hazardous if someone comes through the door
    D. it would be hard to reach the areas that need repair without tipping the ladder off balance

26. Going over the cutting line MORE than once when cutting a pane of glass by hand with a cutting wheel is *usually* 26.____

    A. *advisable;* it gives a straighter line
    B. *advisable;* it gives a cleaner break
    C. *inadvisable;* it gives an uneven break
    D. *inadvisable;* it may blunt the edge of the glass cutter

27. When hammering, it is usually BEST to hold the handle of the hammer 27.____

    A. close to the head because this maximizes the force of the blow
    B. far away from the head because this maximizes the force of the blow
    C. close to the head because this reduces the force of the blow
    D. far away from the head because this reduces the force of the blow

28. Repair crew members should report accidents on the job IMMEDIATELY *primarily* so that 28.____

    A. the proper person will be reprimanded for his carelessness
    B. a correct count can be kept of time lost through accidents
    C. prompt medical care may be given when needed
    D. the correct forms will be filled out

29. Leather gloves should be worn when handling sheet metal *primarily* because 29.____

    A. pressure on the metal might cause it to bend
    B. the edges and corners of the metal may be sharp
    C. natural oil or moisture from hands corrodes the metal
    D. leather provides a more secure grip

30. If a portable ladder does NOT have a nonslip base, the way to overcome this deficiency so that the ladder can be used safely is to 30.____

    A. place the ladder on soft earth
    B. fasten a wooden board across the top of the ladder
    C. splice two short ladders together
    D. tie the bottom of the ladder to a secure structure

KEY (CORRECT ANSWERS)

1. C
2. A
3. B
4. D
5. D

6. D
7. B
8. C
9. C
10. A

11. C
12. D
13. B
14. B
15. D

16. B
17. B
18. A
19. B
20. A

21. D
22. B
23. B
24. D
25. C

26. C
27. B
28. C
29. B
30. D

EXAMINATION SECTION
TEST 1

DIRECTIONS: Each question or incomplete statement is followed by several suggested answers or completions. Select the one that BEST answers the question or completes the statement. *PRINT THE LETTER OF THE CORRECT ANSWEE IN THE SPACE AT THE RIGHT.*

1. As a member of a repair crew, you have been asked by your supervisor to reinforce a door. You have never done this kind of work before and are not certain how to go about it. Of the following, the MOST advisable action to take is to 1.____

   A. tell your supervisor you need assistance
   B. ask the other crew members if they can help you
   C. go ahead and do the best you can
   D. ask another member of your crew if he will do it for you

2. It is BEST to erect a barricade or barrier before repair work begins *mainly* because 2.____

   A. the repair truck can be sent back for additional supplies
   B. the workers can work in more comfortable space
   C. unauthorized persons are kept clear of the work area
   D. a solid platform is provided for workers' use

3. Of the following, the BEST reason for sprinkling water on work areas which have a lot of dust or where the work itself will create a lot of dust is that this action will 3.____

   A. dissolve the dust particles
   B. help the dust to settle
   C. clean away the dust from the area
   D. prevent the dust from drying out

QUESTIONS 4-9.
Questions 4 through 9 are to be answered *solely* on the basis of the following set of instructions.

<u>Patching Simple Cracks in a Built-Up Roof</u>

If there is a visible crack in built-up roofing, the repair is simple and straight forward:

1. With a brush, clean all loose gravel and dust out of the crack, and clean three or four inches around all sides of it.
2. With a trowel or putty knife, fill the crack with asphalt cement and then spread a layer of asphalt cement about 1/8 inch thick over the cleaned area.
3. Place a strip of roofing felt big enough to cover the crack into the wet cement and press it down firmly.
4. Spread a second layer of cement over the strip of felt and well past its edges.
5. Brush gravel back over the patch.

4. According to the above passage, in order to patch simple cracks in a built-up roof, it is necessary to use a 4.____

   A. putty knife and a drill
   B. knife and pliers
   C. tack hammer and a punch
   D. brush and a trowe

5. According to the above passage, the size of the area that should be clear of loose gravel and dust before the asphalt cement is first applied should 5.____

   A. be the exact size of the crack itself
   B. extend three or four inches on all sides of the crack
   C. be 1/8 inch greater than the size of the crack itself
   D. extend the length of the roofing strip

6. According to the above passage, loose gravel and dust in the crack should be removed with a 6.____

   A. brush B. felt pad C. trowel D. dust mop

7. Assume that both layers of asphalt cement needed to patch the crack are of the same thickness. 7.____
   The total thickness of asphalt cement used in the patch should be, *most nearly,* ____ inch.

   A. 1/2 B. 1/3 C. 1/4 D. 1/8

8. According to the instructions in the above passage, how large should the strip of roofing felt be cut? 8.____

   A. Three of four inches square
   B. Smaller than the crack and small enough to be surrounded by cement on all sides of the strip
   C. Exactly the same size and shape of the area covered by the wet cement
   D. Large enough to completely cover the crack

9. The final or finishing action to be taken in patching a simple crack in a built-up roof is to 9.____

   A. clean out the inside of the crack
   B. spread a layer of asphalt a second time
   C. cover the crack with roofing felt
   D. cover the patch of roofing felt and cement with gravel

10. As a repair crew worker, your supervisor tells you that he has in the workshop a piece of glass measuring 5' x 4' from which he wants you to cut a section measuring 4'8" x 3'2". However, you find two pieces of glass in the workshop; one is 5' x 3', and the other is 8' x 5'. 10.____
    Of the following, the BEST action for you to take is to

    A. cut a section measuring 4'8" x 3' from the smaller piece because that is probably what he meant
    B. do NOT cut the glass and wait until he asks you for it
    C. tell him about the differences in measurement and ask him what to do
    D. cut a section measuring 4'8" x 3'2" from the larger piece since that would give you the full size required

11. A floor that is 9' wide by 12' long measures how many square feet? 11.____

    A. 12 B. 21 C. 108 D. 150

12. The sum of 5 1/16, 4 1/4, 4 3/8, and 3 7/16 is 12.____

A. 17 1/8 B. 17 7/16 C. 17 1/4 D. 17 3/8

13. From a length of pipe 6 feet 9 inches long you are asked to cut a piece 4 feet 5 inches long. 13.____
The length of the remainder, in inches, should be

A. 24 B. 26 C. 28 D. 53

QUESTIONS 14-17.
In answering questions 14 through 17 refer to the label pictured below.

LABEL

BREGSON'S CLEAR GLUE HIGHLY FLAMMABLE	PRECAUTIONS
A clear quick-drying glue For temporary bonding, apply glue to one surface and join immediately	Use with adequate ventilation Close container after use
For permanent bonding, apply glue to both surfaces, permit to dry and press together	Keep out of reach of children
Use for bonding plastic to plastic, plastic to wood, and wood to wood only	Avoid prolonged breathing of vapors and repeated contact with skin
Will not bond at temperatures below 60°	

14. Assume that you, as a member of a repair crew, have been asked to repair a wood banister in the hallway of a house. Since the heat has been turned off, the hallway is very cold, except for the location where you have to make the repair. Another repair crew worker is working at that same location using a blow torch to solder a pipe in the wall. 14.____
The temperature at that location is about 67°.
According to the instruction on the above label, the use of this glue to make the necessary repair is

A. *advisable;* the glue will bond wood to wood
B. *advisable;* the heat form the soldering will cause the glue to dry quickly
C. *inadvisable;* the work area temperature is too low
D. *inadvisable;* the glue is highly flammable

15. According to the instructions on the above label, this glue should NOT be used for which of the following applications? 15.____

A. Affixing a pine table leg to a walnut table
B. Repairing leaks around pipe joints
C. Bonding a plastic knob to a cedar drawer
D. Attaching a lucite knob to a lucite drawer

16. According to the instructions on the above label, using this glue to bond ceramic tile to a plaster wall by coating both surfaces with glue, letting the glue dry, and then pressing the tile to the plaster wall is 16.____

A. *advisable;* the glue is quick drying and clear
B. *advisable;* the glue should be permanently affixed to the one surface of the tile only
C. *inadvisable;* the glue is not suitable for bonding ceramic tile to plaster walls
D. *inadvisable;* the bonding should be a temporary one

17. The precaution described in the above label "use with adequate ventilation" means that 17.____

A. the area you are working in should be very cold
B. there should be sufficient fresh air where you are using the glue
C. you should wear gloves to avoid contact with the glue
D. you must apply a lot of glue to make a permanent bond

QUESTIONS 18-20.
Questions 18 through 20 are to be answered *solely* on the basis of the following passage.

A utility plan is a floor plan which shows the layout of a heating, electrical, plumbing, or other utility system. Utility plans are used primarily by the persons responsible for the utilities, but they are important to the craftsman as well. Most utility installations require the leaving of openings in walls, floors, and roofs for the admission or installation of utility features. The craftsman who is, for example, pouring a concrete foundation wall must study the utility plans to determine the number, sizes, and locations of the openings he must leave for piping, electric lines, and the like.

18. The one of the following items of information which is LEAST likely to be provided by a utility plan is the 18.____

A. location of the joists and frame members around
B. stairwells
C. location of the hot water supply and return piping
D. location of light fixtures D. number of openings in the floor for radiators

19. According to the passage, the persons who will *most likely* have the GREATEST need for the information included in a utility plan of a building are those who 19.____

A. maintain and repair the heating system
B. clean the premises
C. paint housing exteriors
D. advertise property for sale

20. According to the passage, a repair crew member should find it MOST helpful to consult a utility plan when information is needed about the 20.____

A. thickness of all doors in the structure
B. number of electrical outlets located throughout the structure
C. dimensions of each window in the structure
D. length of a roof rafter

KEY (CORRECT ANSWERS)

1. A
2. C
3. B
4. D
5. B
6. A
7. C
8. D
9. D
10. C
11. C
12. A
13. C
14. D
15. B
16. C
17. B
18. A
19. A
20. B

TEST 2

DIRECTIONS: Each question or incomplete statement is followed by several suggested answers or completions. Select the one that BEST answers the question or completes the statement. *PRINT THE LETTER OF THE CORRECT ANSWER IN THE SPACE AT THE RIGHT.*

1. Repair crew men should report accidents on the job IMMEDIATELY *primarily* so that 1.____

   A. the proper person will be reprimanded for his carelessness
   B. a correct count can be kept of time lost through accidents on the job
   C. prompt medical care may be given when needed
   D. the correct forms will be filled out

2. In a circulating hot-water heating system, most boilers have an altitude gauge that shows the level of the water in the system. This gauge has two needles, one red, which is set at the proper water level, and one black, which shows the true water level, and which varies with the water-level change. When the red needle is over the black on the gauge, so that they coincide, it means that the system 2.____

   A. has too much water
   B. requires more water
   C. is properly filled with water
   D. should be shut off

3. If a radiator fails to heat properly, the FIRST of the following actions which you should take is to check the 3.____

   A. boiler's steam gauge
   B. boiler's water line
   C. radiator's shut-off valve
   D. pressure reducing valve

4. Assume that you have been asked to remove a door knob. You inspect the door and find that it has a mortise lock, and that the door knob is fastened with a set screw. Which of the following is the FIRST step that you should take in removing the door knob? 4.____

   A. Unscrew the set screw on the slimmest part of the knob
   B. Saw off the knob at its thinnest point
   C. Turn the knob repeatedly to the right and to the left until it finally falls off
   D. Use a pinchbar to spring the lock

5. When preparing a 1:1:6 mix for mortar, how many pails of lime should be added to 3 pails of sand and 1/2 pail of cement? 5.____

   A. 3
   B. 1
   C. 1/2
   D. 1/4

6. If you find that the putty in the can is a little too hard to use, you should add some 6.____

   A. whiting
   B. linseed oil
   C. spackle
   D. glazing compound

7. The purpose of scratching the surface of the first coat of patching stucco is to 7.____

A. spread the patching stucco over a wide area
B. give the surface a textured finish
C. provide a gripping surface for the next coat of patching stucco
D. press the patching stucco into the hole to be repaired

8. When filling in large cracks and holes up to 2 inches in diameter in plaster walls it is BEST to use 8.____

A. spackle
B. patching plaster
C. gypsum wallboard
D. tile

9. Of the following, the MAIN reason for having a vertical distance of about 7 inches between stair treads is that this 9.____

A. makes for the best appearance
B. makes an easy step for the average person
C. allows for the most profitable use of wood
D. cuts out a good deal of unnecessary work

10. When removing a door from its hinges to make repairs, it is ALWAYS best to 10.____

A. remove the pin from the top hinge first
B. keep the door tightly closed
C. remove the pin from the bottom hinge first
D. remove the door knob and lock

11. Dry plaster will absorb water from the patching material, weakening and shrinking it. Based on the information in this statement, it would be *advisable* to take which one of the following actions in the process of patching a plaster crack? 11.____

A. Mix the plaster with a lot of extra water
B. Apply water-eased paint to the wall immediately
C. Apply plaster powder to the crack, then pour water in over it
D. Dampen the area surrounding the patch with a sponge

12. Standard electrical tools which are safe for ordinary use may be unsafe in locations which contain flammable materials because 12.____

A. there may be insufficient ventilation
B. sparks from the tools may start a fire
C. electric current will usually cause fire
D. the automatic sprinkler system may be set off accidentally

13. Of the following, the BEST combination of ingredients to use for good concrete is 13.____

A. cement and water
B. aggregate and water
C. cement, sand, stone, and water
D. gravel, cement, and water

14. If the blade of a screw driver is thicker than the slot at the top of a screw, the way to *properly* drive the screw into wood in this case is to 14.____

A. widen the slot of the screw to fit the larger blade tip
B. tap the end of the screw driver lightly to get a firmer hold into the screw slot
C. get another screw driver which fits the size of the screw slot
D. apply a drop of lubricating oil to the screw slot to get the screw started into the wood

QUESTIONS 15-20.
Questions 15 through 20 are to be answered *solely* on the basis of the following passage.

The basic hand-operated hoisting device is the tackle or purchase, consisting of a line called a fall, reeved through one or more blocks.

To hoist a load of given size, you must set up a rig with a safe working load equal to or in excess of the load to be hoisted. In order to do this, you must be able to calculate the safe working load of a single part of line of given size; the safe working load of a given purchase which contains a line of given size; and the minimum size of hooks or shackles which you must use in a given type of purchase to hoist a given load. You must also be able to calculate the thrust which a given load will exert on a gin pole or a set of shears inclined at a given angle; the safe working load which a spar of a given size, used as a gin pole or as one of a set of shears, will sustain; and the stress which a given load will set up in the back guy of a gin pole, or in the back guy of a set of shears, inclined at a given angle.

15. The above passage refers to the lifting of loads by means of 15.____

A. erected scaffolds
B. manual rigging devices
C. power-driven equipment
D. conveyor belts

16. It can be concluded from the above passage, that a set of shears serves to 16.____

A. absorb the force and stress of the working load
B. operate the tackle
C. contain the working load
D. compute the safe working load

17. According to the above passage, a spar can be used for a 17.____

A. back guy
B. block
C. fall
D. gin pole

18. According to the above passage, the rule that a user of hand-operated tackle MUST follow is to make sure that the safe working load is at LEAST 18.____

A. equal to the weight of the given load
B. twice the combined weight of the block and falls
C. one-half the weight of the given load
D. twice the weight of the given load

19. According to the above passage, the two parts that make up a tackle are 19.____

A. back guys and gin poles
B. blocksm and falls
C. rigs and shears
D. spars and shackles

20. According to the above passage, in order to determine whether it is safe to hoist a particular load, you MUST 20.____

A. use the maximum size hooks
B. time the speed to bring a given load to a desired place
C. calculate the forces exerted on various types of rigs
D. repeatedly lift and lower various loads

KEY (CORRECT ANSWERS)

1.	C	11.	D
2.	C	12.	B
3.	C	13.	C
4.	A	14.	C
5.	C	15.	B
6.	B	16.	A
7.	C	17.	D
8.	B	18.	A
9.	B	19.	B
10.	C	20.	C

EXAMINATION SECTION
TEST 1

DIRECTIONS: Each question or incomplete statement is followed by several suggested answers or completions. Select the one that BEST answers the question or completes the statement. *PRINT THE LETTER OF THE CORRECT ANSWER IN THE SPACE AT THE RIGHT.*

1. A bit is held in a hand drill by means of a(n) 1.____

   A. arbor B. chuck C. collet D. clamp

2. The type of screw that MOST often requires a countersunk hole is a _____ head. 2.____

   A. flat B. round C. fillister D. hexagon

3. Instead of using the ordinary 1 piece screwdriver, a screwdriver bit is MOST often used with a brace because of the 3.____

   A. increased length of the brace
   B. different types of bits available
   C. increased leverage of the brace
   D. ability to work in tight corners

4. A thread gage is usually used to measure the 4.____

   A. thickness of a thread
   B. diameter of a thread
   C. number of threads per inch
   D. height of a thread

5. The wheel of a glass cutter is BEST lubricated with 5.____

   A. kerosene
   B. linseed oil
   C. varnolene
   D. diesel oil

6. A nail set is a 6.____

   A. group of nails of the same size and type
   B. group of nails of different sizes but the same type
   C. tool used to extract nails
   D. tool used to drive nails below the surface of wood

7. To test for leaks in a gas line, it is BEST to use 7.____

   A. a match
   B. soapy water
   C. a colored dye
   D. ammonia

8. Routing is the process of cutting a 8.____

   A. strip out of sheet metal
   B. groove in wood
   C. chamfer on a shaft
   D. core out of concrete

9. A hacksaw frame has a wing nut mainly to 9.____

   A. make it easier to replace blades
   B. increase the strength of the frame
   C. prevent vibration of the blade
   D. adjust the length of the frame

10. A mitre box is usually used with a ______ saw. 10.____

A. hack B. crosscut C. rip D. back

11. A continuous flexible saw blade is MOST often used on a ______ saw. 11.____

A. radial B. band C. swing D. table

12. A pipe reamer is used to 12.____

A. clean out a length of pipe
B. thread pipe
C. remove burrs from the ends of pipe
D. seal pipe joints

13. To lay out a straight cut on a piece of wood at the same angle as the cut on a second piece of wood, the PROPER tool to use is a 13.____

A. bevel B. cope C. butt gauge D. clevis

14. Before drilling a hole in a piece of metal, an indentation should be made with a ______ punch. 14.____

A. pin B. taper C. center D. drift

15. Curved cuts in wood are BEST made with a ______ saw. 15.____

A. jig B. veneer C. radial D. swing

16. A face plate is generally used to 16.____

A. hold material while working with it on a lathe
B. smooth out irregularities in a metal plate
C. protect the finish on a metal plate
D. locate centers of holes to be drilled on a drill press

17. A die would be used to 17.____

A. gage the groove in a splined shaft
B. cut a thread on a metal rod
C. hold a piece to be machined on a milling machine
D. control the depth of a hole to be drilled in a piece of metal

18. Before using a ladle to scoop up molten solder, you should make sure that the ladle is dry.
This is done to prevent 18.____

A. the solder from sticking to the ladle
B. impurities from getting into the solder
C. injuries due to splashing solder
D. cooling of the solder

19. To PROPERLY adjust the gap on a spark plug, you should use a(n) 19.____

A. inside caliper
B. center gauge
C. wire type feeler gauge
D. micrometer

20. The length of the MOST common type of folding wood rule is ______ feet. 20.____

A. 4
B. 5
C. 6
D. 7

21. A four-foot mason's level is usually used to determine whether the top of a wall is level and whether it is 21.____

A. square
B. plumb
C. rigid
D. in line

22. To match a tongue in a board, the matching board MUST have a 22.____

A. rabbet
B. chamfer
C. bead
D. groove

23. When driving screws in close quarters, the BEST type of screwdriver to use is a(n) 23.____

A. Phillips
B. offset
C. butt
D. angled

24. The term 12-24 refers to a ______ screw. 24.____

A. wood
B. lag
C. sheet metal
D. machine

25. To measure the length of a curved line on a drawing or plan, the PROPER tool to use in addition to a ruler is(are) 25.____

A. dividers
B. calipers
C. surface gage
D. radius gage

26. For the standard machine screw, the diameter of a tap drill is generally 26.____

A. *equal* to the diameter of the shaft of the screw at the base of the threads (the root diameter)
B. *larger* than the root diameter, but smaller than the diameter of the screw
C. *equal* to the diameter of the screw
D. *larger* than the diameter of the screw

27. In order to drill a 1" hole accurately with a drill press, you should 27.____

A. drill at high speeds
B. use very little pressure on the drill
C. drill partway down, release pressure on the drill, and then continue drilling
D. drill a pilot hole first

28. Before taking apart an electric motor to repair, punch marks are sometimes placed on the casing near each other. 28.____
The MOST probable reason for doing this is to

A. make sure the parts lock together on reassembly
B. properly line up the parts that are next to each other
C. keep track of the number of parts in the assembly
D. identify all the parts as coming from the one motor

29. To locate a point on a floor directly under a point on the ceiling, the PROPER tool to use is a 29.____

A. square
B. line level
C. height gage
D. plumb bob

Question 30.

DIRECTIONS: Question 30 is based on the diagram appearing below.

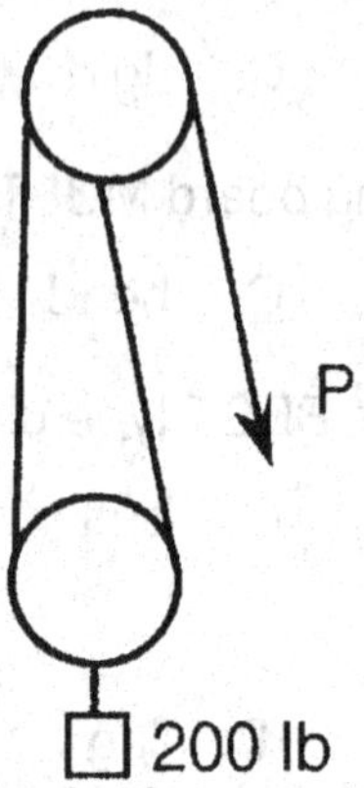

P

200 lb

30. In the above diagram, the full P required to lift the weight a distance of four feet is MOST NEARLY ______ lbs. 30.____

A. 50
B. 67
C. 75
D. 100

31. The EASIEST tool to use to determine whether the edge of a board is at right angles to the face of the board is a 31.____

A. rafter square
B. try square
C. protractor
D. marking gage

32. *Whetting* refers to 32.____

A. tempering of tools by dipping them in water
B. annealing of tools by heating and slow cooling
C. brazing of carbide tips on tools
D. sharpening of tools

33. The MOST difficult part of a plank to plane is the 33.____

A. face
B. side
C. end
D. back

34. To prevent wood from splitting when drilling with an auger, it is BEST to 34.____

A. use even pressure on the bit
B. drill at a slow speed
C. hold the wood tightly in a vise
D. back up the wood with a piece of scrap wood

35. The term *dressing a grinding wheel* refers to 35.____

A. setting up the wheel on the arbor
B. restoring the sharpness of a wheel face that has become clogged
C. placing flanges against the sides of the wheel
D. bringing the wheel up to speed before using it

36. Heads of rivets are BEST cut off with a 36.____

A. hacksaw
B. cold chisel
C. fly cutter
D. reamer

37. A *V-block* is especially useful to 37.____

A. prevent damage to work held in a vise
B. hold round stock while a hole is being drilled into it
C. prevent rolling of round stock stored on the ground
D. shim up the end of a machine so that it is level

38. A full set of taps for a given size usually consists of a ______ tap. 38.____

A. taper and bottoming
B. taper and plug
C. plug and bottoming
D. taper, plug, and bottoming

39. Round thread cutting dies are usually held in stock by means of 39.____

A. wing nuts B. clamps C. set screws D. bolts

40. The one of the following diagrams that shows the plan view and the elevation of a counterbored hole is 40.____

A.

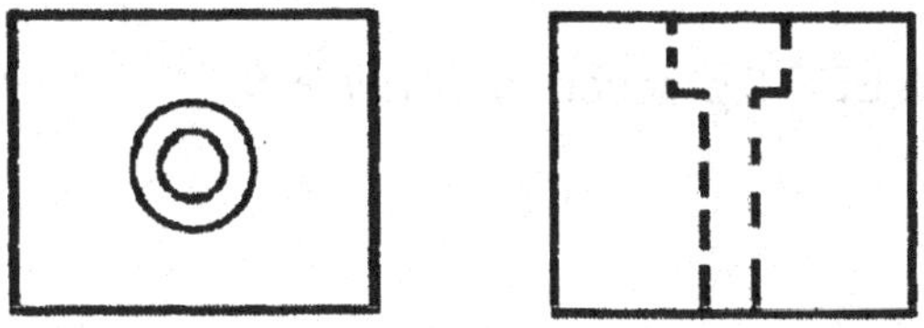

B.

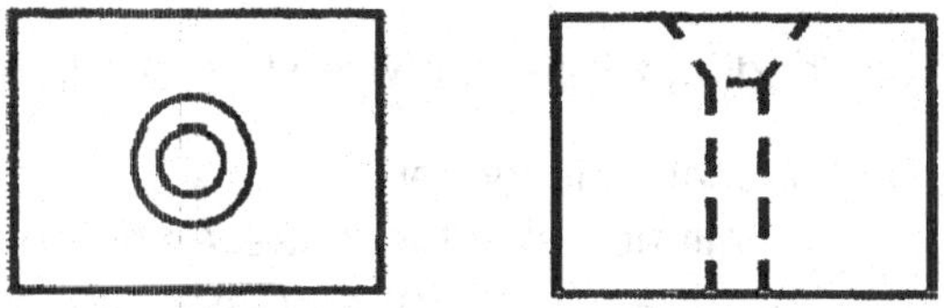

C.

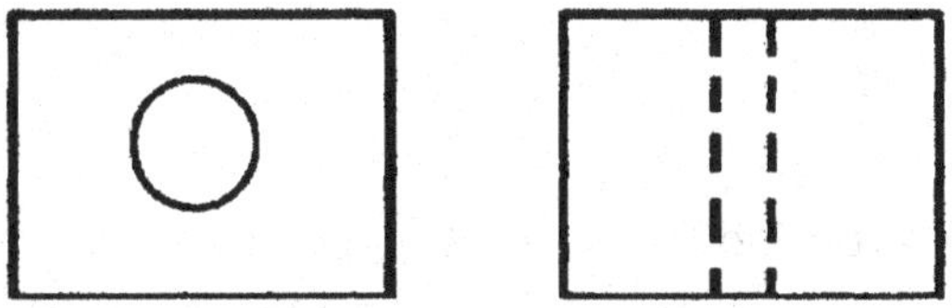

D.

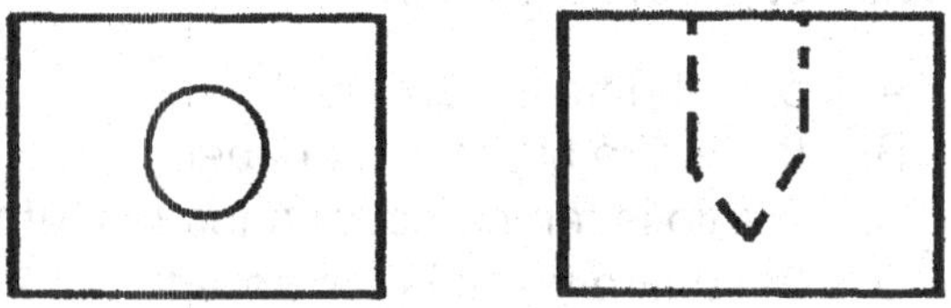

41. With regard to pipe, *I.D.* usually means 41.____

A. inside diameter
B. inside dressed
C. invert diameter
D. installation date

42. A compression fitting is MOST often used to 42.____

A. lubricate a wheel
B. join two pieces of tubing
C. reduce the diameter of a hole
D. press fit a gear to a shaft

43. The shape of a mill file is basically 43.____

A. flat B. half round C. triangular D. square

44. Of the following, the ratio of tin to lead that will produce the solder with the LOWEST melting point is 44.____

A. 30-70 B. 40-60 C. 50-50 D. 60-40

45. A safe edge on a file is one that 45.____

A. is smooth and can not cut
B. has a finer cut than the face of the file
C. is rounded to prevent scratches
D. has a coarser cut than the face of the file

46. The MOST frequent use of a file card is to ______ files. 46.____

A. sort out
B. clean
C. prevent damage to
D. prevent clogging of

47. The BEST way of determining whether a grinding wheel has an internal crack is to 47.____

A. run the wheel at high speed, stop it, and examine the wheel
B. spray lubricating oil on the sides of the wheel and check the amount of absorption of the oil
C. hit the wheel with a rubber hammer and listen to the sound
D. drop the wheel sharply on a table and then check the wheel

48. If a grinding wheel has worn to a smaller diameter, the BEST practice to follow is to 48.____

A. discard the wheel
B. continue using the wheel as before
C. use the wheel, but at a faster speed
D. use the wheel, but at a slower speed

49. With respect to the ordinary awl, 49.____

A. only the tip is hardened
B. the entire blade is hardened
C. the tip is tempered, and the rest of the blade is hardened
D. the entire blade is tempered

50. To prevent overheating of drills, it is BEST to use ______ oil. 50.____

A. cutting
B. lubricating
C. penetrating
D. heating

KEY (CORRECT ANSWERS)

1.	B	11.	B	21.	B	31.	B	41.	A
2.	A	12.	C	22.	D	32.	D	42.	B
3.	C	13.	A	23.	B	33.	C	43.	A
4.	C	14.	C	24.	D	34.	D	44.	D
5.	A	15.	A	25.	A	35.	B	45.	A
6.	D	16.	A	26.	B	36.	B	46.	B
7.	B	17.	B	27.	D	37.	B	47.	C
8.	B	18.	C	28.	B	38.	D	48.	C
9.	A	19.	C	29.	D	39.	C	49.	A
10.	D	20.	C	30.	D	40.	A	50.	A

TEST 2

DIRECTIONS: Each question or incomplete statement is followed by several suggested answers or completions. Select the one that BEST answers the question or completes the statement. *PRINT THE LETTER OF THE CORRECT ANSWER IN THE SPACE AT THE RIGHT.*

1. Crocus cloth is commonly used to 1.____

   A. protect finely machined surfaces from damage while the machines are being repaired
   B. remove rust from steel
   C. protect floors and furniture while painting walls
   D. wipe up oil and grease that has spilled

2. Before using a new paint brush, the FIRST operation should be to 2.____

   A. remove loose bristles
   B. soak the brush in linseed oil
   C. hang the brush up overnight
   D. clean the brush with turpentine

3. When sharpening a hand saw, the FIRST operation is to 3.____

   A. file the teeth down to the same height
   B. shape the teeth to the proper profile
   C. bend the teeth over to provide clearance when sawing
   D. clean the gullies with a file

4. To prevent solder from dripping when soldering a vertical seam, it is BEST to 4.____

   A. hold a waxed rag under the soldering iron
   B. use the soldering iron in a horizontal position
   C. tin the soldering iron on one side only
   D. solder the seam in the order from bottom to top

5. If a round nut has two holes in the face, the PROPER type wrench to use to tighten this nut is a(n) 5.____

   A. Stillson B. monkey C. spanner D. open end

6. A box wrench is BEST used on 6.____

   A. pipe fittings B. flare nuts
   C. hexagonal nuts D. Allen screws

7. To prevent damage to fine finishes on metal work that is to be held in a vise, you should 7.____

   A. clamp the work lightly
   B. use brass inserts on the vise
   C. wrap the work with cloth before inserting it in the vise
   D. substitute a smooth face plate for the serrated plate on the vise

8. The MOST frequent use for a turnbuckle is to 8.____
   A. tighten a guy wire
   B. adjust shims on a machine
   C. bolt a bracket to a wall
   D. support electric cable from a ceiling

9. To form the head of a tinner's rivet, the PROPER tool to use is a rivet 9.____
   A. anvil B. plate C. set D. brake

10. A socket speed handle MOST closely resembles a 10.____
   A. screwdriver B. brace C. spanner D. spin grip

11. Tips of masonry drills are usually made of 11.____
   A. steel B. carbide C. corundum D. monel

12. The BEST flux to use for soldering galvanized iron is 12.____
   A. resin B. sal ammoniac
   C. borax D. muriatic acid

13. The one of the following that is NOT a common type of oilstone is 13.____
   A. silicon carbide B. aluminum oxide
   C. hard Arkansas D. pumice

14. A method of joining metals using temperatures intermediate between soldering and welding is 14.____
   A. corbelling B. brazing C. annealing D. lapping

15. When an unusually high degree of accuracy is required with woodwork, lines should be marked with a 15.____
   A. pencil ground to a chisel point
   B. pencil line over a crayon line
   C. sharp knife point
   D. scriber

16. The MOST important difference between pipe threads and *V* threads on bolts is that pipe threads are usually 16.____
   A. longer B. sharper
   C. tapered D. more evenly spaced

17. A street elbow differs from the ordinary elbow in that the street elbow has 17.____
   A. different diameter threads at each end
   B. male threads at one end and female threads at the other
   C. female threads at both ends
   D. male threads at both ends

18. Water hammer in a pipe line can MOST often be stopped by the installation of a(n) 18.____
   A. pressure reducing valve B. expansion joint
   C. flexible coupling D. air chamber

19. If water is leaking from the top part of a bibcock, the part that should be replaced is MOST likely the 19.____

A. bibb washer
B. packing
C. seat
D. bibb screw

20. When joining electric wires together in a fixture box, the BEST thing to use are wire 20.____

A. connectors B. couplings C. clamps D. bolts

21. If the name plate of a motor indicates that it is a split phase motor, it is LIKELY that this motor 21.____

A. is a universal motor
B. operates on DC only
C. operates on AC only
D. operates either on DC at full power or on AC at reduced power

22. To make driving of a screw into hard wood easier, it is BEST to lubricate the threads of the screw with 22.____

A. varnoline
B. penetrating oil
C. beeswax
D. cutting oil

23. Assume that a thermostatically controlled oil heater fails to operate. To determine whether it is the thermostat that is at fault, you should 23.____

A. check the circuit breaker
B. connect a wire across the terminals of the thermostat
C. replace the contacts on the thermostat
D. put an ammeter on the line

24. The function of the carburetor on a gasoline engine is to 24.____

A. mix the air and gasoline properly
B. filter the fuel
C. filter the air to engine
D. pump the gasoline into the cylinder

25. If a car owner complains that the battery in his car is constantly running dry, the item that should be checked FIRST is the 25.____

A. fan belt
B. generator
C. voltage regulator
D. relay

26. On MOST modern automobiles, foot brake pressure is transmitted to the brake drums by 26.____

A. air pressure
B. mechanical linkage
C. hydraulic fluid
D. electro-magnetic force

27. Assume that the engine of a car remains cold even though it is run for a period of time. The part that is MOST likely at fault is the 27.____

A. heat by-pass valve
B. thermostat
C. heater control
D. choke

28. To permit easy stripping of concrete forms, they should be 28.____

A. dried B. oiled C. wet down D. cleaned

29. To prevent honey combing in concrete, the concrete should be 29.____

A. vibrated
B. cured
C. heated in cold weather
D. protected from the rain

30. The MAIN reason for using wire mesh in connection with concrete work is to 30.____

A. strain the impurities from the sand
B. increase the strength of the concrete
C. hold the forms together
D. protect the concrete till it hardens

31. Segregation of concrete is MOST often caused by pouring concrete 31.____

A. in cold weather
B. from too great a height
C. too rapidly
D. into a form in which the concrete has already begun to harden

32. Headers in carpentry are MOST closely associated with 32.____

A. trimmers
B. cantilevers
C. posts
D. newels

33. Joists are very often supported by 33.____

A. suspenders
B. base plates
C. anchor bolts
D. bridal irons

34. At outside corners, the type of joint MOST frequently used on a baseboard is the 34.____

A. plowed
B. mitered
C. mortise and tenon
D. butt

35. The vehicle used with latex paints is usually 35.____

A. linseed oil
B. shellac
C. varnish
D. water

36. *Boxing* of paint refers to the ______ of paints. 36.____

A. mixing B. storage C. use D. canning

37. When painting wood, nail holes should be puttied 37.____

A. *before* applying the prime coat
B. *after* applying the prime coat but before the second coat
C. *after* applying the second coat but before the third coat
D. *after* applying the third coat

38. In laying up a brick wall, you find that at the end of the wall there is not enough space for a full brick. 38.____
You should use a

A. stretcher B. bat C. corbel D. bull nose

39. Pointing a brick wall is the same as 39.____

A. truing up the wall
B. topping the wall with a waterproof surface
C. repairing the mortar joints in the wall
D. providing a foundation for the wall

40. The pigment MOST often used in a prime coat of paint on steel to prevent rusting is 40.____

A. lampblack
B. calcimine
C. zinc oxide
D. red lead

41. If you find a co-worker lying unconscious across an electric wire, the FIRST thing you should do is 41.____

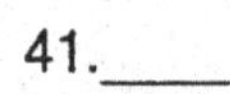

A. get him off the wire
B. call the foreman
C. get a doctor
D. shut off the power

42. 42.____

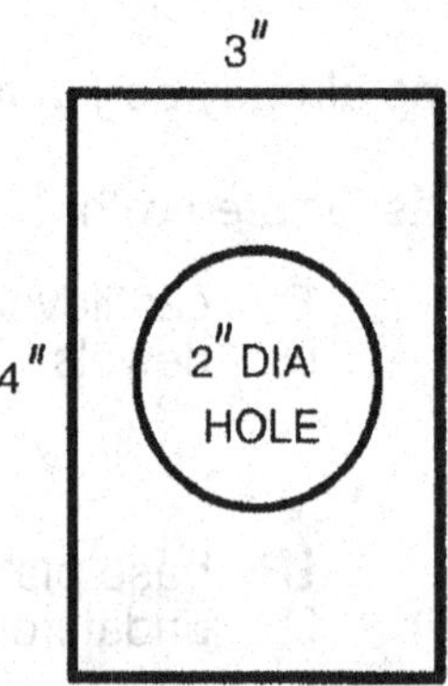

The area of the metal plate shown above, minus the hole area, is MOST NEARLY ______ square inches.

A. 8.5
B. 8.9
C. 9.4
D. 10.1

43. 43.____

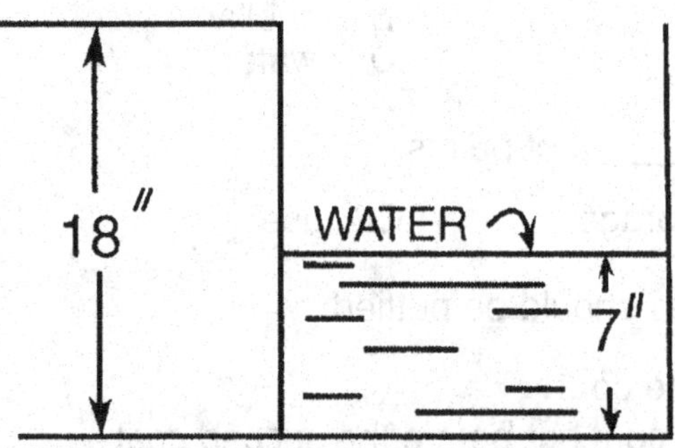

The percentage of the above tank that is filled with water is MOST NEARLY

A. 33
B. 35
C. 37
D. 39

44. 44.____

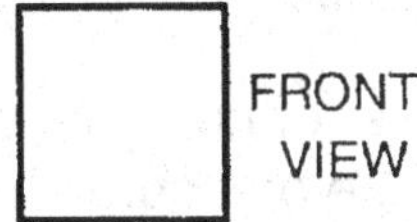

The top and front view of an object are shown above.The right side view will MOST likely look like

A. 

B. 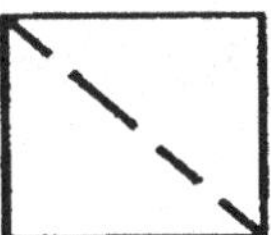

C. 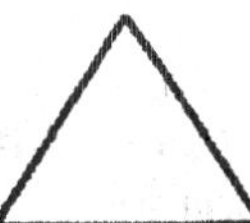

D. 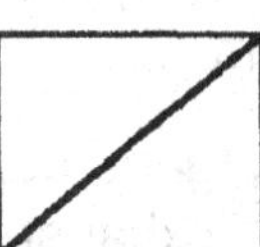

45. 45.____

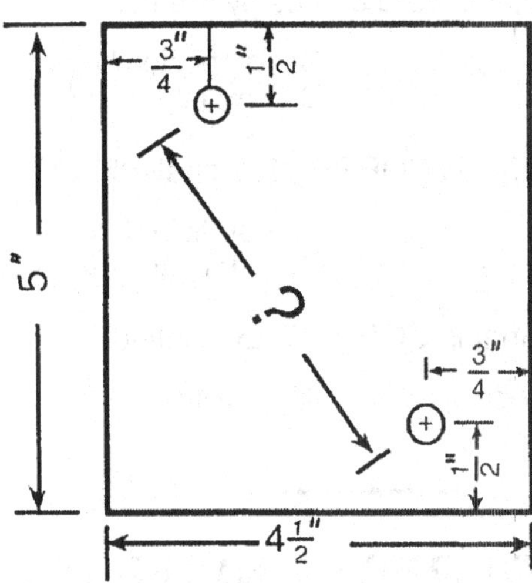

The distance between centers of the holes in the above diagram is MOST NEARLY

A. $4\frac{1}{2}$" B. 4 3/4" C. 5" D. $5\frac{1}{4}$"

Questions 46-48.

DIRECTIONS: Questions 46 through 48, inclusive, are to be answered in accordance with the paragraph below.

A steam heating system with steam having a pressure of less than 10 pounds is called a low-pressure system. The majority of steam-heating systems are of this type. The steam may be provided by low-pressure boilers installed expressly *for the purpose, or it may be gener-*

ated in boilers at a higher pressure and reduced in pressure before admitted to the heating mains. In other instances, it may be possible to use exhaust steam which has been made to run engines and other machines and which still contains enough heat to be utilized in the heating system. The first case represents the system of heating used in the ordinary residence or other small building; the other two represent the systems of heating employed in industrial buildings where a power plant is installed for general power purposes.

46. According to the above paragraph, whether or not a steam heating system is considered a low pressure system is determined by the pressure 46.____

 A. generated by the boiler
 B. in the heating main
 C. at the inlet side of the reducing valve
 D. of the exhaust

47. According to the above paragraph, steam used for heating is sometimes obtained from steam 47.____

 A. generated principally to operate machinery
 B. exhausted from larger boilers
 C. generated at low pressure and brought up to high pressure before being used
 D. generated by engines other than boilers

48. As used in the above paragraph, the word *expressly* means 48.____

 A. rapidly B. specifically
 C. usually D. mainly

49. Of the following words, the one that is CORRECTLY spelled is 49.____

 A. suficient B. sufficiant
 C. sufficient D. suficiant

50. Of the following words, the one that is CORRECTLY spelled is 50.____

 A. fairly B. fairley C. farely D. fairlie

KEY (CORRECT ANSWERS)

1. B	11. B	21. C	31. B	41. D
2. A	12. D	22. C	32. A	42. B
3. A	13. D	23. B	33. D	43. D
4. C	14. B	24. A	34. B	44. A
5. C	15. C	25. C	35. D	45. C
6. C	16. C	26. C	36. A	46. B
7. B	17. B	27. B	37. B	47. A
8. A	18. D	28. B	38. B	48. B
9. C	19. B	29. A	39. C	49. C
10. B	20. A	30. B	40. D	50. A

EXAMINATION SECTION
TEST 1

DIRECTIONS: Each question or incomplete statement is followed by several suggested answers or completions. Select the one that BEST answers the question or completes the statement. *PRINT THE LETTER OF THE CORRECT ANSWER IN THE SPACE AT THE RIGHT.*

Questions 1-8.

DIRECTIONS: Questions 1 through 8 involve tests on the fuse box arrangement shown below. All tests are to be performed with a neon tester or a lamp test bank consisting of two 6-watt, 120-volt lamps connected in series. Do not make any assumptions about the conditions of the circuits. Draw your conclusions only from the information obtained with the neon tester or the two-lamp test bank, applied to the circuits as called for.

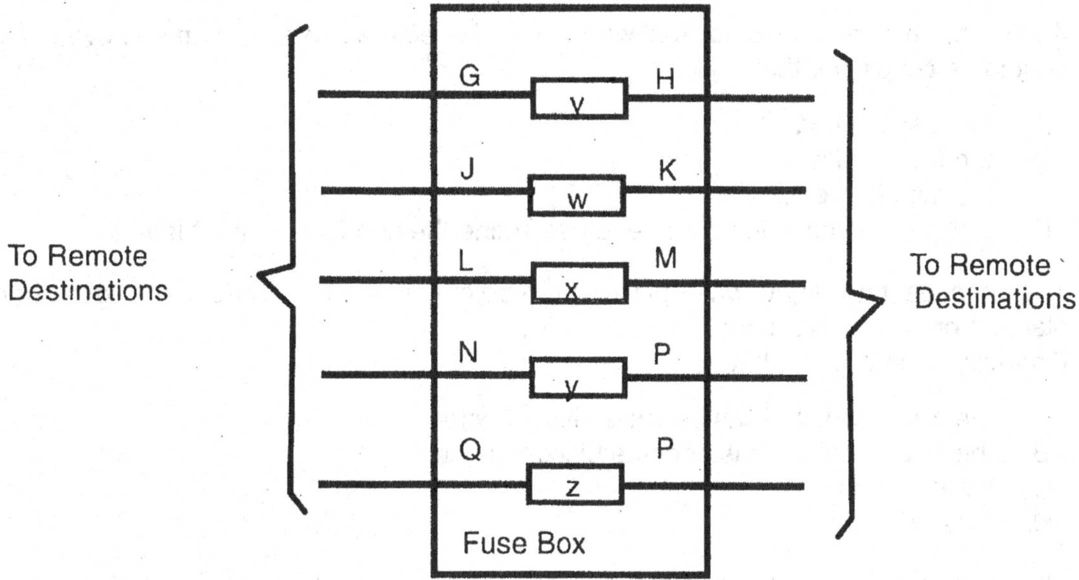

1. The two lamp test bank is placed from point *G* to joint *J*, and both lamps light. One of the lamps is momentarily removed from its socket; during that instant, the other lamp in the series-connected test bank should 1.____

   A. go dark
   B. get dimmer
   C. remain at same brightness
   D. get brighter

2. The test bank with two 60-watt, 120-volt lamps in series should be used on circuits with 2.____

   A. wattages only from 60 to 120 watts
   B. wattages only from 0 to 120 watts
   C. voltages only from 120 to 240 volts
   D. voltages only from 0 to 240 volts

3. The neon tester is placed from point *G* to point *J* and only one-half of the neon tester lights. 3.____
It should be concluded that

   A. half of the tester has gone bad
   B. a wire has become disconnected in the circuit
   C. the voltage is AC
   D. the voltage is DC

4. If both lamps in the test bank light when placed directly across one of the above fuses, it should be concluded that 4.____

   A. the fuse is good
   B. the fuse is blown
   C. the fuse is overrated
   D. further tests have to be made to determine the condition of the fuse

5. If the lamp test bank does not light when placed directly across one of the above fuses, it should be concluded that 5.____

   A. the fuse is good
   B. the fuse is blown
   C. the fuse is overrated
   D. further tests have to be made to determine the condition of the fuse

6. The lamp test bank lights when placed from point *G* to point *J* but does not light when placed from point *H* to point *J*. 6.____
It should be concluded that

   A. the wire to point *H* has become disconnected
   B. the wire to point *J* has become disconnected
   C. fuse *υ* is bad
   D. fuse *w* is bad

7. The lamp test bank lights when placed from point *L* to point *N* but does not light when placed from point *M* to point *P*. 7.____
It should be concluded that

   A. both fuses *x* and *y* are bad
   B. either fuse *x* or fuse *y* is bad or both are bad
   C. both fuses *x* and *y* are good
   D. these tests do not indicate the condition of any fuse

8. The lamp test bank is placed from point *L* to point *N*, then from *N* to point Q, and finally from point *L* to point Q. In each case, both lamps light to full brightness. 8.____
It should be concluded that points *L*, *N*, and Q have

   A. three-phase, 120 volts, AC, line-to-line
   B. plus and minus 120 volts, DC
   C. three-phase, 208 volts, AC
   D. plus and minus 240 volts, DC

9. An automatic device used for regulating air temperature is a(n) 9.____

A. rheostat B. aquastat C. thermostat D. duostat

10. Assume that you have just completed a certain maintenance job which you feel is satisfactory, but your foreman asks you to make certain changes. 10.____
The BEST procedure for you to follow is to

A. request the foreman to assign this work to someone else
B. have another maintainer verify that the job was done properly
C. ask the foreman the reasons for the changes
D. complain to the foreman's superior of this waste of time

11. The PROPER set of tools and equipment to be used to clean and adjust the ignition points of an automobile consists of a 11.____

A. screwdriver, feeler gauge, and point file
B. wrench, micrometer, and sandpaper
C. scraper, micrometer, and emery cloth
D. V-block, pliers, and sandpaper

12. The voltage developed in each cell of an automobile battery is ______ volts. 12.____

A. 2 B. 4 C. 6 D. 12

13. The one of the following tools that is NOT used to clear plumbing stoppages is a 13.____

A. force-cup B. drain auger
C. snake D. pick-out iron

14. Eyebolts are generally fastened to the shells of machinery in order to 14.____

A. act as a leveling device
B. facilitate lifting
C. permit easy tagging of the equipment
D. reinforce the machine shells

15. When grinding a weld smooth, it is MOST important to avoid 15.____

A. grinding too slowly
B. overheating the surrounding metal
C. grinding away too much of the weld
D. grinding after the weld has cooled off

16. A cold chisel whose head has become *mushroomed* should NOT be used because 16.____

A. it is impossible to hit the head squarely
B. the chisel will not cut accurately
C. chips might fly from the head
D. the chisel has lost its *temper*

17. The type of screwdriver specially made to be used in tight spots is the 17.____

A. Phillips B. offset
C. square shank D. truss

18. An indication that a fluorescent lamp in a fixture should be replaced is 18.____

A. humming in the fixture
B. the ends of the lamp remain black when the lamp is lit
C. poor or slow starting
D. the lamp does not shut off each time the OFF button is pressed

19. Asbestos is used as a covering on electrical wires to provide protection from 19.____

A. high voltage
B. high temperatures
C. water damage
D. electrolysis

20. Many electric power tools, such as drills, have a third conductor in the line cord which should be connected to a grounded part of the power receptacle. 20.____
The reason for this is to

A. have a spare wire in case one power wire should break
B. strengthen the power lead so that it cannot be easily damaged
C. protect the user of the tool from electrical shocks
D. allow use of the tool for extended periods of time without overheating

21. Employees are responsible for the good care, proper maintenance, and serviceable condition of the property issued or assigned for their use. 21.____
As used above, *serviceable condition* means the property is in a state where it is

A. capable of being repaired
B. easily handled
C. fit for use
D. least expensive

22. A brush that has been used in shellac should be cleaned by washing it in 22.____

A. water
B. linseed oil
C. lacquer thinner
D. alcohol

23. Excessive moisture on a surface being painted would MOST likely result in 23.____

A. alligatoring
B. blistering
C. cracking
D. sagging

24. In order to reverse the direction of rotation of a series motor, the 24.____

A. connections to the armature should be reversed
B. connections to both the armature and the series field should be reversed
C. connections of the motor to the power lines should be reversed
D. series field should be placed in shunt with the armature

25. A megger is an instrument used to measure 25.____

A. capacitance
B. insulation resistance
C. power
D. illumination levels

26. The first aid treatment for chemical burns on the skin is 26.____

A. treatment with ointment and then bandaging
B. washing with large quantities of water and then treating as heat burns
C. treatment with a neutralizing agent and no bandaging
D. application of sodium bicarbonate and then bandaging

27. The chemical MOST frequently used to clean drains clogged with grease is 27.____

A. muriatic acid
B. soda ash
C. ammonia
D. caustic soda

28. When tapping a blind hole in a steel plate, the FIRST type of tap to use is a ______ tap. 28.____

A. plug B. taper C. lead D. bottoming

29. A common handshaving tool used in woodwork is a(n) 29.____

A. trammel B. router C. auger D. plane

30. *Dressing* a grinding wheel refers to 30.____

A. making the wheel thinner
B. replacing with a new wheel
C. repairing a crack in the wheel
D. making the wheel round

31. The maintainer who is MOST valuable is the one who 31.____

A. offers to do the heavy lifting
B. asks many questions about the work
C. listens to instructions and carries them out
D. makes many suggestions on work procedures

32. Of the following, turpentine is used for thinning 32.____

A. latex paint
B. red lead paint
C. calcimine
D. shellac

33. Of the following, the hacksaw blade BEST suited for cutting thin-walled tubing is one which has ______ teeth/inch. 33.____

A. 14 B. 18 C. 24 D. 32

34. Because of its weather-resistant properties, a varnish commonly used on exterior surfaces is ______ varnish. 34.____

A. spar B. flat C. rubbing D. hard oil

35. A trip spring or spring cylinder on a snow plow assembly is a device that 35.____

A. absorbs the shock of impact when the plow strikes an obstacle in the road
B. provides for snap-action in the lowering of the plow blade
C. allows for quick removal or attachment of the snow plow supporting frame
D. detaches the plow blade and lets it hang free when the plow blade is dragged backwards

36. The term *preventative maintenance* is used to identify a plan whereby 36.____

A. equipment is serviced according to a regular schedule
B. equipment is serviced as soon as it fails
C. equipment is replaced as soon as it becomes obsolete
D. all equipment is replaced periodically

37. The ratio of air to gasoline in an automobile engine is controlled by the 37.____

A. gas filter
B. fuel pump
C. carburetor
D. intake manifold

38. *Energizer* is another name given to the 38.____

A. automobile battery
B. fluorescent fixture ballast
C. battery charger
D. generator shunt field

39. Wearshoes may be found on 39.____

A. circuit breakers
B. automobile brake systems
C. snow plows
D. door sills

40. When moving heavy equipment by means of pipe rollers, it is MOST important to 40.____

A. use solid steel rollers
B. use rollers with different diameters
C. see that the trailing roller does not slip out from under the equipment
D. use more than three rollers at all times

41. The one of the following storage areas that is BEST for the storage of paint is one which is 41.____

A. unheated and not ventilated
B. cool and ventilated
C. sunny and ventilated
D. warm and not ventilated

42. The leverage that can be obtained with a wrench is determined mainly by the 42.____

A. material of which the wrench is made
B. gripping surface of the jaw
C. length of the handle
D. thickness of the wrench

43. A star drill is used to bore holes in 43.____

A. steel
B. concrete
C. wood
D. sheet metal

44. The one of the following actions of a maintainer that is MOST likely to contribute to a good working relationship between him and his assistant is for him to 44.____

A. observe the same rules of conduct that he expects his assistant to observe
B. freely give advice on his assistant's personal problems
C. always be frank and outspoken to his assistant in pointing out his faults
D. expect his assistant to perform with equal efficiency on any job assigned

45. Three common types of windows are 45.____

A. batten, casement, and awning
B. batten, casement, and double-hung
C. batten, double-hung, and awning
D. casement, double-hung, and awning

46. A staircase has twelve risers, each 6 3/4" high. The TOTAL rise of the staircase is 46.____

A. 6' $2\frac{1}{4}$" B. 6'9" C. 7'0" D. 7'3 3/4"

47. A twenty-foot straight ladder placed at an angle against a wall should be at a distance from the wall equal to ______ feet. 47.____

A. 3 B. 5 C. 7 D. 9

48. Reflective sheeting traffic signs that have become dirty should be wiped with kerosene or gasoline FOLLOWED by a 48.____

A. wiping with a soft cloth soaked in thin oil
B. hand rub with very fine sandpaper
C. wash with detergent and a rinse with water
D. coating of shellac applied with a brush

49. A temporary wooden fence carrying red flags and built around an opening in a pavement to warn oncoming traffic is known as a 49.____

A. batter board B. bulkhead
C. bollard D. barricade

50. *Four-ply belted* is used to describe the construction of 50.____

A. belt-drive pulleys
B. auto tires
C. electrical wiring insulation
D. seat belts

KEY (CORRECT ANSWERS)

1. A	11. A	21. C	31. C	41. B
2. D	12. A	22. D	32. B	42. C
3. D	13. D	23. B	33. D	43. B
4. B	14. B	24. A	34. A	44. A
5. D	15. C	25. B	35. A	45. D
6. C	16. C	26. B	36. A	46. B
7. B	17. B	27. D	37. C	47. B
8. C	18. B	28. B	38. A	48. C
9. C	19. B	29. D	39. C	49. D
10. C	20. C	30. D	40. C	50. B

TEST 2

DIRECTIONS: Each question or incomplete statement is followed by several suggested answers or completions. Select the one that BEST answers the question or completes the statement. *PRINT THE LETTER OF THE CORRECT ANSWER IN THE SPACE AT THE RIGHT.*

1. An oil bath filter is MOST often used on a(n) 1.____

   A. air compressor B. auto engine
   C. electric generator D. steam boiler

2. A 3-ohm resistor placed across a 12-volt battery will dissipate ______ watts. 2.____

   A. 3 B. 4 C. 12 D. 48

3. Instead of using fuses, modern electric wiring uses 3.____

   A. quick switches B. circuit breakers
   C. fusible links D. lag blocks

4. The MOST common combination of gases used for welding is 4.____

   A. carbon dioxide and acetylene
   B. nitrogen and hydrogen
   C. oxygen and acetylene
   D. oxygen and hydrogen

5. If a wheel has turned through an angle of 180, then it has made ______ revolution(s). 5.____

   A. 1/4 B. 1/2 C. 1/8 D. 18

6. Sewer gas is prevented from backing up through a plumbing fixture by a 6.____

   A. water trap B. return elbow
   C. check valve D. float valve

7. Putty that is too stiff is made workable by adding 7.____

   A. gasoline B. linseed oil
   C. water D. lacquer thinner

8. A vertical wood member in the wall of a wood frame house is known as a 8.____

   A. A stringer B. ridge member
   C. stud D. header

9. A 10-to-1 step-down transformer has an input of 1 ampere at 120 volts AC. If the losses are negligible, the output of the transformer is ______ volts. 9.____

   A. 1 ampere at 12 B. .1 ampere at 1200
   C. 10 amperes at 12 D. 10 amperes at 120

10. An oscilloscope is an instrument used in 10.____

    A. measuring noise levels
    B. displaying waveforms of electrical signals
    C. indicating the concentrations of pollutants in air
    D. photographing high-speed events

11. Assume that a brake pedal of a truck goes to the floorboard when depressed. The one of the following that could cause this condition is 11.____

    A. a leak in the hydraulic lines
    B. a clogged hydraulic line
    C. scored drums
    D. glazed linings

12. The universal joints of an automobile are located on the 12.____

    A. suspension springs
    B. steering linkages
    C. wheel cylinders
    D. drive shaft

13. The MAIN purpose of a flexible coupling is to connect two shafts which are 13.____

    A. of different diameters
    B. of different shapes
    C. not in exact alignment
    D. of different material

14. When using a standard measuring micrometer, starting with a zero reading, one complete counterclockwise revolution of the sleeve will give a reading of ______ inch. 14.____

    A. .001
    B. .010
    C. .025
    D. .250

15. If a nut is to be tightened to an exact specified value of inch-lbs., the wrench to use is a ______ wrench. 15.____

    A. spanner
    B. box
    C. lock-jaw
    D. torque

16. Common permanent type anti-freezes for automobile cooling systems are MAINLY 16.____

    A. alcohol
    B. methanol
    C. ethylene glycol
    D. trychloroethylene

17. Plexiglas is also called 17.____

    A. mylar
    B. lucite
    C. isinglass
    D. PVC

18. Long, curved lines are BEST cut in 1/4" plexiglas with a ______ saw. 18.____

    A. rip
    B. jig
    C. keyhole
    D. coping

19. The specific gravity of storage battery cells can be measured with a(n) 19.____

    A. odometer
    B. hydrometer
    C. ammeter
    D. dwell meter

20. A nail set is a tool used for 20.____

    A. straightening bent nails
    B. measuring nail sizes
    C. cutting nails to specified size
    D. driving a nail head into wood

21. To cut a number of 2" x 4" lengths of wood accurately at an angle of 45°, it is BEST to use a 21.____

    A. protractor
    B. mitre-box
    C. triangle
    D. square

22. The type of fastener MOST commonly used when bolting to concrete uses a(n) 22.____

A. expansion shield
B. U-bolt
C. toggle bolt
D. turnbuckle

23. When an automobile engine does not start on a damp day, the trouble is MOST likely in the ______ system. 23.____

A. ignition B. cooling C. fuel D. lubricating

24. The battery of an automobile is prevented from discharging back through the alternator by the blocking action of the 24.____

A. commutator B. diodes C. brushes D. slip rings

25. The master cylinder in an automobile is actuated by the 25.____

A. steering column
B. brake pedal
C. clutch plate
D. cam shaft

26. The FINEST sandpaper from among the following is No. 26.____

A. 3 B. 1 C. 2/0 D. 6/0

27. A screw whose head is buried below the surface of the wood that it is screwed into is said to be 27.____

A. countersunk
B. scalloped
C. expanded
D. flushed

28. The one of the following devices which is used to measure angles is the 28.____

A. caliper
B. protractor
C. marking gauge
D. divider

29. Before a new oil stone is used, it should be 29.____

A. heated
B. soaked in oil
C. coated with shellac
D. washed with soapy water

30. Dies are used for 30.____

A. threading the outside ends of metal pipes
B. making sweated joints on lead pipes
C. cutting nipples to exact lengths
D. caulking cast-iron pipe joints

31. The energy stored by a storage battery is commonly given in 31.____

A. volts
B. amperes
C. ampere-hours
D. kilowatts

32. *Vapor lock* occurs in automobile 32.____

A. gas tanks
B. crankcases
C. transmissions
D. carburetors

33. A woodworking tool used to bore odd-size holes for which there is no standard auger bit is a(n) 33.____

A. single twist auger
B. double twist auger
C. expansive bit
D. straight fluted drill

34. Soap is sometimes applied to wood screws in order to 34.____

A. prevent rust
B. make a tight fit
C. make insertion easier
D. prevent wood splitting

35. On a long run of copper tubing, the tubing is often bent in the shape of a horseshoe rather than being run in a straight line. 35.____
The MAIN reason for this is to

A. allow an excess that could be used in future repairs
B. make it easier to install the tubing
C. permit the tubing to expand and contract with changes in temperature
D. eliminate the need for accurate measurements in cutting the tubing

36. Loss of seal water in a house water trap is prevented by the use of a 36.____

A. drainage tee B. faucet C. hose bibb D. vent

37. BX is a designation for a type of 37.____

A. flexible armored electric cable
B. flexible gas line
C. rigid conduit
D. electrical insulation

38. *WYE-WYE* and *DELTA-WYE* are two 38.____

A. types of DC motor windings
B. arrangements of 3-phase transformer connections
C. types of electrical splices
D. shapes of commutator bars

39. Green lumber should NOT be used in the building of scaffolding because it 39.____

A. will not hold nails well
B. easily splits when nailed
C. may warp on drying
D. is too expensive

40. *Scotchlite* ready-made traffic sign faces with heat-activated adhesive backings are applied to backing blanks by use of a 40.____

A. temperature-controlled oven
B. vacuum applicator
C. hot water bath
D. heated roller assembly

41. *Scotchcal* is a(n) 41.____

A. reflective sheeting
B. epoxy protective paint
C. fluorescent film
D. high temperature lubricant

42. Wooden ladders should NOT be painted because the paint 42.____

A. is inflammable
B. may cover defects in the wood
C. makes the rungs slippery
D. may deteriorate the wood

43. To prevent ladders from slipping, the bottoms of the ladder side rails are OFTEN fitted with 43.____

A. automatic locks
B. ladder shoes
C. ladder hooks
D. stirrups

44. A bowline is 44.____

A. the sag that a scaffold develops when men get on it
B. a knot with a loop that does not run
C. a temporary telephone wire strung during emergencies
D. the reference line established in ditch excavations

45. A method sometimes used to prevent a pipe from buckling during a bending operation is to 45.____

A. bend the pipe very quickly
B. keep the seam of the pipe on the outside of the bend
C. nick the pipe at the center of the bend
D. pack the inside of the pipe with sand

46. A rectifier changes 46.____

A. DC to AC
B. AC to DC
C. single-phase power to three-phase power
D. battery power to three-phase power

47. Continuity in a de-energized electrical circuit may be checked with a(n) 47.____

A. voltmeter
B. ohmmeter
C. neon tester
D. rheostat

48. Of the following crankcase oils, the one that should be used in sub-zero weather is SAE 48.____

A. 10W
B. 20W
C. 20
D. 30

49. Caster in an automobile is an adjustment in the 49.____

A. ignition system
B. drive-shaft
C. rear differential
D. front suspension

50. If the spark plugs in an engine run too hot, the result is MOST likely that 50.____

A. oil and carbon compounds will accumulate on the insulators
B. the electrodes will wear rapidly
C. the timing will be retarded
D. the ignition coil may become damaged

KEY (CORRECT ANSWERS)

1. B	11. A	21. B	31. C	41. C
2. B	12. D	22. A	32. D	42. B
3. B	13. C	23. A	33. C	43. B
4. C	14. C	24. B	34. C	44. B
5. B	15. D	25. B	35. C	45. D
6. A	16. C	26. D	36. D	46. B
7. B	17. B	27. A	37. A	47. B
8. C	18. B	28. B	38. B	48. A
9. C	19. B	29. B	39. C	49. D
10. B	20. D	30. A	40. B	50. B

EXAMINATION SECTION
TEST 1

DIRECTIONS: Each question or incomplete statement is followed by several suggested answers or completions. Select the one that BEST answers the question or completes the statement. *PRINT THE LETTER OF THE CORRECT ANSWER IN THE SPACE AT THE RIGHT.*

1. The combustion efficiency of a boiler can be determined with a CO_2 indicator and the 1.____

   A. under fire draft
   B. boiler room humidity
   C. flue gas temperature
   D. outside air temperature

2. A quick, practical method of determining if the cast-iron waste pipe delivered to a job has been damaged in transit is to 2.____

   A. hydraulically test it
   B. "ring" each length with a hammer
   C. drop each length to see whether it breaks
   D. visually examine the pipe for cracks

3. An electrostatic precipitator is used to 3.____

   A. filter the air supply
   B. remove sludge from the fuel oil
   C. remove particles from the fuel gas
   D. supply samples for an Orsat analysis

4. The PRIMARY cause of cracking and spalling of refractory lining in the furnace of a steam generator is *most likely* due to 4.____

   A. continuous over-firing of boiler
   B. slag accumulation on furnace walls
   C. change in fuel from solid to liquid
   D. uneven heating and cooling within the refractory brick

5. The term "effective temperature" in air conditioning means 5.____

   A. the dry bulb temperature
   B. the average of the wet and dry bulb temperatures
   C. the square root of the product of wet and dry bulb temperatures
   D. an arbitrary index combining the effects of temperature, humidity, and movement

6. The piping in all buildings having dual water distribution systems should be identified by a color coding of ______ for potable water lines and ______ for non-potable water lines. 6.____

   A. green; red
   B. green; yellow
   C. yellow; green
   D. yellow; red

7. The breaking of a component of a machine subjected to excessive vibration is called 7.____

   A. tensile failure
   B. fatigue failure
   C. caustic embrittlement
   D. amplitude failure

8. The TWO MOST important factors to be considered in selecting fans for ventilating systems are 8.____

   A. noise and efficiency
   B. space available and weight
   C. first cost and dimensional bulk
   D. construction and arrangement of drive

9. In the modern power plant deaerator, air is removed from water to 9.____

   A. reduce heat losses in the heaters
   B. reduce corrosion of boiler steel due to the air
   C. reduce the load of the main condenser air pumps
   D. prevent pumps from becoming vapor bound

10. The abbreviations BOD, COD, and DO are associated with 10.____

   A. flue gas analysis
   B. air pollution control
   C. boiler water treatment
   D. water pollution control

11. The piping of a newly installed drainage system should be tested upon completion of the rough plumbing with a head of water of NOT LESS THAN ______ feet. 11.____

   A. 10 B. 15 C. 20 D. 25

12. Of the following statements concerning aquastats, the one which is CORRECT is: 12.____

   A. Aquastats may be obtained with either a narrow or wide range of settings
   B. Aquastats have a mercury tube switch which is controlled by the stack switch
   C. An aquastat is a device used to shut down the burner in the event of low water in the boiler
   D. An aquastat should be located about 4 inches above the normal water line of the boiler

13. The SAFEST way to protect the domestic water supply from contamination by sewage or non-potable water is to insert 13.____

   A. air gaps
   B. swing connections
   C. double check valves
   D. tanks with overhead discharge

14. The MAIN function of a back-pressure valve which is sometimes found in the connection between a water drain pipe and the sewer system is to 14.____

   A. equalize the pressure between the drain pipe and the sewer
   B. prevent sewer water from flowing into the drain pipe
   C. provide pressure to enable waste to reach the sewer
   D. make sure that there is not too much water pressure in the sewer line

15. Boiler water is neutral if its pH value is 15.____

   A. 0 B. 1 C. 7 D. 14

16. A domestic hot water mixing or tempering valve should be preceded in the hot water line by a 16.____

A. strainer
B. foot valve
C. check valve
D. steam trap

17. Between a steam boiler and its safety valve there should be 17.____

A. no valve of any type
B. a gate valve of the same size as the safety valve
C. a swing check valve of at least the same size as the safety valve
D. a cock having a clear opening equal in area to the pipe connecting the boiler and safety valve

18. A diagram of horizontal plumbing drainage lines should have cleanouts shown 18.____

A. at least every 25 feet
B. at least every 100 feet
C. wherever a basin is located
D. wherever a change in direction occurs

19. When a Bourdon gauge is used to measure steam pressures, some form of siphon or water seal must be maintained.
The reason for this is to 19.____

A. obtain "absolute" pressure readings
B. prevent steam from entering the gage
C. prevent condensate from entering the gage
D. obtain readings below atmospheric pressure

20. In a closed heat exchanger, oil is cooled by condensate which is to be returned to a boiler. In order to avoid the possibility of contaminating the condensate with oil should a tube fail in the oil cooler, it would be good practice to 20.____

A. cool the oil by air instead of water
B. treat the condensate with an oil solvent
C. keep the oil pressure in the exchanger higher than the water pressure
D. keep the water pressure in the exchanger higher than the oil pressure

21. A radiator thermostatic trap is used on a vacuum return type of heating system to 21.____

A. release the pocketed air only
B. reduce the amount of condensate
C. maintain a predetermined radiator water level
D. prevent the return of live steam to the return line

22. According to the color coding of piping, fire protection piping should be painted 22.____

A. green
B. yellow
C. purple
D. red

23. The MAIN purpose of a standpipe system is to 23.____

A. supply the roof water tank
B. provide water for firefighting

C. circulate water for the heating system
D. provide adequate pressure for the water supply

24. The name "Saybolt" is associated with the measurement of 24.____

A. viscosity
B. Btu content
C. octane rating
D. temperature

25. Recirculation of conditioned air in an air-conditioned building is done MAINLY to 25.____

A. reduce refrigeration tonnage required
B. increase room entrophy
C. increase air specific humidity
D. reduce room temperature below the dewpoint

26. In a plumbing installation, vent pipes are GENERALLY used to 26.____

A. prevent the loss of water seal from traps by evaporation
B. prevent the loss of water seal due to several causes other than evaporation
C. act as an additional path for liquids to flow through during normal use of a plumbing fixture
D. prevent the backflow of water in a cross-connection between a drinking water line and a sewage line

27. The designation "150 W" cast on the bonnet of a gate valve is an indication of the 27.____

A. water working temperature
B. water working pressure
C. area of the opening in square inches
D. weight of the valve in pounds

28. In the city, the size soil pipe necessary in a sewage drainage system is determined by the 28.____

A. legal occupancy of the building
B. vertical height of the soil line
C. number of restrooms connected to the soil line
D. number of "fixture units" connected to the soil line

29. Fins or other extended surfaces are used on heat exchanger tubes when 29.____

A. the exchanger is a water-to-water exchanger
B. water is on one side of the tube and condensing steam on the other side
C. the surface coefficient of heat transfer on both sides of the tube is high
D. the surface coefficient of heat transfer on one side of the tube is low compared to the coefficient on the other side of the tube

30. A fusible plug may be put in a fire tube boiler as an emergency device to indicate low water level. The fusible plug is installed so that under normal operating conditions, 30.____

A. both sides are exposed to steam
B. one side is exposed to water and the other side to steam
C. one side is exposed to steam and the other side to hot gases
D. one side is exposed to the water and the other side to hot gases

31. Extra strong wrought-iron pipe, as compared to standard wrought-iron pipe of the same nominal size, has 31.____

A. the same outside diameter but a smaller inside diameter
B. the same inside diameter but a larger outside diameter
C. a larger outside diameter and a smaller inside diameter
D. larger inside and outside diameters

32. Fans may be rated on a dynamic or a static efficiency basis. The dynamic efficiency would *probably* be 32.____

A. lower in value because of the energy absorbed by the air velocity
B. the same as the static in the case of centrifugal blowers running at various speeds
C. the same as the static in the case of axial flow blowers running at various speeds
D. higher in value than the static

33. The function of the stack relay in an oil burner installation is to 33.____

A. regulate the draft over the fire
B. regulate the flow of fuel oil to the burner
C. stop the motor if the oil has not ignited
D. stop the motor if the water or steam pressure is too high

34. The type of centrifugal pump which is inherently balanced for hydraulic thrust is the 34.____

A. double suction impeller type
B. single suction impeller type
C. single stage type
D. multistage type

35. The specifications for a job using sheet lead calls for "4-lb. sheet lead." This means that each sheet should weigh 35.____

A. 4 lbs.
B. 4 lbs. per square
C. 4 lbs. per square foot
D. 4 lbs. per cubic inch

36. The total cooling load design conditions for a building are divided for convenience into two components.
These are: 36.____

A. infiltration and radiation
B. sensible heat and latent heat
C. wet and dry bulb temperatures
D. solar heat gain and moisture transfer

37. The function of a Hartford loop used on some steam boilers is to 37.____

A. limit boiler steam pressure
B. limit temperature of the steam
C. prevent high water levels in the boiler
D. prevent back flow of water from the boiler into the return main

38. Vibration from a ventilating blower can be prevented from being transmitted to the duct work by 38.____

A. installing straighteners in the duct
B. throttling the air supply to the blower
C. bolting the blower tightly to the duct
D. installing a canvas sleeve at the blower outlet

39. A specification states that access panels to suspended ceiling will be of metal. The MAIN reason for providing access panels is to 39.____

A. improve the insulation of the ceiling
B. improve the appearance of the ceiling
C. make it easier to construct the building
D. make it easier to maintain the building

40. A plumber on a job reports that the steamfitter has installed a 3" steam line in a location at which the plans show the house trap. On inspecting the job, you should 40.____

A. tell the steamfitter to remove the steam line
B. study the condition to see if the house trap can be relocated
C. tell the plumber and steamfitter to work it out between themselves and then report to you
D. tell the plumber to find another location for the trap because the steamfitter has already completed his work

41. In the installation of any heating system, the MOST important consideration is that 41.____

A. all elements be made of a good grade of cast iron
B. all radiators and connectors be mounted horizontally
C. the smallest velocity of flow of heating medium be used
D. there be proper clearance between hot surfaces and surrounding combustible material

42. Which one of the following is the PRIMARY object in drawing up a set of specifications for materials to be purchased? 42.____

A. Control of quality
B. Outline of intended use
C. Establishment of standard sizes
D. Location and method of inspection.

43. The drawing which should be used as a LEGAL reference when checking completed construction work is the ______ drawing. 43.____

A. contract
B. assembly
C. working or shop
D. preliminary

Questions 44-50.

DIRECTIONS: Questions 44 through 50 refer to the plumbing drawing shown below.

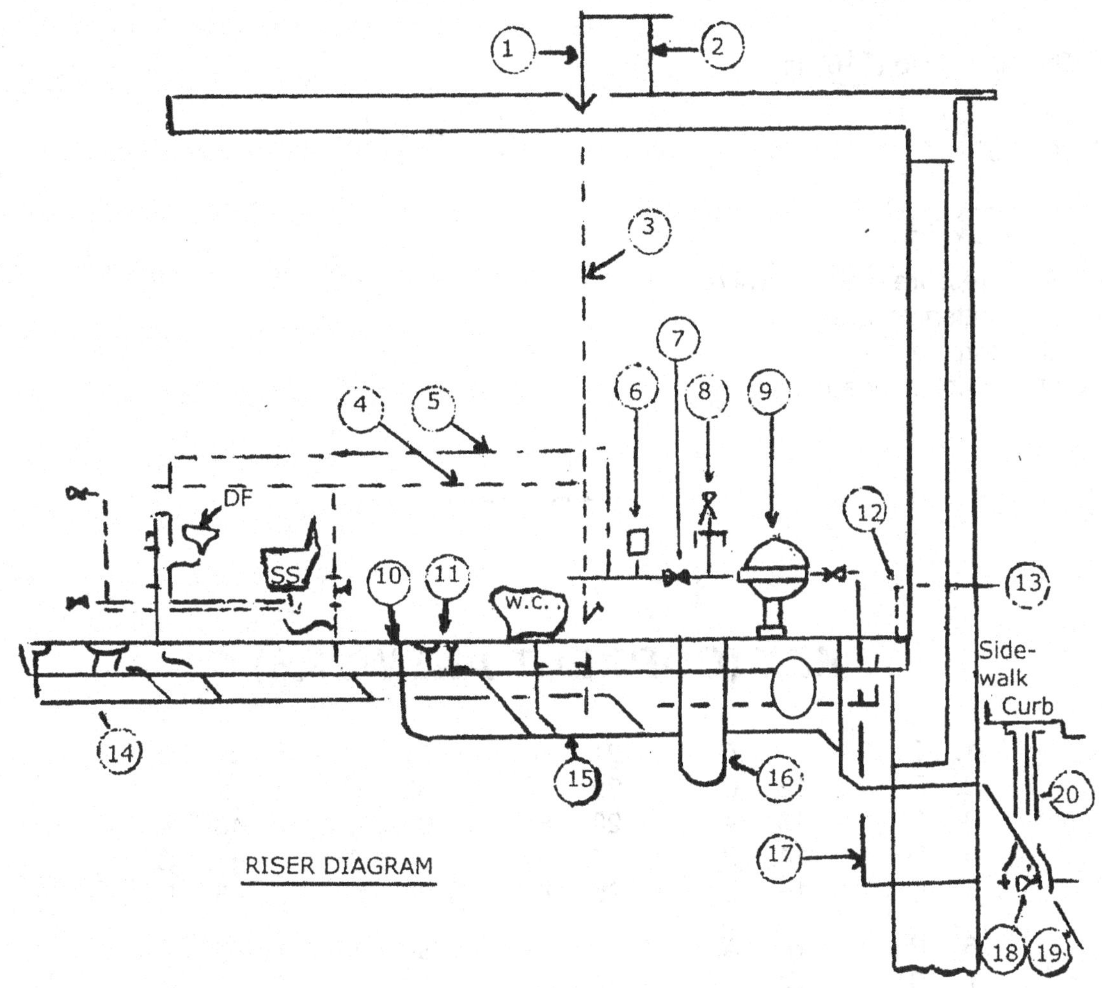

44. According to the building code, the MINIMUM diameter of No. (1) and its minimum height, No. (2) respectively, are 44.____

A. 2" and 12"
B. 3" and 18"
C. 4" and 24"
D. 6" and 36"

45. No (6) is a 45.____

A. relief valve
B. shock absorber
C. testing connection
D. drain

46. No. (9) is a 46.____

A. strainer
B. float valve
C. meter
D. pedestal

47. No. (11) is a 47.____

A. floor drain
B. cleanout
C. trap
D. vent connection

48. No. (13) is a 48.____

A. standpipe
B. air inlet
C. sprinkler head
D. cleanout

49. The size of No. (16) is 49.____

A. 2" x 2"
B. 2" x 3"
C. 3" x 3"
D. 4" x 4"

50. No. (18) is a 50.____

A. pressure reducing valve
B. butterfly valve
C. curb cock
D. sprinkler head

KEY (CORRECT ANSWERS)

1.	C	11.	A	21.	D	31.	A	41.	D
2.	B	12.	C	22.	D	32.	D	42.	A
3.	C	13.	A	23.	B	33.	C	43.	A
4.	D	14.	B	24.	A	34.	A	44.	C
5.	D	15.	C	25.	A	35.	C	45.	B
6.	B	16.	A	26.	B	36.	B	46.	C
7.	B	17.	A	27.	B	37.	D	47.	A
8.	A	18.	D	28.	D	38.	D	48.	B
9.	B	19.	B	29.	D	39.	D	49.	D
10.	D	20.	D	30.	D	40.	B	50.	C

EXAMINATION SECTION
TEST 1

DIRECTIONS: Each question or incomplete statement is followed by several suggested answers or completions. Select the one that BEST answers the question or completes the statement. *PRINT THE LETTER OF THE CORRECT ANSWER IN THE SPACE AT THE RIGHT.*

1. Leaks from the stem of a faucet can GENERALLY be stopped by replacing the 1.____

   A. bibb washer B. seat
   C. packing D. gasket

2. Of the following, the BEST procedure to follow with a frozen water pipe is to 2.____

   A. allow the pipe to thaw out by itself as the weather gets warmer
   B. put anti-freeze into the pipe above the section that is frozen
   C. turn on the hot water heater
   D. open the faucet closest to the frozen pipe and warm the pipe with a blow torch, starting at this point

3. Rubber will deteriorate FASTEST when it is constantly in contact with 3.____

   A. air B. water C. oil D. soapsuds

4. Stoppage of water flow is often caused by dirt accumulating in an elbow. 4.____
   As used in the above sentence, the word *accumulating* means MOST NEARLY

   A. clogging B. collecting
   C. rusting D. confined

5. The symbol shown at the right on a plumbing plan MOST likely represents a 5.____

   A. check valve
   B. vent
   C. sump
   D. trap

6. Of the following outside lines entering a building, the one for which grades must be MOST carefully controlled is the 6.____

   A. sewer line B. water line
   C. gas line D. electric cable

7. Threads are cut on the ends of a length of steel pipe by the use of a 7.____

   A. brace and bit B. counterbore
   C. stock and die D. doweling jig

8. When installing a catch basin, the outlet should be located 8.____

   A. at the same level as the inlet
   B. above the inlet
   C. below the inlet
   D. at the invert

9. The copper float in a low down water tank is perforated so that water enters the ball. As a result, the tank will 9.____

A. flush once, and then will not operate again
B. not flush at all
C. not flush completely
D. continue to flush, but water will be wasted

10. If water leaks from the stem of a faucet when the faucet is opened, the ______ should be ______. 10.____

A. faucet; replaced
B. cap nut; rethreaded
C. seat; reground
D. packing; replaced

11. Which of the following would ordinarily occur FIRST in a toilet tank after the handle is pushed down to flush the toilet? 11.____

A. Float ball drops with water level, opening the ball-cock assembly through which fresh water flows into the tank.
B. Tank ball sinks slowly into place.
C. Rising water pushes the float ball up until it closes the ballcock assembly, shutting off the supply of fresh water when the tank is full.
D. The tank ball lifts, opening the outlet so water can flow from tank to bowl.

12. When repairing a hole in a leaking pipe, which of the following should be done FIRST? 12.____

A. Wrap tape around the hole
B. Turn off the water supply
C. Tighten a clamp around the hole
D. Seal the hole with epoxy

13. If water is leaking from the top part of a bibcock, the part that should be replaced is MOST likely the 13.____

A. bibb washer
B. packing
C. seat
D. bibb screw

14. The pipe fitting that would be used to connect a 2" pipe at a 45° angle to another 2" pipe is called a(n) 14.____

A. tee
B. orifice flange
C. reducer
D. elbow

15. An order of 600 feet of 1-inch pipe is shipped in 24-foot lengths. The number of 7-foot pieces that can be cut from this shipment is 15.____

A. 25
B. 72
C. 75
D. 85

16. The tool shown at the right is a 16.____

A. countersink
B. counterbore
C. star drill
D. burring reamer

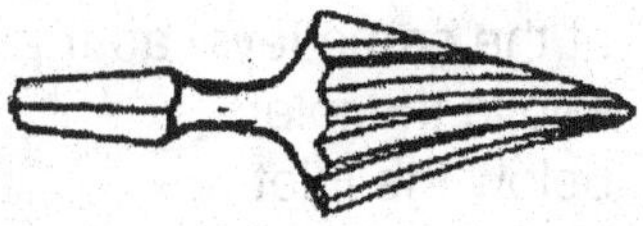

17. The temperature of a domestic hot water system is MOST often controlled by a(n) 17.____

    A. relief valve
    B. aquastat
    C. barometer
    D. thermostat

18. Insulation of steam pipes was MOST often done with 18.____

    A. asbestos
    B. celotex
    C. alundum
    D. sheathing

19. The BEST tool to use to remove the burr and sharp edge resulting from cutting tubing with a tube cutter is a 19.____

    A. file
    B. scraper
    C. reamer
    D. knife

20. Gaskets are seldom made of 20.____

    A. rubber
    B. lead
    C. asbestos
    D. vinyl

21. The composition of plumber's solder for wiping is APPROXIMATELY (ratio of tin to lead) 21.____

    A. 40-60
    B. 50-50
    C. 60-40
    D. 70-30

22. A device used to lift sewage to the level of a sewer from a floor below the sewer grade is known as a(n) 22.____

    A. elevator
    B. ejector
    C. sump
    D. conveyer

23. A check valve in a piping system will 23.____

    A. permit excessive pressures in a boiler
    B. eliminate water hammer
    C. permit water to flow in only one direction
    D. control the rate of flow of water

24. The chemical MOST frequently used to clean drains clogged with grease is 24.____

    A. muriatic acid
    B. soda ash
    C. ammonia
    D. caustic soda

25. A full thread cutting set would have both taps and 25.____

    A. cutters
    B. bushings
    C. dies
    D. plugs

KEY (CORRECT ANSWERS)

1. C
2. D
3. C
4. B
5. D
6. A
7. C
8. C
9. D
10. D
11. D
12. B
13. B
14. D
15. C
16. D
17. B
18. A
19. C
20. D
21. A
22. B
23. C
24. D
25. C

TEST 2

DIRECTIONS: Each question or incomplete statement is followed by several suggested answers or completions. Select the one that BEST answers the question or completes the statement. *PRINT THE LETTER OF THE CORRECT ANSWER IN THE SPACE AT THE RIGHT.*

1. To test for leaks in a newly installed C.I. waste stack, 1.____

   A. oil of peppermint is poured into the top of the stack
   B. smoke under pressure is pumped into the stack
   C. a water meter is used to measure the water flow
   D. dye is placed in the system at the top of the stack

2. 2.____

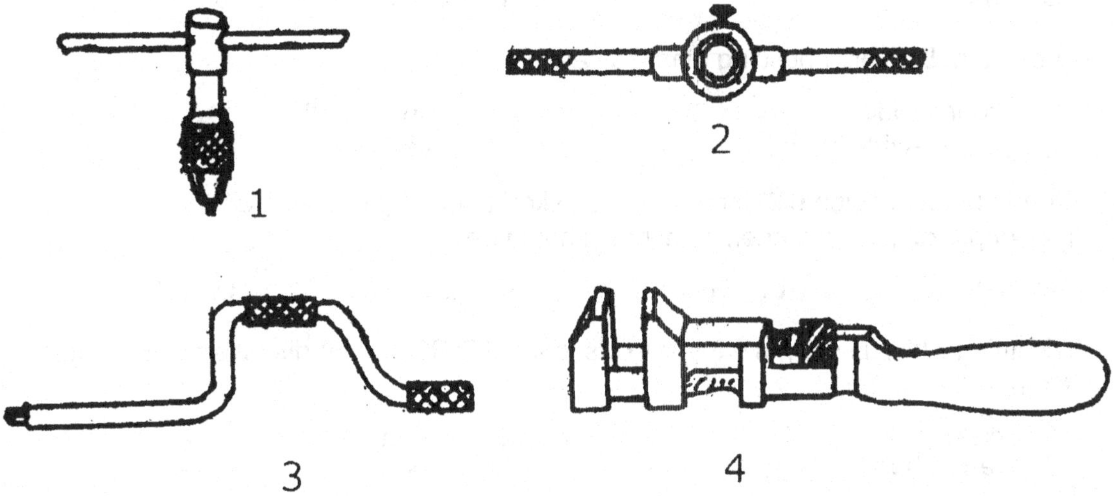

1 2

3 4

   The wrench whose PRINCIPAL purpose is to hold taps for threading is numbered

   A. 1 B. 2 C. 3 D. 4

3. An alloy used where resistance to corrosion is important is 3.____

   A. tungsten B. mild steel
   C. monel D. tin

4. The size of iron pipe is given in terms of its nominal 4.____

   A. weight B. inside diameter
   C. outside diameter D. wall thickness

5. When preparing surfaces to be soldered, the FIRST step is 5.____

   A. tinning B. sweating C. heating D. cleaning

6. To test for leaks in an acetylene torch, it is BEST that one use 6.____

   A. soapy water
   B. a match
   C. a gas with a strong odor
   D. a pressure gauge

7. To close off one opening in a pipe tee when the line connecting into it is to be temporarily removed, it is necessary to use a 7.____

A. pipe cap B. pipe plug C. nipple D. bushing

8. A 1-inch pipe is to span exactly 12 inches between the faces of two fittings. If a pipe thread table shows that 1-inch pipe has good threads extending for a distance of 11/16 inch at each end, then the necessary piece of 1-inch pipe must be cut to a total length of 8.____

A. 12 11/32" B. 12 11/16" C. 13 1/32" D. 13 3/8"

9. The letters W.C. on a building plan indicate 9.____

A. water closet
B. wet concrete
C. wire coil
D. workman's cloakroom

10. The letters D.S. on a building plan indicate a 10.____

A. door saddle
B. down spout
C. dumbwaiter shaft
D. dead space

11. From a length of pipe 6'9" long, you are asked to cut a piece 4'5" long. The length of the remainder, in inches, should be 11.____

A. 24 B. 26 C. 28 D. 53

12. The fitting which usually is easiest to disconnect FIRST when disassembling a piping run is a(n) 12.____

A. cross
B. union
C. return bend
D. elbow

13. For convenience in case of future repairs to a long pipe line, it is DESIRABLE to fit the pipe together with several 13.____

A. street ells
B. elbows
C. return bends
D. unions

14. If four pipes are to be connected to each other at a common point, it would be NECESSARY to use a(n) 14.____

A. tee fitting
B. street ell
C. cross
D. offset

15. Rubber gaskets are frequently placed between the faces of the flanges when making up a flanged joint in a pipe line in order to 15.____

A. prevent corrosion of the machined faces
B. permit full tightening of the flange bolts without danger of thread stripping
C. eliminate the necessity for accurate alignment of the pipe
D. make a tight joint

16. The percentage of the tank shown at the right that is filled with water is MOST NEARLY 16.____
   A. 33
   B. 35
   C. 37
   D. 39

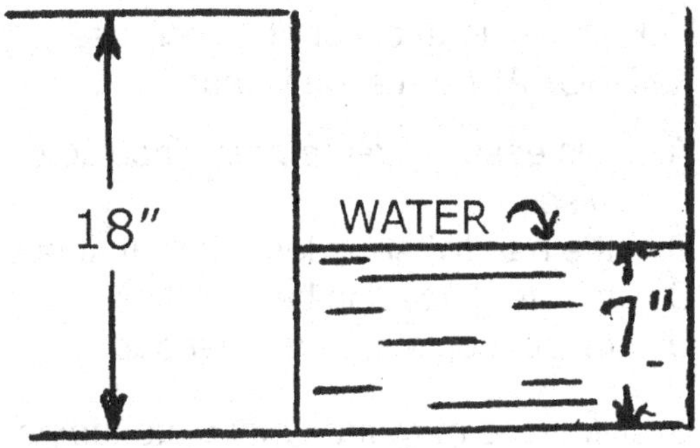

18″
WATER
7″

17. Of the following statements, the one that MOST closely identifies the term *house sewer* is: The house sewer is 17.____
   A. located outside the building area and connects to the public sewer in the street
   B. located inside the building area and ends at the outside of the front wall of the building
   C. the pipe which carries the discharge from the plumbing fixtures to the house drain
   D. the house drain

18. Of the following, the BEST tool to use to remove a chrome-plated bonnet from a faucet is a(n) 18.____
   A. vise-grip plier
   B. open end wrench
   C. stillson wrench
   D. chisel

19. The BEST flux to use for soldering galvanized iron is 19.____
   A. resin
   B. sal ammoniac
   C. borax
   D. muriatic acid

20. The one of the following that is NOT a common type of oilstone is 20.____
   A. silicon carbide
   B. aluminum oxide
   C. hard Arkansas
   D. pumice

21. A method of joining metals using temperatures intermediate between soldering and welding is 21.____
   A. corbelling
   B. brazing
   C. annealing
   D. lapping

22. The specifications of piping require the use of graphite on cleanout plugs. Of the following, the BEST reason for the use of graphite is to 22.____
   A. facilitate installing the plug
   B. facilitate removing the plug
   C. make the plug watertight
   D. give the plug a dark color for identification purposes

23. Practically all valves used in plumbing work are made so that the handwheel is turned clockwise instead of counterclockwise to close the valve. 23.____
The PROBABLE reason is that

A. it is easier to remember since screws and nuts move inward when turned clockwise
B. the handwheel is less likely to loosen
C. greater force can be exerted
D. most people are right-handed

24. Specifications may state that a standpipe system will be provided in each building. 24.____
The MAIN purpose of a standpipe system is to

A. supply the roof water tank
B. provide water for firefighting
C. circulate water for the heating system
D. provide adequate pressure for the water supply

25. A cast iron soil pipe-bend having an angle of 45 is COMMONLY called a ______ bend. 25.____

A. 1/16 B. 1/8 C. 1/4 D. return

KEY (CORRECT ANSWERS)

1.	B	11.	C
2.	A	12.	B
3.	C	13.	D
4.	B	14.	C
5.	D	15.	D
6.	A	16.	D
7.	B	17.	A
8.	D	18.	B
9.	A	19.	D
10.	B	20.	D

21. B
22. B
23. A
24. B
25. B

TEST 3

DIRECTIONS: Each question or incomplete statement is followed by several suggested answers or completions. Select the one that BEST answers the question or completes the statement. *PRINT THE LETTER OF THE CORRECT ANSWER IN THE SPACE AT THE RIGHT.*

1. Faucet leakage in a large building is BEST controlled by periodic 1.____

   A. faucet replacement
   B. addition of a sealing compound to the water supply
   C. packing replacement
   D. faucet inspection and repair

2. The one of the following that is the MOST practical method to use in making a temporary repair in a straight portion of a water pipe which has a small leak is to 2.____

   A. attach a clamped patch over the leak
   B. weld or braze the pipe, depending on the material
   C. drill and tap the pipe, then insert a plug
   D. fill the hole with an epoxy sealer

3. When constructing a tall reinforced concrete building, the pipeline system that should be built FIRST is the 3.____

   A. drainage plumbing
   B. standpipe system
   C. hot water system
   D. cold water system

4. The coefficient of expansion for brass pipe is 0.00001 inch per $^{\circ}$F. 4.____
   When the temperature of the water in a 110-foot length of brass pipe increases from 40° to 140° F, the increase in the length of the pipe is ______ inches.

   A. 0.32
   B. 1.32
   C. 2.31
   D. 21.2

5. The pipe taking water from a roof supply tank should extend at least six inches above the bottom of the tank PRIMARILY in order to 5.____

   A. allow some water to remain in the tank at all times
   B. prevent sediment from being carried into the plumbing
   C. provide sufficient pressure to the top floors of the building
   D. avoid corrosion of the bottom of the tank

6. The PROPER wrench to use in installing or tightening brass or chrome plated fittings is a(n) 6.____

   A. alligator
   B. stillson
   C. S
   D. strap

7. Which one of the wrenches pictured below is designed to grip round pipes in making plumbing repairs? 7.____

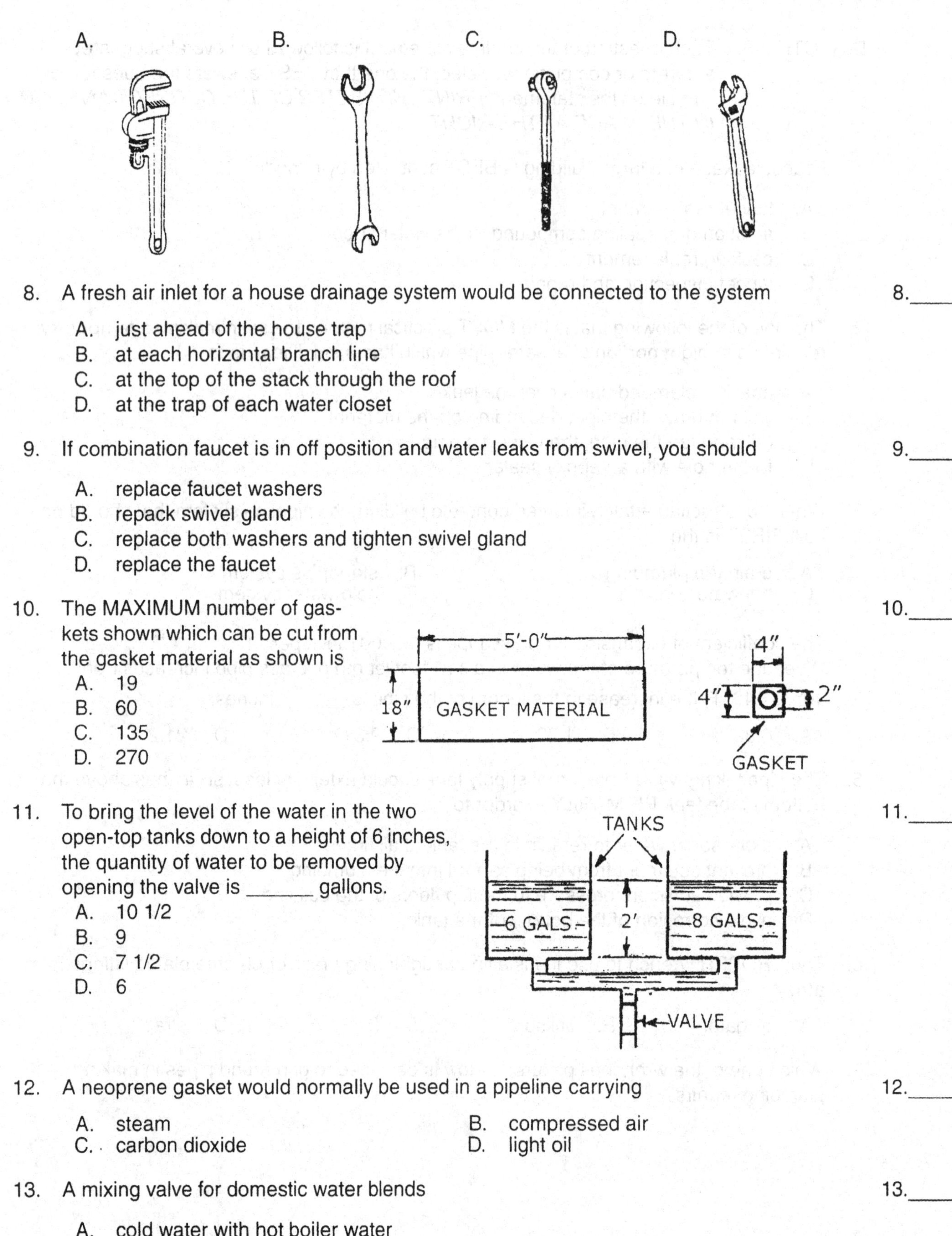

A. B. C. D.

8. A fresh air inlet for a house drainage system would be connected to the system 8.____

   A. just ahead of the house trap
   B. at each horizontal branch line
   C. at the top of the stack through the roof
   D. at the trap of each water closet

9. If combination faucet is in off position and water leaks from swivel, you should 9.____

   A. replace faucet washers
   B. repack swivel gland
   C. replace both washers and tighten swivel gland
   D. replace the faucet

10. The MAXIMUM number of gaskets shown which can be cut from the gasket material as shown is 10.____

   A. 19
   B. 60
   C. 135
   D. 270

11. To bring the level of the water in the two open-top tanks down to a height of 6 inches, the quantity of water to be removed by opening the valve is ______ gallons. 11.____

   A. 10 1/2
   B. 9
   C. 7 1/2
   D. 6

12. A neoprene gasket would normally be used in a pipeline carrying 12.____

   A. steam
   B. compressed air
   C. carbon dioxide
   D. light oil

13. A mixing valve for domestic water blends 13.____

   A. cold water with hot boiler water
   B. hot and cold water

C. cold water and hot water from coil submerged in boiler water
D. hot and cold water from cooling coil

14. In accordance with the uniform method of identifying piping in public buildings, pipes carrying materials classified as being dangerous are colored 14.____

A. blue
B. red
C. orange and yellow
D. green and white

15. The MAIN reason for preventing sewer gas from entering buildings through the plumbing system is because the gas 15.____

A. is highly inflammable and explosive in nature and could result in a fire hazard
B. has an eroding effect on plumbing fixtures and pipe lines
C. is highly infectious and contagious in nature
D. has a nuisance effect on occupants

16. In a multi-story building, standpipes are installed FIRST by the plumber for 16.____

A. water supply
B. sanitary facilities
C. fire protection
D. steam supply

17. A plumber's friend operates by 17.____

A. oscillation of water and air in the pipe
B. density of water and pressure
C. snake action
D. water pressure *only*

18. Compound is applied to pipe thread. 18.____
When threading pipe, where would you apply compound?

A. Male and female thread
B. Female *only*
C. Male *only*
D. At the end of the male connection *only*

19. In reference to domestic gas piping, 19.____

A. couplings with running threads are used to join pipes
B. risers must have a drip leg and cap at bottom
C. gasketed unions may be used in joining pipe
D. composition disc globe valves are used to throttle the gas

20. In the sketch at the right, the measurement of the inside diameter is MOST NEARLY ______ inches. 20.____

A. 2 1/2
B. 3
C. 3 1/2
D. 4

21. The FIRST item which should be checked when a sump pit overflows because the automatic electric sump pump is not operating properly is the 21.____

A. feedwater pressure
B. ficat switch mechanism
C. stat switch
D. discharge line check valve

22. The plumbing fixture that contains a ball cock is the 22.____

A. trap B. water closet
C. sprinkler D. dishwasher

23. A plumbing sketch is drawn to a scale of 1/8" = 1 foot. A horizontal water line measuring 63/4 inches on the sketch would be equivalent to ______ feet of water pipe. 23.____

A. 27 B. 41 C. 54 D. 64

24. The tool that holds the die when threading a 2" pipe is called a 24.____

A. yoke B. punch C. vise D. stock

25. The type of valve that permits fluid to flow in one direction ONLY in a pipe run is a ______ valve. 25.____

A. check B. gate C. globe D. cross

KEY (CORRECT ANSWERS)

1.	C	11.	A
2.	A	12.	D
3.	B	13.	B
4.	B	14.	C
5.	B	15.	D
6.	D	16.	C
7.	A	17.	A
8.	A	18.	C
9.	A	19.	B
10.	B	20.	B

21. B
22. B
23. C
24. D
25. A

MECHANICAL APTITUDE
TOOLS AND THEIR USE

EXAMINATION SECTION
TEST 1

Questions 1-16.

DIRECTIONS: Questions 1 through 16 refer to the tools shown below. The numbers in the answers refer to the numbers beneath the tools.
NOTE: These tools are NOT shown to scale

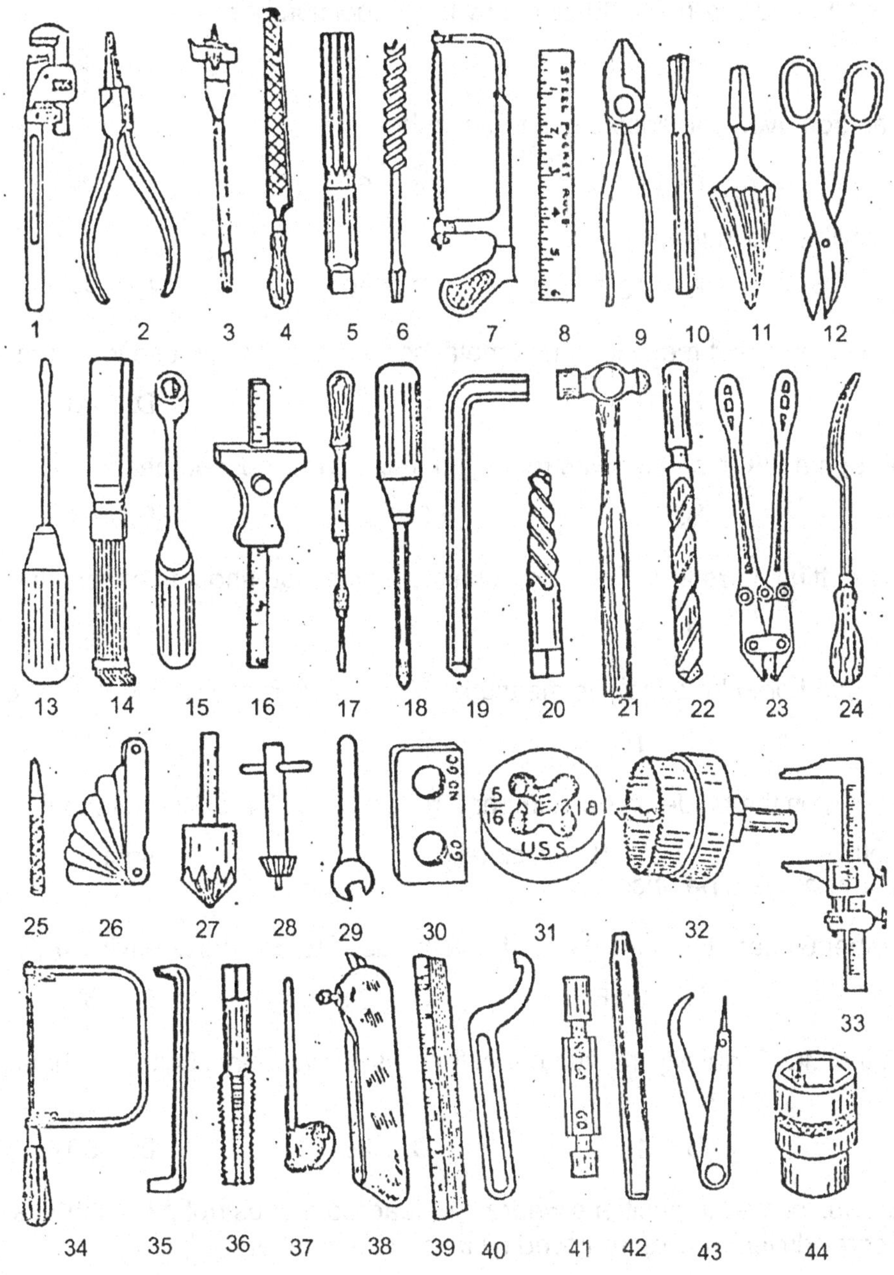

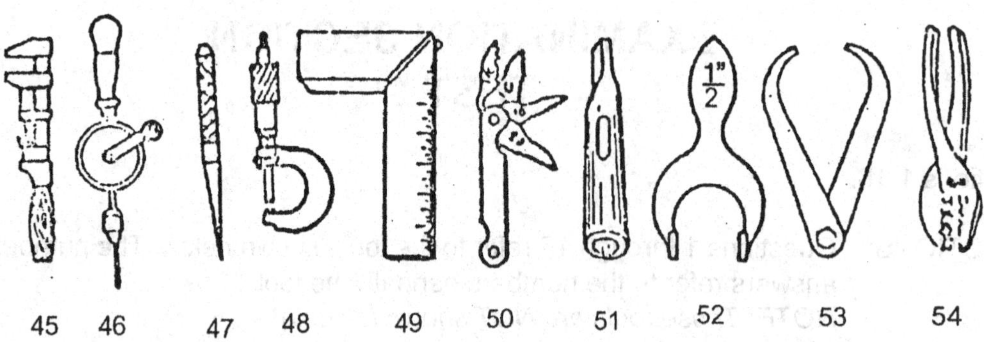

1. A 1" x 1" x 1/8" angle iron should be cut by using tool number 1.____

   A. 7 B. 12 C. 23 D. 42

2. To peen an iron rivet, you should use tool number 2.____

   A. 4 B. 7 C. 21 D. 43

3. The star "drill" is tool number 3.____

   A. 5 B. 10 C. 20 D. 22

4. To make holes in sheet metal for sheet metal screws, you should use tool number . 4.____

   A. 6 B. 10 C. 36 D. 46

5. To cut through a 3/8" diameter wire rope, you should use tool number 5.____

   A. 12 B. 23 C. 42 D. 54

6. To remove cutting burrs from the inside of a steel pipe, you should use tool number 6.____

   A. 5 B. 11 C. 14 D. 20

7. The depth of a bored hole may be measured MOST accurately with tool number 7.____

   A. 8 B. 16 C. 26 D. 41

8. If the marking on the blade of tool number 7 reads:12"-32", the 32 refers to the 8.____

   A. length B. thickness C. weight
   D. number of teeth per inch

9. If tool number 6 bears the mark "5", it should be used to drill holes having a diameter of 9.____

   A. 5/32" B. 5/16" C. 5/8" D. 5"

10. To determine MOST quickly the number of threads per inch on a bolt, you should use tool number 10.____

    A. 8 B. 16 C. 26 D. 50

11. Wood screws, located in positions where the headroom does not permit the use of an ordinary screwdriver, may be removed by using tool number 11.____

    A. 17 B. 28 C. 35 D. 46

12. To remove a broken-off piece of 1/2" diameter pipe from a fitting, you should use tool number 12.____

A. 5 B. 11 C. 20 D. 36

13. The outside diameter of a bushing may be measured MOST accurately with tool number 13.____

A. 8 B. 26 C. 33 D. 43

14. To re-thread a stud hole in the casting of an elevator motor, you should use tool number 14.____

A. 5 B. 20 C. 22 D. 36

15. To enlarge slightly a bored hole in a steel plate, you should use tool number 15.____

A. 5 B. 11 C. 20 D. 36

16. The term "16 oz." should be applied to tool number 16.____

A. 1 B. 12 C. 21 D. 42

KEYS (CORRECT ANSWERS)

1. A	9. B
2. C	10. D
3. B	11. C
4. D	12. C
5. B	13. C
6. B	14. D
7. B	15. A
8. D	16. C

TEST 2

Questions 1-11.

DIRECTIONS: Questions 1 through 11 refer to the instruments listed below. Each instrument is listed with an identifying number in front of it.

1 - Hygrometer	6 - Oscilloscope	11 - 6-foot folding rule
2 - Ammeter	7 - Frequency meter	12 - Architect's scale
3 - Voltmeter	8 - Micrometer	13 - Planimeter
4 - Wattmeter	9 - Vernier calliper	14 - Engineer's scale
5 - Megger	10 - Wire gage	15 - Ohmmeter

1. The instrument that should be used to *accurately* measure the resistance of a 4,700-ohm resistor is number 1.____

   A. 3 B. 4 C. 7 D. 15

2. To measure the current in an electrical circuit, the instrument that should be used is number 2.____

   A. 2 B. 7 C. 8 D. 15

3. To measure the insulation resistance of a rubber-covered electrical cable, the instrument that should be used is number 3.____

   A. 4 B. 5 C. 8 D. 15

4. An AC motor is hooked up to a power distribution box. In order to check the voltage at the motor terminals, the instrument that should be used is number 4.____

   A. 2 B. 3 C. 4 D. 7

5. To measure the shaft diameter of a motor *accurately* to one-thousandth of an inch, the instrument that should be used is number 5.____

   A. 8 B. 10 C. 11 D. 14

6. The instrument that should be used to determine whether 25 Hz. or 60 Hz. is present in an electrical circuit is number 6.____

   A. 4 B. 5 C. 7 D. 8

7. Of the following, the *proper* instrument to use to determine the diameter of the conductor of a piece of electrical hookup wire is number 7.____

   A. 10 B. 11 C. 12 D. 14

8. The amount of electrical power being used in a balanced three-phase circuit should be measured with number 8.____

   A. 2 B. 3 C. 4 D. 5

9. The electrical wave form at a given point in an electronic circuit can be observed with number 9.____

   A. 2 B. 3 C. 6 D. 7

10. The *proper* instrument to use for measuring the width of a door is number 10.____

A. 11 B. 12 C. 13 D. 14

11. A one-inch hole with a tolerance of plus or minus three-thousandths is reamed in a steel block. The *proper* instrument to accurately check the diameter of the hole is number 11.____

A. 8 B. 9 C. 11 D. 14

12. An oilstone is LEAST likely to be used correctly to sharpen a 12.____

A. scraper B. chisel C. knife D. saw

13. To cut the ends of a number of lengths of wood at an angle of 45 degrees, it would be BEST to use a 13.____

A. mitre-box B. protractor C. triangle D. wooden rule

14. A gouge is a tool used for 14.____

A. planing wood smooth
B. grinding metal
C. drilling steel
D. chiseling wood

15. Holes are usually countersunk when installing 15.____

A. carriage bolts
B. lag screws
C. flat-head screws
D. square nuts

16. A tool that is *generally* used to slightly elongate a round hole in scrap-iron is a 16.____

A. rat-tail file B. reamer C. drill D. rasp

17. When the term "10-24" is used to specify a machine screw, the number 24 refers to the 17.____

A. number of screws per pound
B. diameter of the screw
C. length of the screw
D. number of threads per inch

18. If you were unable to tighten a nut by means of a ratchet wrench because, although the nut turned on with the forward movement of the wrench, it turned off with the backward movement, you should 18.____

A. make the nut hand-tight before using the wrench
B. reverse the ratchet action
C. put a few drops of oil on the wrench
D. use a different socket in the handle

19. If you were installing a long wood screw and found you were unable to drive this screw more than three-quarters of its length by the use of a properly-fitting straight-handled screwdriver, the *proper* SUBSEQUENT action would be for you to 19.____

A. take out the screw and put soap on it
B. change to the use of a screwdriver-bit and brace
C. take out the screw and drill a shorter hole before redriving
D. use a pair of pliers on the blade of the screwdriver

20. Good practice requres that the end of a pipe to be installed in a plumbing system be reamed to remove the inside burr after it has been cut to length. The *purpose* of this reaming is to 20.____

A. restore the original inside diameter of the pipe at the end
B. remove loose rust
C. make the threading of the pipe easier
D. finish the pipe accurately to length

KEYS (CORRECT ANSWERS)

1.	D	11.	B
2.	A	12.	D
3.	B	13.	A
4.	B	14.	D
5.	A	15.	C
6.	C	16.	A
7.	A	17.	D
8.	C	18.	A
9.	C	19.	A
10.	A	20.	A

MECHANICAL APTITUDE
TOOL RECOGNITION AND USE

EXAMINATION SECTION
TEST 1

DIRECTIONS: Each question or incomplete statement below is followed by several suggested answers or completions. Select the one that *BEST* answers the question or completes the statement.

KEY : CORRECT ANSWERS APPEAR AT THE END OF THIS TEST.

1. 1.____

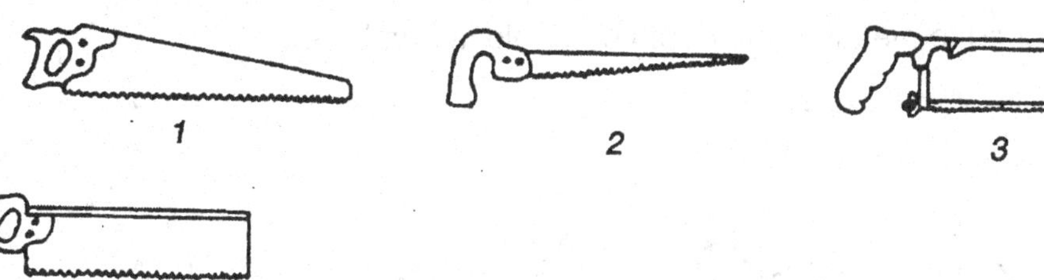

The saw that is used principally where curved cuts are to be made is numbered

1. 1 2. 2 3. 3 4. 4

2. 2.____

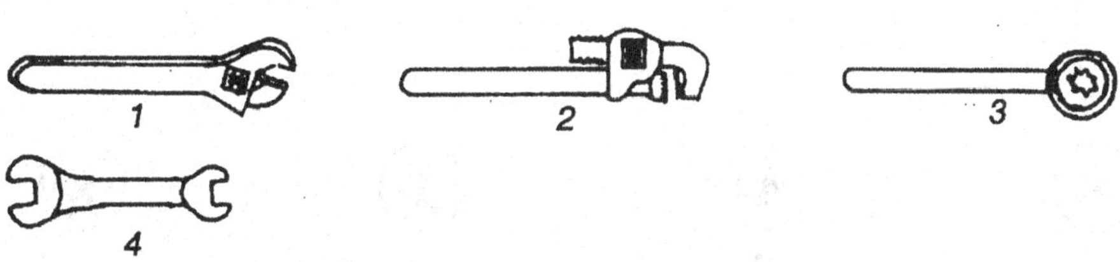

The wrench that is used principally for pipe work is numbered

1. 1 2. 2 3. 3 4. 4

3. 3.____

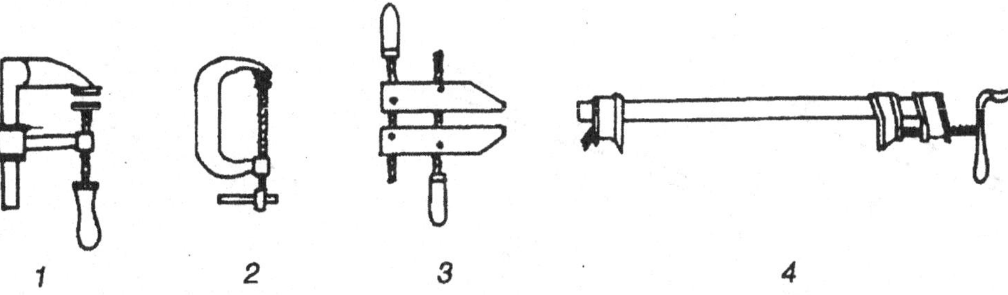

The carpenter's "hand screw" is numbered

1. 1 2. 2 3. 3 4. 4

4. 4.____

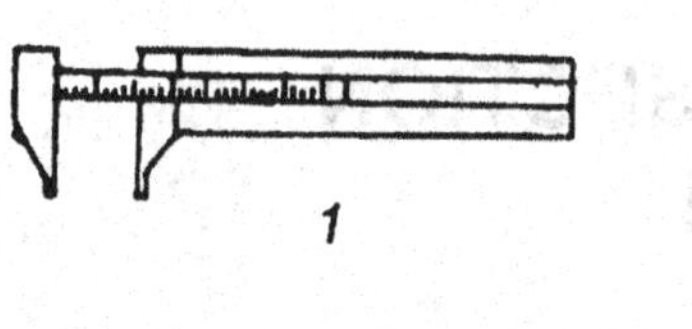
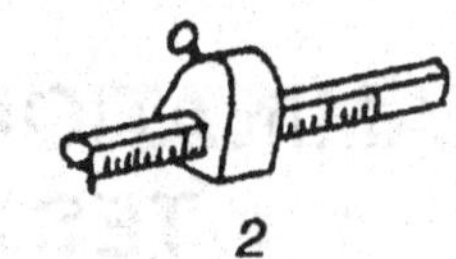

1 2

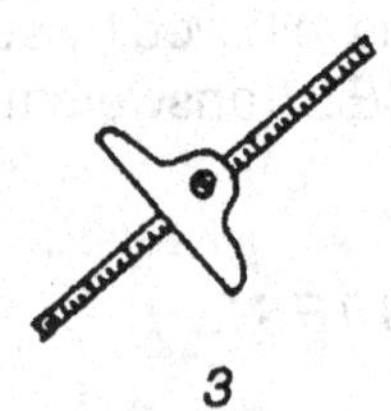
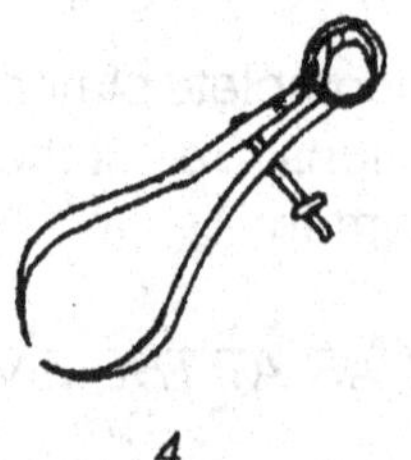

3 4

The tool used to measure the depth of a hole is numbered

1. 1 2. 2 3. 3 4. 4

5. 5.____

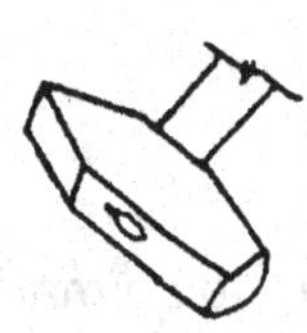

1 2 3 4

The tool that is best suited for use with a wood chisel is numbered

1. 1 2. 2 3. 3 4. 4

6. 6.____

1 2 3 4

The screw head that would be tightened with an "Allen" wrench is numbered

1. 1 2. 2 3. 3 4. 4

7. 7.____

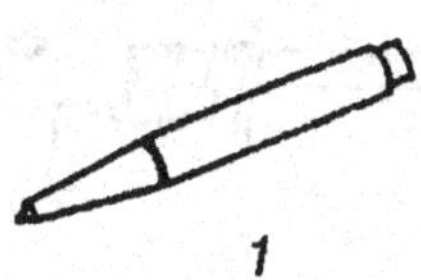
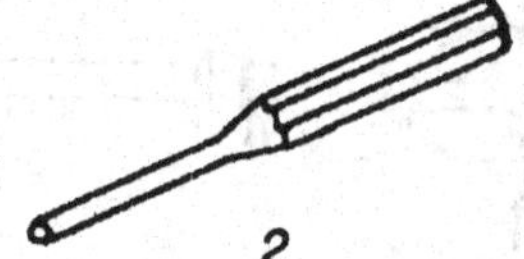
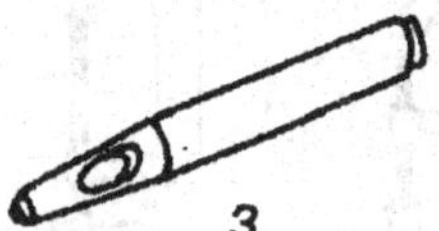

1 2 3

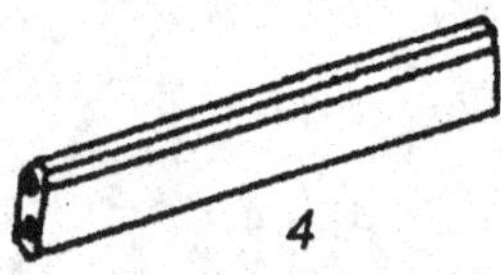

4

The center punch is numbered

1. 1 2. 2 3. 3 4. 4

8. 8.____

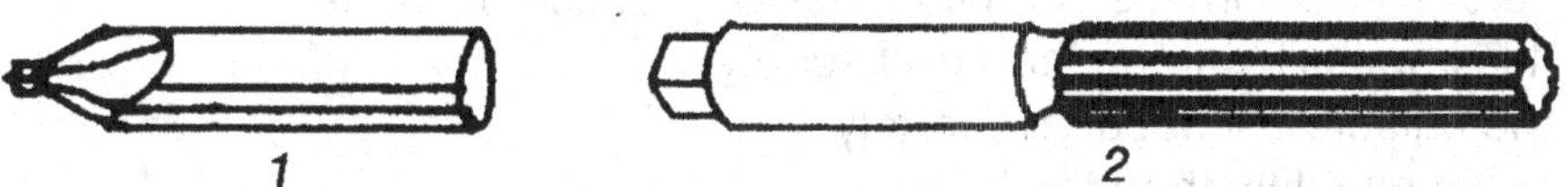

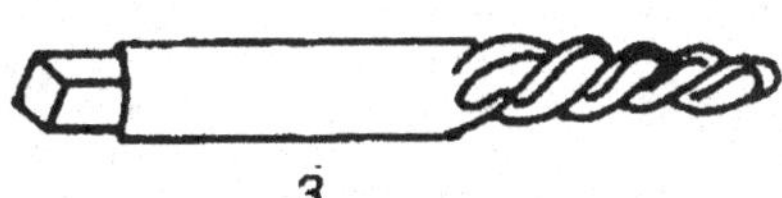

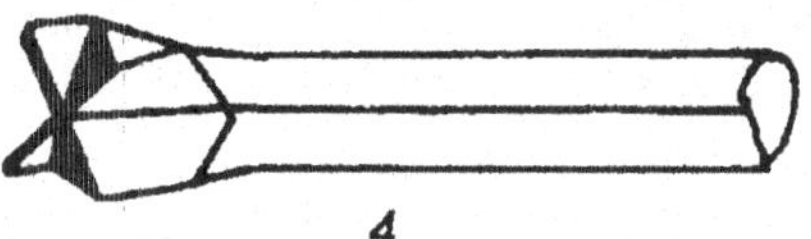

The tool used to drill a hole in concrete is numbered

1. 1 2. 2 3. 3 4. 4

9. 9.____

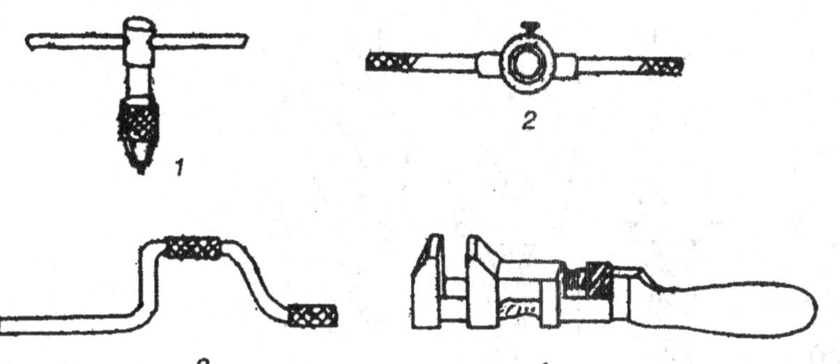

The wrench whose principal purpose is to hold taps for threading is numbered

1. 1 2. 2 3. 3 4. 4

10. 10.____

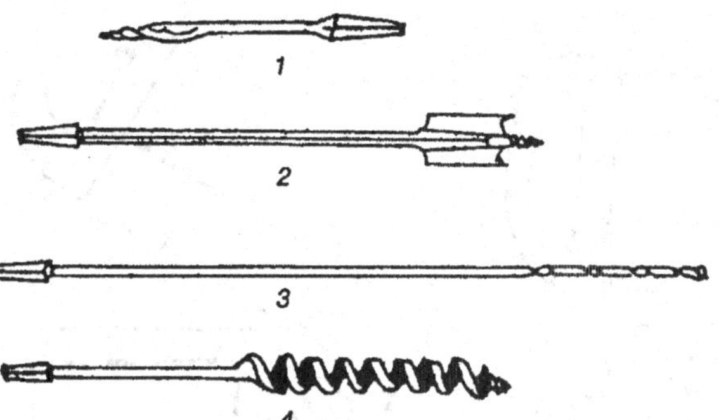

The electrician's bit is indicated by the number

1. 1 2. 2 3. 3 4. 4

11. The head of a cold chisel is "mushroomed" as shown in the sketch. The use of a chisel in this condition is poor practice because 11.____
   1. it is impossible to hit the head squarely
   2. the chisel will not cut accurately
   3. chips might fly from the head
   4. the chisel has lost its "temper"

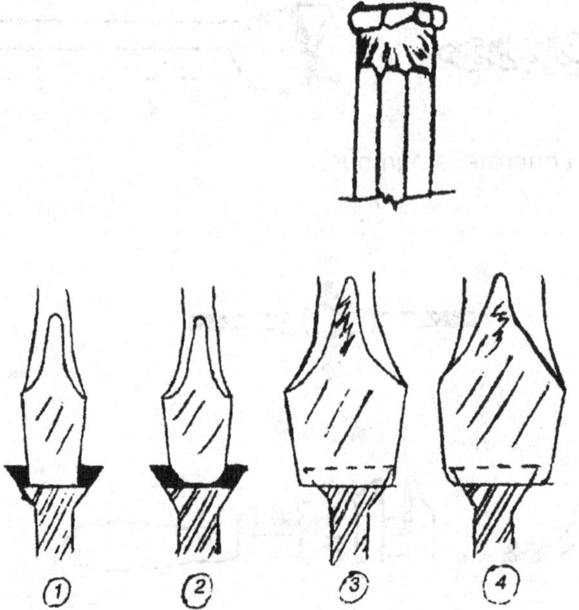

12. The above diagrams show a section of a screw with a screwdriver that is to be used with the screw. The one of the diagrams that shows the correct shape of screwdriver is 12.____

   1. 1   2. 2   3. 3   4. 4

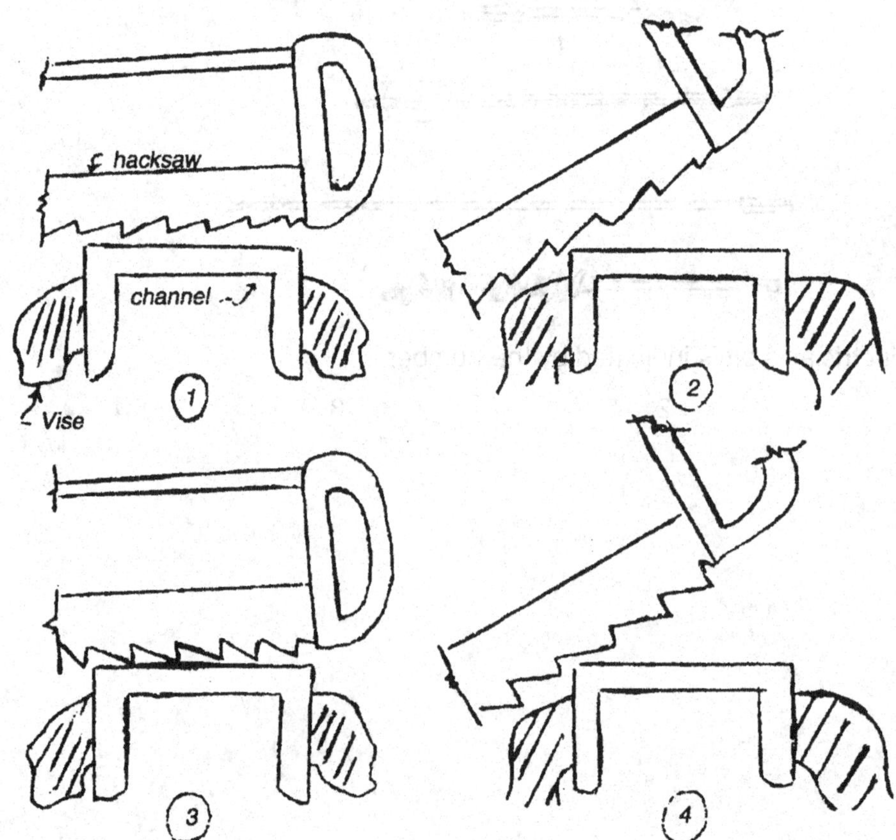

13. A steel channel is to be cut through with a hacksaw. The correct method for doing this is shown in the diagram numbered (diagrams above) 13.____

1. 1   2. 2   3. 3   4. 4

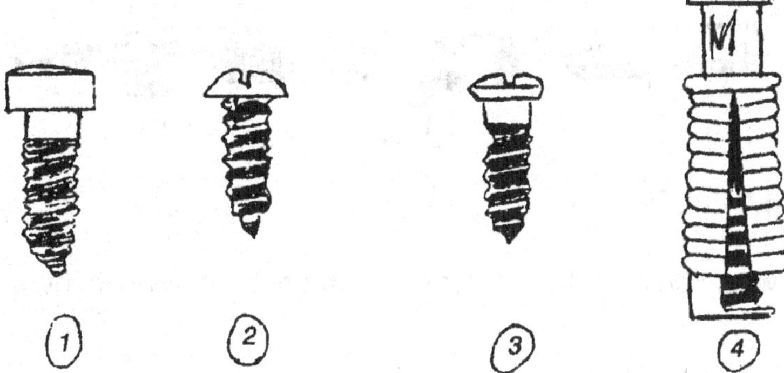

14. The screw above that is most frequently used for sheet metal work is numbered 14.

1. 1   2. 2   3. 3   4. 4

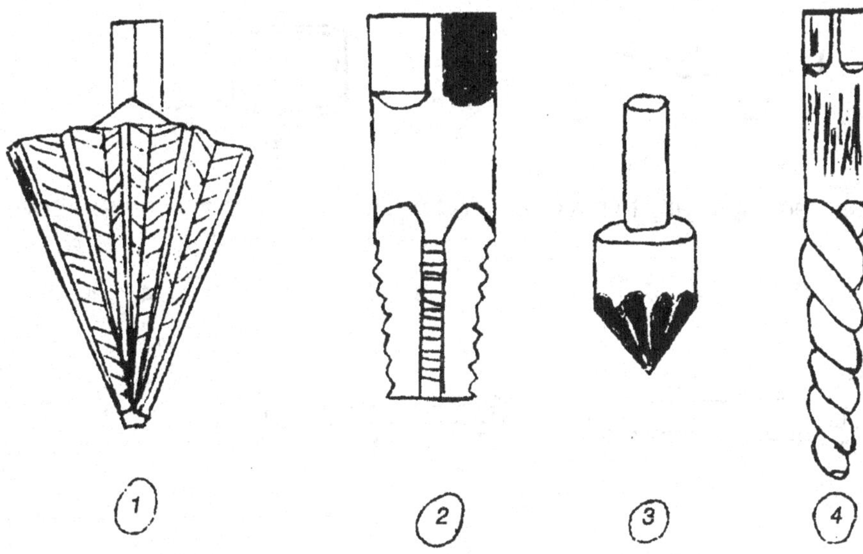

15. The tool used to ream the ends of pipe after the pipe has been cut is shown above in the diagram numbered 15.____

1. 1 2. 2 3. 3 4. 4

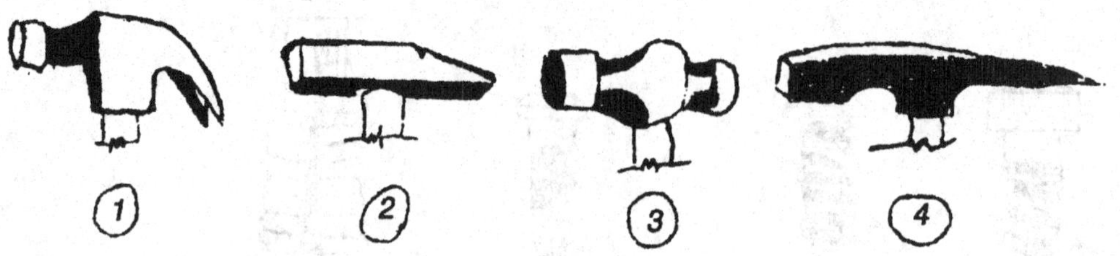

16. The hammer that would be used by a mason to trim brick is shown in the above diagram numbered 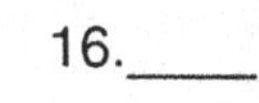

1. 1 2. 2 3. 3 4. 4

17. The saw intended especially to make accurate miter cuts is shown in the above diagram numbered 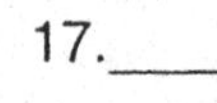

1. 1 2. 2 3. 3 4. 4

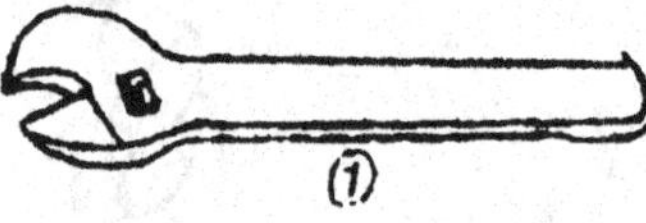

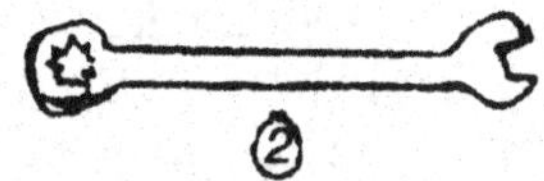

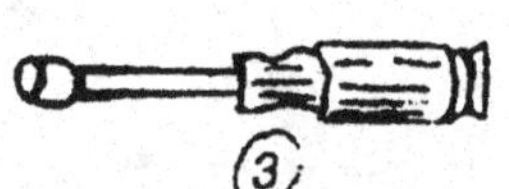

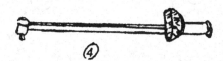

18. A wrench used to tighten cylinder head bolts to a specified torque is shown in the above diagram numbered 18.____

1. 1 2. 2 3. 3 4. 4

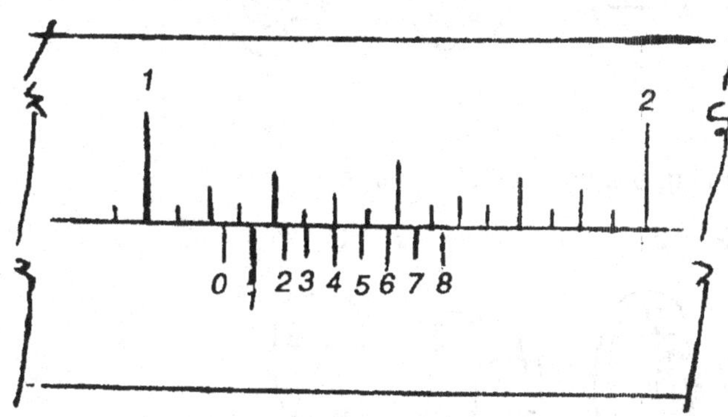

19. A section of the scale of a vernier caliper is shown above. The reading of this caliper setting is most nearly 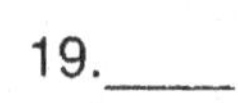

1. 1 3/8 2. 1 5/64 3. 1 5/32 4. 1 7/64

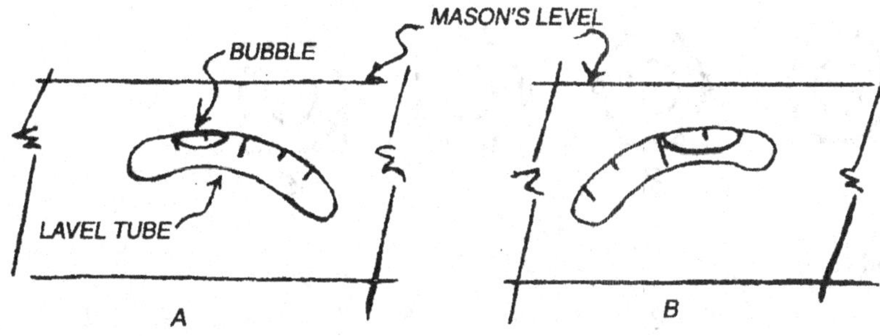

20. A level is placed on a table and the bubble moves to the position indicated in diagram A above. The level is then turned end for end and placed in the same location on the table as before. The bubble now appears as shown in diagram B. The one of the following statements that is correct is 

1. the left end of the table is higher than the right end
2. the right end of the table is higher than the left end
3. it is impossible to tell which end of the table is higher
4. the level tube is not set properly in the level

21. The flat-head screw is No. 

1. 1 2. 2 3. 3 4. 4

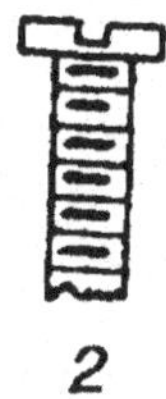

22. The "Phillips" head is No. 22. 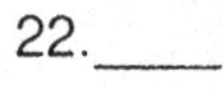

1. 1 2. 2 3. 3 4. 4

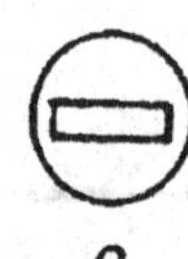

23. The standard coupling for rigid electrical conduit is 23.____

1. 1 2. 2 3. 3 4. 4

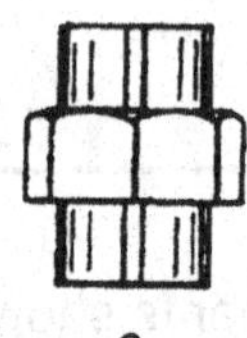

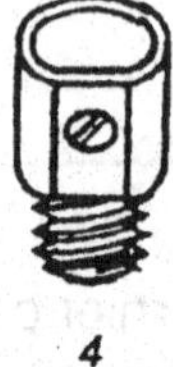

24. The shape of nut most commonly used on electrical terminals is 24.____

1. 1 2. 2 3. 3 4. 4

25. The stove bolt is 25. 

1. 1 2. 2 3. 3 4. 4

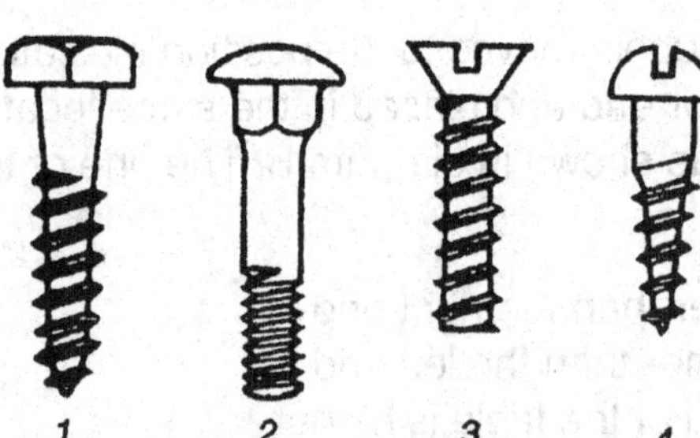

KEY (CORRECT ANSWERS)

1. 2
2. 2
3. 3
4. 3
5. 4
6. 3
7. 1
8. 4
9. 1
10. 3
11. 3
12. 1
13. 1
14. 2
15. 1
16. 4
17. 3
18. 4
19. 3
20. 4
21. 3
22. 4
23. 1
24. 2
25. 3

THE USE AND CARE OF TOOLS

CONTENTS

d. Scrapers
e. Punches
f. Awls
g. Shears, Nippers, and Pincers h. Bolt, Cable, and Glass Cutters
i. Pipe and Tube Cutters, and Flaring Tools
j. Reamers
k. Taps and Dies
l. Thread Chasers
m. Screw and Tap Extractors

THE USE AND CARE OF TOOLS

I. INTRODUCTION

1. Definitions

   a. Handtools are defined as hand powered and hand operated tools that are designed to perform mechanical operations.

   b. Measuring tools are defined as tools that will measure work. Measuring tools can be classed as precision and non-precision tools.

2. Safety Precautions

   It is extremely important for all concerned to recognize the possibilities of injury when using handtools and measuring tools.

   The following safety precautions are included as a guide to prevent or minimize personal injury:

   a. Make certain all tool handles are securely attached before using them.

   b. Exercise extreme caution when handling edged tools.

   c. Do not use a tool for a purpose other than that for which it was intended.

   d. Do not handle tools carelessly carelessly piling tools in drawers, dropping tools on hard surfaces, etc., can damage tools. Damaged tools can cause mishaps.

   e. Keep your mind on your work so that you do not strike yourself or someone else with a hammer or sledge.

   f. Do not carry edged or pointed tools in your pocket.

   g. Always wear goggles when chipping metal and when grinding edges on tools.

   h. Hold driving tools correctly so that they will not slip off the work surface.

   i. Use the right tool for the job. The wrong tool may damage materials, injure workers, or both,

   j. Do not use punches with improper points or mushroomed heads,

   k. Do not use a tool that is oily or greasy. It may slip out of your hand, causing injury.

   l. When using jacks, make certain to use blocking or other supports when lifting a vehicle, in case of jack failure.

   m. Make sure work to be cut, sheared, chiseled, filed, etc., is steadied and secure, to prevent the tool from slipping.

   n. When using a knife, always cut away from your body, except in the case of a spoke shave or draw knife.

   o. Use torches and soldering irons with extreme care to prevent burns and explosions. The soldering iron must be so placed that the hot point cannot come in contact with flammable material or with the body.

   p. Familiarize yourself with the composition and hardness of the material to be worked.

II. MEASURING TOOLS

1. General

Measuring tools are designed for measuring work accurately. They include level indicating devices (levels), noncalibrated measuring tools (calipers, dividers, trammels) for transferring dimensions and/or layouts from one medium to another, calibrated measuring tools (rules, precision tapes, micrometers) designed to measure distances in accordance with one of several standards of measurement, gages (go and no-go gages, thread gages) which are machined to pre-determined shapes and/or sizes for measurement by comparison, and combination tools such as a combination square which is designed to perform two or more types of operation.

2. Standards of Measurement

a. Standards of Length

Two systems, the English and Metric, are commonly used in the design of measuring tools for linear measurements. The English system uses inches, feet, and yards, while the Metric system uses millimeters, centimeters, and meters. In relation to each other, 1 inch is equivalent to 25.4 millimeters, or 1 millimeter is equivalent to 0.039370 inch.

b. Standards of Screw Threads

There are several screw thread systems that are recognized as standards throughout the world. All threaded items for Ordnance use in the United States, Great Britain, and Canada are specified in the Unified System. The existing inch-measure screw-thread systems should be understood despite the existence of the Unified System.

(1) Inch-measure systems

(a) Whitworth

Introduced in England in 1941. The thread form is based on a 55 thread angle, and the crests and roots are rounded.

(b) American National

The American National screw-thread system was developed in 1933. This system is based on the 60 thread angle and the flat crests and roots and is included in the following series:

1. Coarse thread sizes of 1 to 12 and 1/4 to 4".
2. The fine thread series in sizes 0 to 12 and 1/4 to 1 1/2".
3. The extra-fine thread series in sizes 0 to 12 and 1/2 to 2".
4. The 8-pitch series in sizes from 1 to 6".
5. The 12-pitch series from 1/2 to 6".
6. The 16-pitch series from 3/4 to 4".

(c) Classes of fit

The American National screw-thread system calls for four regular classes of fit.

Class 1. - Loose fit, with no possibility for interference between screw and tapped hole.

2. - Medium or free fit, but permitting slight interference in the worst combination of maximum screw and maximum nut.
3. - Close tolerances on mating parts may require this fit, applied to the highest grade of interchangeable work.
4. - A fine snug fit, where a screwdriver or wrench may be necessary for assembly.

NOTE: An additional Class 5, or jaw fit, is recognized for studs.

(2) Unified system

Since the whitworth and American National thread forms do not assemble because of the difference in thread angle, the 60 thread angle was adapted in 1949; however, the British may still use rounded crests and roots and their products will assemble with those made in United States plants. In the Unified system, class signifies tolerance, or tolerance and allowance. It is determined by the selected combination of classes for mating external and internal threads. New classes of tolerance are listed below: 3 for screws, 1A, 2A, and 3A; and 3 for nuts, IB, 2B, and 3B.

(a) Classes 1A and 1B, loose fit

A fit giving quick and easy assembly, even when threads are bruised or dirty. Applications: Ordnance and special uses.

(b) Classes 2A and 2B, medium fit

This fit permits wrenching with minimum galling and seizure. This medium fit is suited for the majority of commercial fasteners and is interchangeable with the American National Class 2 fit.

(c) Classes 3A and 3B, close fit

No allowance is provided. Applications are those where close fit and accuracy of lead and thread angle are required.

c. Standards of Wire and Sheet Metal

Sheet metal, strip, wire, and tubing are produced with thickness diameters or wall thicknesses, according to several gaging systems, depending on the article and metal. This situation is the result of natural development and preferences of the industries that produce these products. No single standard for all manufacturers has been established, since practical considerations stand in the way of adoption. In the case of steel, large users are thoroughly familiar with the behavior of existing gages in tooling, especially dies, and do not intend that their shop personnel be burdened with learning how preferred thicknesses behave. Another important factor is the sum total of orders of warehouse stock manufactured with existing gages. You must keep abreast of any change in availability of metals in these common gaging systems, as opposed to simplified systems.

For example; in the brass industry, the American Standards Association (ASA) numbers are said to be preferred for simplicity of stocking, but actually most of the metal is still made to Brown and Sharpe (B&S) gage numbers.

(1) Sheet metal gaging systems

Several gaging systems are used for sheet and strip metal.

(a) Manufacturer's standard gaging system (Mfr's std)

This gaging system is currently used for carbon and alloy sheets. This system is based on steel weighing 41.82 psf, 1 inch thick. Gage thickness equivalents are based on 0.0014945 in. per oz. per sq. ft.; 0.023912 in. per lb. per sq. ft. (reciprocal of 41.82 lb. per sq. ft. per in. thick); 3.443329 in. per lb. per sq. in.

(b) U.S. standard gaging system (U.S. std)

This gaging system is obsolete except for stainless steel sheets, cold-rolled steel strip (both carbon and alloy), stainless steel tubing, and nickel-alloy sheet and strip.

(c) Birmingham wire gaging system (BWG)

This gaging system is also called the Stubs iron wire gaging system, and is used for hot-rolled steel carbon and alloy strip and steel tubing.

(d) Brown and Sharpe, or American wire gaging system (B&S or AWG)

This gaging system is used for copper strip, brass and bronze sheet and strip, and aluminum and wire magnesium sheet.

(2) Wire gaging systems

(a) Steel wire gaging system (SWG) or washburn & Moen gaging system

This gaging system is used for steel wire, carbon steel mechanical spring wire, alloy-steel spring wire, stainless steel wire, and so forth. Carbon steel or music wire (wire used in the manufacture of musical instruments) is nominally specified to the sizes in the American Steel & Wire Company music wire sizes, although it is referred to by a number of other names found in steel catalogs.

(b) Brown & Sharpe (B&S) or American wire gaging system (AWG)

This gaging system is used for copper, copper alloy, aluminum, magnesium, nickel alloy, and other nonferrous metal wires used commercially.

(3) Rod gaging systems

The Brown & Sharpe gaging system is used for copper,brass, and aluminum rods. Steel rods are nominally listed in fractional sizes, but drill rod may be listed in stubs steel wire gage or the twist drill and steel wire gage. It is preferable to refer to twist drill sizes in inch equivalents instead of the Stubs or twist drill numbers.

d. Standards of Weight

Two standards of weight that are most commonly used are the Metric and English weight measures.

(1) Metric standards

The principal unit of weight in the Metric system is the gram (gm). Multiples of grams are obtained by prefixing the Greek words deka (10), hekto (100), and kilo (1,000). Divisions are obtained by prefixing the Latin words deci (1/10), centi (1/100), and milli (1/1000). The gram is the weight of 1 cubic centimeter of puje distilled water at a temperature of 39.2° F.; the kilogram is the weight of 1 liter (one cubic decimeter) of pureQdistilled water at a temperature of 39.2° F.; the metric ton is the weight of 1 cubic meter of pyre distilled water at a temperature of 39.2° F.

(2) English standards

The principal unit of weight in the English system is the grain (gr). We are more familiar with the ounce (oz), which is equal to 437.5 grains.

3. Useful Measuring Tools

a. Levels

(1) Purpose

Levels are tools designed to prove whether a plane or surface is true horizontal or true vertical. Some levels are calibrated so that they will indicate the angle inclination in relation to a horizontal or vertical surface in degrees, minutes, and seconds.

b. Plumb Bobs

(1) Purpose

The common plumb bob is used to determine true verticality. It is used in carpentry when erecting vertical uprights and corner posts of framework. Surveyors use it for transferring and lining up points. Special plumb bobs are designed for use with steel tapes or line to measure tank contents (oil, water, etc.).

c. Scribers

(1) Purpose

Scribers are used to mark and lay out a pattern of work, to be followed in subsequent machining operations. Scribers are made for scribing, scoring, or marking many different materials such as glass, steel, aluminium, copper, and so forth.

d. Rules or Scales

(1) Purpose

All rules (scales) are used to measure linear dimensions. They are read by a comparison of the etched lines on the scale with an edge or surface. Most scale dimensions are read with the naked eye, although a magnifying glass can be used to read graduations on a scale smaller than 1/64 inch.

e. Precision Tapes

(1) Purpose

Precision tapes are used for measuring circumferences and long distances where rules cannot be applied.

f. Squares

(1) Purpose

The purpose of a square is to test work for squareness and trueness. It is also used as a guide when marking work for subsequent machining, sawing, planing, and chiseling operations.

g. Calipers and Dividers

(1) Purpose

Dividers are used for measuring distances between two points, for transferring or comparing measurements directly from a rule, or for scribing an arc, radius, or circle. Calipers are used for measuring diameters and distances, or for comparing dimensions or sizes with standards such as a graduated rule,

h. Micrometers

(1) Purpose

Micrometers are used for measurements requiring precise accuracy. They are more reliable and more accurate than the calipers listed in the preceding section.

i. Surface, Depth, and Height Gages

(1) Purpose

(a) Surface Gage

A surface gage is a measuring tool generally used to transfer measurements to work by scribing a line, and to indicate the accuracy or parallelism of surfaces.

(b) Depth Gage

A depth gage is an instrument adapted to measuring the depth of holes, slots, counterborers, recesses, and the distance from a surface to some recessed part.

(c) Height Gage

A height gage is used in the layout of jigs and fixtures, and on a bench, where it is used to check the location of holes and surfaces. It accurately measures and marks off vertical distances from a plane surface.

(d) Surface Plate

A surface plate provides a true, smooth, plane surface. It is often used in conjunction with surface and height gages as a level base on which the gages and parts are placed to obtain accurate measurements,

j. Plug, Ring, and Snap Gages and Gage Blocks

(1) Purpose

Plug, ring, and snap gages, and precision gage blocks are used as standards to determine whether or not one or more dimensions of a manufactured part are within specified limits. Their measurements are included in the construction of each gage, and they are called fixed gages; however, some snap gages are adjustable. In the average shop, gages are used for a wide range of work, from rough machining to the finest tool and die making. The accuracy required of the same type gage will be different, depending on the application. The following classes of gages and their limits of accuracy are standard for all makes:

Class XX(Male gages only).

Precision lapped to laboratory tolerances. For master or setup standards.

Class X

Precision lapped to close tolerances for many types of masters and the highest quality working and inspection gages.

Class Y

Good lapped finish to slightly increased tolerances for inspection and working gages.

Class Z

Commercial finish (ground and polished, but not fully lapped) for a large percentage of working gages in which tolerances are fairly wide, and where production quantities are not so large.

Class ZZ(Ring gages only)

Ground only to meet the demand for an inexpensive gage, where quantities are small and tolerances liberal.

k. Miscellaneous Measuring Gages

(1) Purpose

(a) Thickness (Feeler) Gages

These gages are fixed in leaf form, which permits the checking and measuring of small openings such as contact points, narrow slots, and so forth. They are widely used to check the flatness of parts in straightening and grinding operations and in squaring objects with a try square.

(b) Wire and Drill Gages

The wire gage is used for gaging metal wire, and a similar gage is also used to check the size of hot and cold rolled steel, sheet and plate iron, and music wire. Drill gages determine the size of a drill and indicate the correct size of drill to use for given tap size. Drill number and decimal size are also shown in this type gage.

(c) Drill Rods or Blanks

Drill rods or blanks are used on line inspection work to check the size of drilled holes in the same manner as with plug gages. They are also used for setup inspection to check the location of holes.

(d) Thread Gages

Among the many gages used in connection with the machining and inspection of threads are the center gage and the screw pitch gages.

1. Center gage

The center gage is used to set thread cutting tools. Four scales on the gage are used for determining the number of threads per inch.

2. Screw pitch gage

Screw pitch gages are used to determine the pitch of an unknown thread. The pitch of a screw thread is the distance between the center of one tooth to the center of the next tooth.

(e) Small Hole Gage Set

This set of 4 or more gages is used to check dimensions of small holes, slots, groves etc., from approximately 1/8 to 1/2" in diameter.

(f) Telescoping Gages

These gages are used for measuring the inside size of slots or holes up to 6" in width or diameter.

(g) Thread Cutting Tool Gages

These gages provide a standard for thread cutting tools. They have an enclosed angle of 29 and include a 29 setting tool. One gage furnishes the correct form for square threads and the other for Acme standard threads.

(h) Fillet and Radius Gages

These gages are used to check convex and concave radii in corners or against shoulders.

(i) Drill Point Gage

This gage is used to check the accuracy of drill cutting edges after grinding. It is also equipped with a 6" hook rule. This tool can be used as a drill point gage, hook rule, plain rule, and a slide caliper for taking outside measurements.

(j) Marking Gages

A marking gage is used to mark off guidelines parallel to an edge, end, or surface of a piece of wood. It has a sharp spur or pin that does the marking.

(k) Tension Gage

This type of gage is used to check contact point pressure and brush spring tension in 1 ounce graduations.

(l) Saw Tooth Micrometer Gage

This special gage checks the depth of saw teeth in thousandths of an inch from 0 to 0.075 inch.

III. NONEDGED TOOLS

1. General

This title encompasses a large group of general purpose hand-tools. These tools are termed nonedged hand-tools because they are not used for cutting purposes and do not have sharpened or cutting edges. They are designed to facilitate mechanical operations such as clamping, hammering, twisting, turning, etc. This group includes such tools as hammers, mallets, and screwdrivers; which are commonly referred to as driving tools. Other types of nonedged tools are wrenches, pliers, clamps, pullers, soldering irons, torches, and many others of similar nature. Several types of pliers have cutting edges (exceptions to the rule).

2. Useful Nonedged Tools

a. Hammers and Mallets

(1) Purpose

Hammers and mallets are used to drive nails, spikes, drift pins, bolts, and wedges. They are also used to strike chisels, punches, and to shape metals. Sledge hammers are used to drive spikes and large nails, to break rock and concrete, and to drift heavy timbers.

b. Screwdrivers

(1) Purpose

Screwdrivers are used for driving or removing screws or bolts with slotted or special heads.

c. Wrenches

(1) Purpose

Wrenches are used to tighten or loosen nuts, bolts, screws, and pipe plugs. Special wrenches are made to grip round stock, such as pipe, studs, and rods. Spanner wrenches are used to turn cover plates, rings and couplings.

d. Pliers and Tongs

(1) Purpose

Pliers are used for gripping, cutting, bending, forming, or holding work, and for special jobs. Tongs look like long-handled pliers and are mainly used for holding or handling hot pieces of metal work to be forged or quenched, or hot pieces of glass.

e. Clamping Devices

(1) Purpose

Vises are used for holding work on the bench when it is being planed, sawed, drilled, shaped, sharpened, riveted, or when wood is being glued. Clamps are used for holding work that cannot be satisfactorily held in a vise because of its shape or size, or when a vise is not available. Clamps are generally used for light work.

f. Jacks

(1) Purpose

Jacks are used to raise or lower work and heavy loads short distances. Some jacks are used for pushing and pulling operations, or for spreading and clamping.

g. Bars and Mattock

(1) Purpose

Bars are heavy steel tools used to lift and move heavy objects and to pry where leverage is needed. They are also used to remove nails and spikes during wrecking operations. The mattock is used for digging in hard ground, cutting Toots irnderground, und to loosen clay formations in which there is little or no rock. The mattock may also be used for light prying when no bars are available,

h. Soldering Irons

(1) Purpose

Soldering is joining two pieces of metal by adhesion. The soldering iron is the source of heat by melting solder and heating the parts to be joined to the proper temperature.

i. Grinders and Sharpening Stones

(1) Purpose

Grinders are devices that are designed to mount abrasive wheels that will wear away other materials to varying degrees. Special grinders are designed to receive engine valves. Sharpening stones are used for whetting or final sharpening of sharp edged tools that have been ground to shape or to a fine point on a grinder,

j. Benders and Pullers

(1) Purpose

Benders are designed to facilitate bending brass or copper pipe and tubing.Pullers are designed to facilitate pulling operations such as removing bearings, gears, wheels, pulleys, sheaves, bushings, cylinder sleeves, shafts, and other close-fitting parts.

k. Torches

(1) Purpose

Torches are used as sources of heat in soldering, sweating, tinning, burning, and other miscellaneous jobs where heat is required.

l. Blacksmith's Anvils and Iron Working Tools

(1) Purpose

Blacksmith's anvils are designed to provide a working surface when punching holes through metal and for supporting the metal when it is being forged and shaped. Iron working tools such as flatters, fullers, swages, hardies, and set hammers are used to form or shape forgings. Heading tools are used to shape bolts.

m. Breast Drill and Ratchet Bit Brace

(1) Purpose

The breast drill and ratchet bit brace are used to hold various kinds of bits and twist drills used in boring and reaming holes and to drive screws, nuts, and bolts.

n. Sheet Metal Tools

(1) Purpose

Sheet metal working tools consist of stakes, dolly blocks, calking tools, rivet sets, and dolly bars. Punches, shears, and hammers are also sheet metal working tools. However, they are covered in other sections of this text. Rivet sets and dolly bars are used to form heads on rivets after joining sections of sheet metal and steel work. Stakes are used to support sheet metal while the metal is being shaped. Calking tools are used to shape joints of sheet metal. Dolly blocks are used conjunction with bumping body hammers to straighten out damaged sheet metal.

IV. EDGED HANDTOOLS

1. General

Edged handtools are designed with sharp edges for working on metal, wood, plastic, leather, cloth, glass, and other materials. They are used to remove portions from the work or to separate the work into sections by cutting, punching, scraping, chiseling, filing, and so forth.

2. Useful Edged Eandtools

a. Chisels

(1) Purpose

Chisels are made to cut wood, metal hard putty, and other materials. Woodworker's chisels are used to pare off and cut wood. Cold chisels are used to chip and cut cold metal. Some blacksmith's chisels are used to cut hot metal. A special chisel that is available is used to cut hard putty so that glass may be removed from its frame channel.

b. Files

(1) Purpose

Files are used for cutting, smoothing off, or removing small amounts of metal.

c. Knives

(1) Purpose

Most knives are used to cut, pare, notch, and trim wood, leather, rubber, and other materials. Some knives used by glaziers are called putty knives; these are used to apply and spread putty when installing glass.

d. Scrapers

(1) Purpose

Some scrapers are used for trueing metal, wood, and plastic surfaces which have previously been machined or filed. Other scrapers are made to remove paint, stencil markings, and other coatings from various surfaces.

e. Punches

(1) Purpose

Punches are used to punch holes in metal, leather, paper, and other materials; mark metal, drive pins or rivets; to free frozen pins from their holes; and aline holes in different sections of metal. Special punches are designed to install grommets and snap fasteners. Bench mounted punching machines are used to punch holes in metal one at a time, or up to 12 holes simultaneously.

f. Awls

(1) Purpose

A saddler's awl is used for forcing holes in cloth or leather to make sewing easier. A scratch awl is used for making a center point or a small hole and for scribing lines on wood and plastics.

g. Shears, Nippers, and Pincers

(1) Purpose

Shears are used for cutting sheet metal and steel of various thicknesses and shapes. Nippers are used to cut metal off flush with a surface, and likewise to cut wire, light metal bars, bolts, and nails. Pincers are used to pull out nails, bolts, and pins.

h. Bolt, Cable, and Glass Cutters

(1) Purpose

Cutters or clippers are used to cut bolts, rods, wire rope, cable, screws, rivets, nuts, bars, strips, and wire. Special cutters are made to cut glass.

i. Piper and Tube Cutters, and Flaring Tools

(1) Purpose

Pipe cutters are used to cut pipe made of steel, brass, copper, wrought iron, and lead. Tube cutters are used to cut tube made of iron, steel, brass, copper, and aluminum. The essential difference is that tubing has considerably thinner walls are compared to pipe. Flaring tools are used to make single or double flares in the ends of tubing,

j. Reamers

(1) Purpose

Reamers are used to smoothly enlarge drilled holes to an exact size and to finish the hole at the same time. Reamers are also used to remove burrs from the inside diameters of pipe and drilled holes,

k. Taps and Dies

(1) Purpose

Taps and dies are used to cut threads in metal, plastics, or hard rubber. The taps are used for cutting internal threads, and the dies are used to cut external threads.

l. Thread Chasers

(1) Purpose

Thread chasers are used to re-thread damaged external or internal threads,

m. Screw and Tap Extractors

(1) Purpose

Screw extractors are used to remove broken screws without damaging the surrounding material or the threaded hole. Tap extractors are used to remove broken taps.

HEATING AND ENVIRONMENTAL CONTROL

CONTENTS

HEATING AND ENVIRONMENTAL CONTROL

I. Introduction

The function of a heating system is to provide for human comfort. The variables to be controlled are temperature, air motion, and relative humidity. Temperature must be maintained uniformly throughout the heated area. Field experience indicates a variation from 6 to 10 degrees F from floor to ceiling. The adequacy of the heating device and the tightness of the structure or room determine the degree of personal comfort within the dwelling.

Coal, wood, oil, gas, and electricity are the main sources of heat energy. Heating systems commonly used are steam, hot water, and hot air. The housing inspector should have a knowledge of the various heating fuels and systems to be able to determine their adequacy and safety in operation. To cover fully all aspects of the heating system, the entire area and physical components of the system must be considered.

II. Definitions

A **Anti-flooding Control** — A safety control that shuts off fuel and ignition when excessive fuel accumulates in the appliance.

B **Appliance:**

1 **High-heat** — a unit that operates with flue entrance temperature of combustion products above 1,500°F.

2 **Medium heat** — same as high-heat, except above 600°F.

3 **Low heat** — same as high heat, except below 600°F.

C **Boiler:**

1 **High pressure** – a boiler furnishing pressure at 15 psi or more.

2 **Low pressure** — (hot water or steam) — a boiler furnishing steam at a pressure less than 15 psi or hot water not more than 30 psi.

D **Burner** — A device that provides the mixing of fuel, air, and ignition in a combustion chamber.

E **Chimney** — A vertical shaft containing one or more passageways.

1 **Factory-built chimney** — a tested and accredited flue for venting gas appliances, incinerators and solid or liquid fuel-burning appliances.

2 **Masonry chimney** — a field-constructed chimney built of masonry and lined with terra cotta flue or firebrick.

3 **Metal chimney** — a field-constructed chimney of metal.

4 **Chimney Connector** — A pipe or breeching that connects the heating appliance to the chimney.

F **Clearance** — The distance separating the appliance, chimney connector, plenum, and flue from the nearest surface of combustible material.

G **Central Heating System** – A boiler or furnace, flue connected, installed as an integral part of the structure and designed to supply heat adequately for the structure.

H **Controls:**

1 **High-low limit control** — an automatic control that responds to liquid level changes and pressure or temperature changes and that limits operation of the appliance to be controlled.

2 **Primary safety control** — the automatic safety control intended to prevent abnormal discharge of fuel at the burner in case of ignition failure or flame failure.

3 **Combustion safety control** — a primary safety control that responds to flame properties, sensing the presence of flame and causing fuel to be shut off in event of flame failure.

I **Convector** — A convector is a radiator that supplies a maximum amount of heat by convection, using many closely-spaced metal fins fitted onto pipes that carry hot water or steam and thereby heat the circulating air.

J **Conversion** — a boiler or furnace, flue connected, originally designed for solid fuel but converted for liquid or gas fuel.

K **Damper** — a valve for regulating draft. Generally located on the exhaust side of the combustion chamber, usually in the chimney connector.

L **Draft Hood** — a device placed in and made a part of the vent connector (chimney connector or smoke pipe) from an appliance, or in the appliance itself, that is designed to (a) ensure the ready escape of the products of combustion in the event of no draft, back-draft, or stoppage beyond the draft hood; (b) prevent backdraft from entering the appliance; (c) neutralize the effect of stack action of the chimney flue upon appliance operation.

M **Draft Regulator** — a device that functions to maintain a desired draft in oil-fired appliances by automatically reducing the chimney draft to the desired value. Sometimes this device is referred to, in the field, as air-balance, air-stat, or flue velocity control.

N **Fuel Oil** — a liquid mixture or compound derived from petroleum that does not emit flammable vapor below a temperature of 125°F.

O **Heat** — the warming of a building, apartment, or room by a stove, furnace, or electricity.

P **Heating Plant** — the furnace, boiler, or the other heating devices used to generate steam, hot water, or hot air, which then is circulated through a distribution system. It uses coal, gas, oil, or wood as its source of heat.

Q **Limit Control** — a thermostatic device installed in the duct system to shut off the supply of heat at a predetermined temperature of the circulated air.

R **Oil Burner** — a device for burning oil in heating appliances such as boilers, furnaces, water heaters, and ranges. A burner of this type may be a pressure-atomizing gun type, a horizontal or vertical rotary type, or a mechanical or natural draft-vaporizing type.

S **Oil Stove** — a flue-connected, self-contained, self-supporting oil-burning range or room heater equipped with an integral tank not exceeding 10 gallons; it may be designed to be connected to a separate oil supply tank.

T **Plenum Chamber** — an air compartment to which one or more distributing air ducts are connected.

U **Pump, Automatic Oil** — a device that automatically pumps oil from the supply tank and delivers it in specific quantities to an oil-burning appliance. The pump or device is designed to stop pumping automatically in case of a breakage of the oil supply line.

V **Radiant Heat** — a method of heating a building by means of electric coils, hot water, or steam pipes installed in the floors, walls, or ceilings.

W Register — a grille-covered opening in a floor or wall through which hot or cold air can be introduced into a room. It may or may not be arranged to permit closing of the grille.

X Room Heater — a self-contained, free-standing heating appliance intended for installation in the space being heated and not intended for duct connection (space heater).

Y Smoke Detector — a device installed in the plenum chamber or in the main supply air duct of an air-conditioning system to shut off the blower automatically and close a fire damper in the presence of smoke.

Z Tank — a separate tank connected, directly or by pump, to an oil-burning appliance.

AA Thimble — a term applied to a metal or terra cotta lining for a chimney or furnace pipe.

BB Valve — Main Shut-off Valve — a manually operated valve in an oil line for the purpose of turning on or off the oil supply to the burner.

CC Vent System — the gas vent or chimney and vent connector, if used, assembled to form a continuous, unobstructed passageway from the gas appliance to the outside atmosphere for the purpose of removing vent gases.

III. Fuels

A Coal

Classification and composition — the four types of coal are: anthracite, bituminous, sub-bituminous, and lignitic.

Coal is prepared in many sizes and combinations of sizes. The combustible portions of the coal are fixed carbons, volatile matter (hydrocarbons), and small amounts of sulfur. In combination with these are non-combustible elements composed of moisture and impurities that form ash. The various types differ in heat content. The heat content is determined by analysis and is expressed in British Thermal Units (BTU) per pound.The type and size of coal used are determined by the availability and by the equipment in which it is burned.

The type and size of coal must be proper for the particular heating unit; that is, the furnace grate and flue size must be designed for the particular type of coal. Excessive coal gas can be generated through improper firing as a result of improper fuel or improper furnace design, or both.

The owner should be questioned about his procedure for adding coal to his furnace. It should be explained that a period of time must be allowed to pass before damping to prevent the release of excessive coal gas. This should also be done before damping for the night or other periods when full draft is not required.

Improper coal furnace operation can result in an extremely hazardous and unhealthful occupancy — the inspector should be able to offer helpful operational procedures. Ventilation of the area surrounding the furnace is very important in order to prevent heat buildup and to supply air for combustion.

B Fuel Oil

Fuel oils are derived from petroleum, which consists primarily of compounds of hydrogen and carbon (hydrocarbons) and smaller amounts of nitrogen and sulfur.

Classification of fucl oils Domestic fuel oils are controlled by rigid specifications. Six grades of fuel oil arc generally used in healing systems; the lighter two grades arc used primarily for domestic heating.

These grades are:

1 **Grade Number 1** — A volatile, distillate oil for use in burners that prepare fuel for burning solely by vaporization (oil-fired space heaters).

2 **Grade Number 2** — A moderate-weight, volatile, distillate oil used for burners that prepare oil for burning by a combination of vaporization and atomization. This grade of oil is commonly used in domestic heating furnaces.

3 **Grade Number 3** — A low-viscosity, distillate oil used in burners wherein fuel and air are prepared for burning solely by atomization.

4 **Grade Number 4** — A medium-viscosity oil used in burners without preheating. (Small industrial or apartment house applications.)

5 **Grade Number 5** — A medium-viscosity oil used in burners with preheaters that require an oil of lower viscosity than Grade Number 6. (Industrial or apartment house application.)

6 **Grade Number 6** — A high-viscosity oil for use in burners with preheating facilities adequate for handling oil of high viscosity. (Industrial applications.)

7 **Heat content** — Heating values of oil vary from approximately 152,000 BTU per gallon for Number 6 oil to 136,000 BTU per gallon for Number 1.

Oil is more widely used today than coal and provides a more automatic source of heat and comfort. It also requires more complicated systems and controls.

If the oil supply is used within the basement or cellar area, certain basic regulations must be followed (see Figure 1). No more than two 275-gallon tanks may be installed above ground in the lowest story of any one building. The tank shall not be closer than 7 feet horizontally to any boiler, furnace, stove, or exposed flame. Fuel oil lines should be embedded in a concrete or cement floor or protected against damage if they run across the floor. Bach tank must have a shutoff valve that will stop the flow from each tank if a leak develops in the line to or in the burner itself.

The tank or tanks must be vented to the outside, and a gauge showing the quantity of oil in the tank or tanks must be tight and operative. Tanks must be off the floor and on a stable base to prevent settlement or movement that may rupture the connections.

A buried outside tank installation is shown in Figure 2.

C Gas

Commercial gas fuels are colorless gases. Some have a characteristic pungent odor, while others are odorless and cannot be detected by smell. Although gas fuels are easily handled in heating equipment, their presence in air in appreciable quantities becomes a serious health hazard. Gases diffuse readily in the air, making explosive mixtures possible. (A proportion of combustible gas and air that is ignited burns with such a high velocity that an explosive force is created.) Because of these characteristics of gas fuels, precautions must be taken to prevent leaks, and care must be exercised when gas-fired equipment is lit.

Classification of gas - Gas is broadly classified as natural or manufactured.

1. **Manufactured Gas** — This gas as distributed is usually a combination of certain proportions of gases produced by two or more processes as obtained from coke, coal, and petroleum. Its BTU value per cubic foot is generally closely regulated, and costs are determined on a guaran-

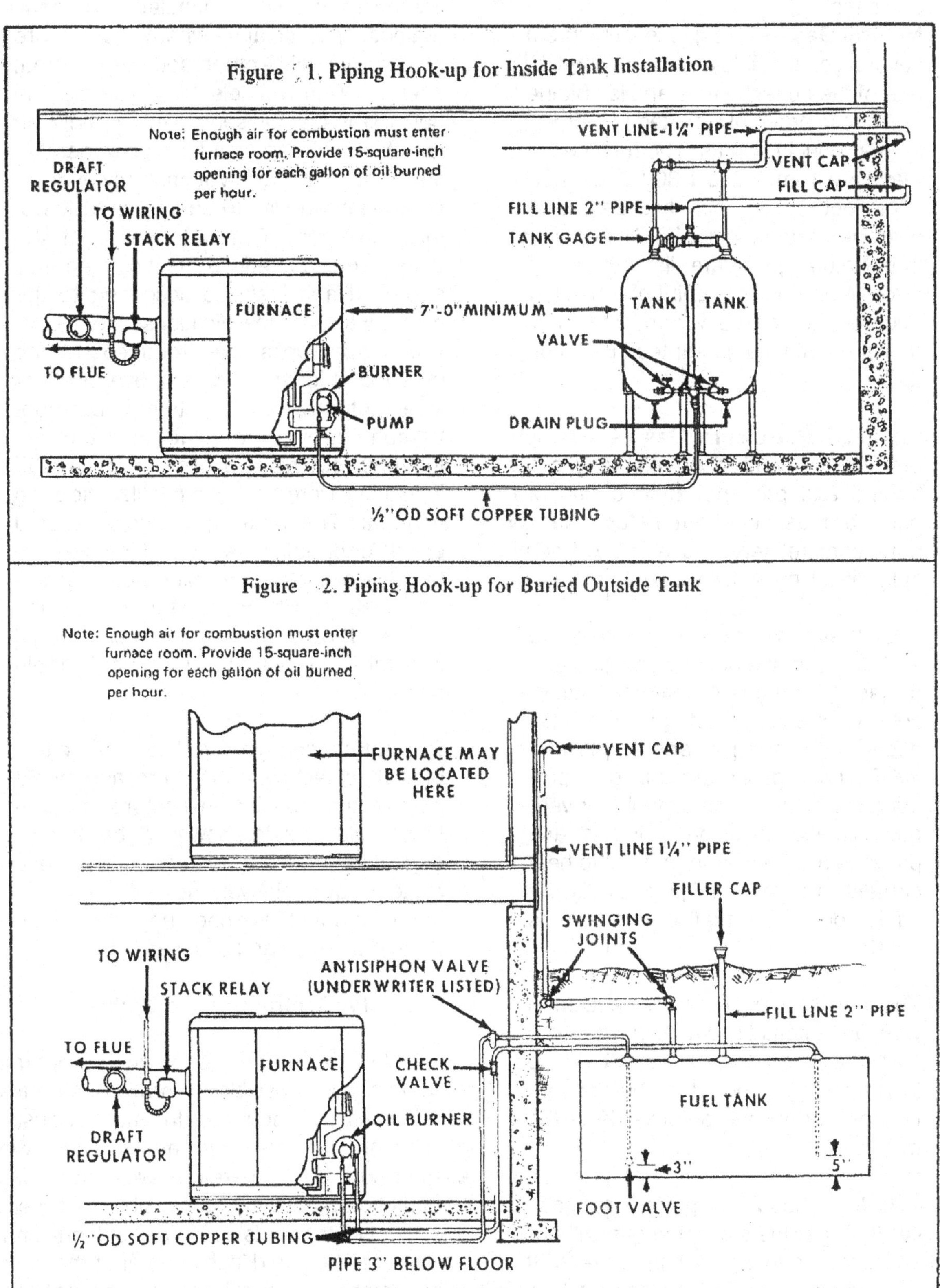

Figure 1. Piping Hook-up for Inside Tank Installation

Figure 2. Piping Hook-up for Buried Outside Tank

teed BTU basis, usually 520 to 540 per cubic foot.

2. **Natural Gas** — This gas is a mixture of several combustible and inert gases. It is one of the richest gases and is obtained from wells ordinarily located in petroleum-producing areas. The heat content may vary from 700 to 1,300 BTU's per cubic foot with a generally accepted average figure of 1,000 BTU's per cubic foot. Natural gases are distributed through pipe lines to point of utilization and are often mixed with manufactured gas to maintain a guaranteed BTU content.

3. **Liquified Petroleum Gas** — Principal products of liquified petroleum gas are butane and propane. Butane and propane are derived from natural gas or petroleum refinery gas and are chemically classified as hydrocarbon gases.

   Specifically, butane and propane are on the borderline between a liquid and a gaseous state. At ordinary atmospheric pressure butane is a gas above 33°F and propane a gas at -42°F. These gases are mixed to produce commercial gas suitable for various climatic conditions. Butane and propane are heavier than air. The heat content of butane is 3,274 BTU's per cubic foot while that of propane is 2,519.

   The gas burner should be equipped with an automatic cutoff in case the flame fails. Shutoff valves should be located within 1 foot of the burner connection and on the output side of the meter.

CAUTION — Liquified petroleum gas is heavier than air; therefore, the gas will accumulate at the bottom of confined areas. If a leak should develop, care should be taken to ventilate the appliance before lighting.

D Electricity

Electricity is gaining popularity in many regions, particularly where costs are competitive with other sources of heat energy. With an electric system, the housing inspector should rely mainly on the electrical inspector for proper installation. There are a few items, however, to be concerned with to ensure safe use of the equipment. Check to see that the units are accredited testing agency approved and installed according to the manufacturer's specifications. Most convector-type units are required to be installed at least 2 inches above the floor level, not only to ensure that proper convection currents are established through the unit, but also to allow sufficient air insulation from any combustible flooring material. The housing inspector should check for curtains that extend too close to the unit or loose, long pile rugs that are too close. A distance of 6 inches on the floor and 12 inches on the walls should separate rug or curtains from the appliance.

Radiant heating plastered into the ceiling or wall is technical in nature and not a part of the housing inspector's competence. He should, however, be knowledgeable about the system used. These systems are relatively new. If wires are bared in the plastering they should be treated as open and exposed wiring.

IV. Central Heating Units

The boiler should be placed in a separate room whenever possible; in new construction this is usually required. In most housing inspections, however, we are dealing with existing conditions; therefore, we must adapt the situation as closely as possible to acceptable safety standards. In many old buildings the furnace is located in the center of the cellar or basement, and this location does not lend itself for practical conversion to a boiler room.

A Boiler Location

Consider the physical requirements for a boiler room.

1 Ventilation — More circulating air is required for the boiler room than for a habitable room, in order to reduce the heat buildup caused by the boiler or furnace as well as to supply oxygen for combustion.

2 Fire Protection Rating — As specified by various codes (fire code, building code, and insurance underwriters) the fire regulations must be strictly adhered to in areas surrounding the boiler or furnace. This minimum dimension from which a boiler or furnace is to be spaced from a wall or ceiling is shown in Figure 3.

   Many times the enclosure of the furnace or boiler creates a problem of providing adequate air supply and ventilation for the room. Where codes and local authority permit, it may be more practical to place the furnace or boiler in an open area. The ceiling above the furnace should be fire protected to a distance of 3 feet beyond all furnace or boiler appurtenances and this area should be free of all storage material. The furnace or boiler should be set on a firm foundation of concrete if located in the cellar or basement. If the codes permit furnace installations on the first floor, then the building code must be consulted for proper setting and location.

B Heating Boilers

Boilers may be classified according to several kinds of characteristics. The material may be cast iron or steel. Their construction may be section, portable, fire-tube, water-tube, or special. Domestic heating boilers are generally of low-pressure type with a maximum working pressure of 15 pounds per square inch for steam and 30 pounds per square inch for hot water.

All boilers have a combustion chamber for burning fuel. Automatic fuel-firing devices help supply the fuel and control the combustion. Handfiring is accomplished by the provision of a grate, ash pit, and controllable drafts to admit air under the fuel bed and over it through slots in the firing door. A check draft is required at the smoke pipe connection to control chimney draft. The gas passes from the combustion chamber to the flue, passages (smoke pipe) designed for maximum possible transfer of heat from the gas. Provisions must be made for cleaning flue passages.

The term boiler is applied to the single heat source that can supply either steam or hot-water (boiler is often called a heater).

Cast iron boilers are generally classified as:

1 Square or rectangular boilers with vertical sections.
2 Round, square, or rectangular boilers with horizontal pancake sections.

Cast iron boilers are usually shipped in sections and assembled at the site.

C Steel Boilers

Most steel boilers are assembled units with welded steel construction and are called portable boilers. Larger boilers are installed in refractory brick settings built on the site. Above the combustion chamber a group of tubes is suspended, usually horizontally, between two headers. If flue gases pass through the tubes and water surrounds them, the boiler is designated as the fire-tube type. When water flows through the tubes, it is termed water-tube. Fire-tube is the predominant type.

D Heating Furnaces

Heating furnaces are the heat sources used when air is the heat-carrying medium. When air circulates because of the different densities of the heated and cooled air, the furnace is a gravity type. A fan may be included for the air circulation; this type is called a mechanical warm-air furnace. Furnaces may be of cast iron or steel and burn various types of fuel.

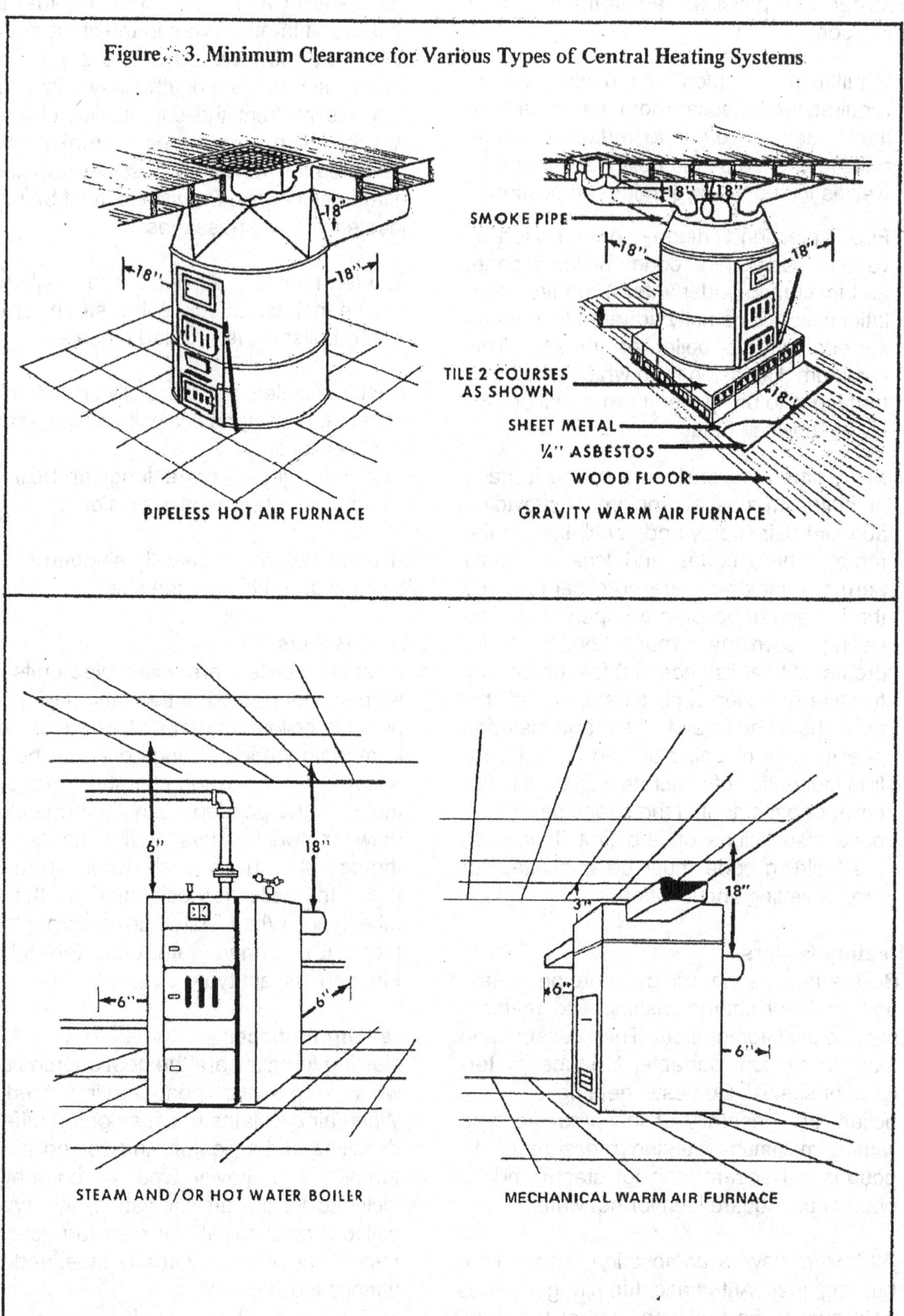

Figure 3. Minimum Clearance for Various Types of Central Heating Systems

V. Fuel-Burning Procedures and Automatic Firing Equipment

A **Coal** — Many localities throughout the nation still use coal as a heating fuel.

1 **Hand Stoking** - In many older furnaces, the coal is stoked or fed into the fire box by hand.

2 **Automatic Stokers** - The single-retort, underfeed-type bituminous coal stoker is the most commonly used domestic-type steam or hot water boiler (see Figure 4). The stoker consists of a coal hopper, a screw for conveying coal from hopper to retort, a fan that supplies air for combustion, a transmission for driving coalfeed and fan, and an electric motor for supplying power. The air for combustion is admitted to the fuel through tuyeres at the top of the retort. The stoker feeds coal to the furnace intermittently in accordance with the temperature or pressure demands.

B **Oil Burners** — Oil burners are broadly designated as distillate, domestic, and commercial or industrial. Distillate burners are usually found in oil-fired space heaters. Domestic oil burners are usually power driven and are used in domestic heating plants. Commercial or industrial burners are used in larger central-heating plants for steam or power generation.

1 **Domestic Oil Burners** — Thesevaporize and atomize the oil, and deliver a predetermined quantity of oil and air to the combustion chambers. Domestic oil burners operate automatically to maintain a desired temperature.

a **Gun-type burners** — These burners atomize the oil either by oil pressure or by low-pressure air forced through a nozzle.

The oil system pressure atomizing burner (see Figure 5) consists of a strainer, pump, pressure-regulating valve, shutoff valve, and atomizing nozzle. The air system consists of a power-drive fan and an air tube that surrounds the nozzle and electrode assembly. The fan and oil pump are generally connected directly to the motor. Oil pressures normally used are about 100 pounds per square inch, but pressures con-

Figure 4. Typical Underfeed Coal Stoker Installation in Small Boiler

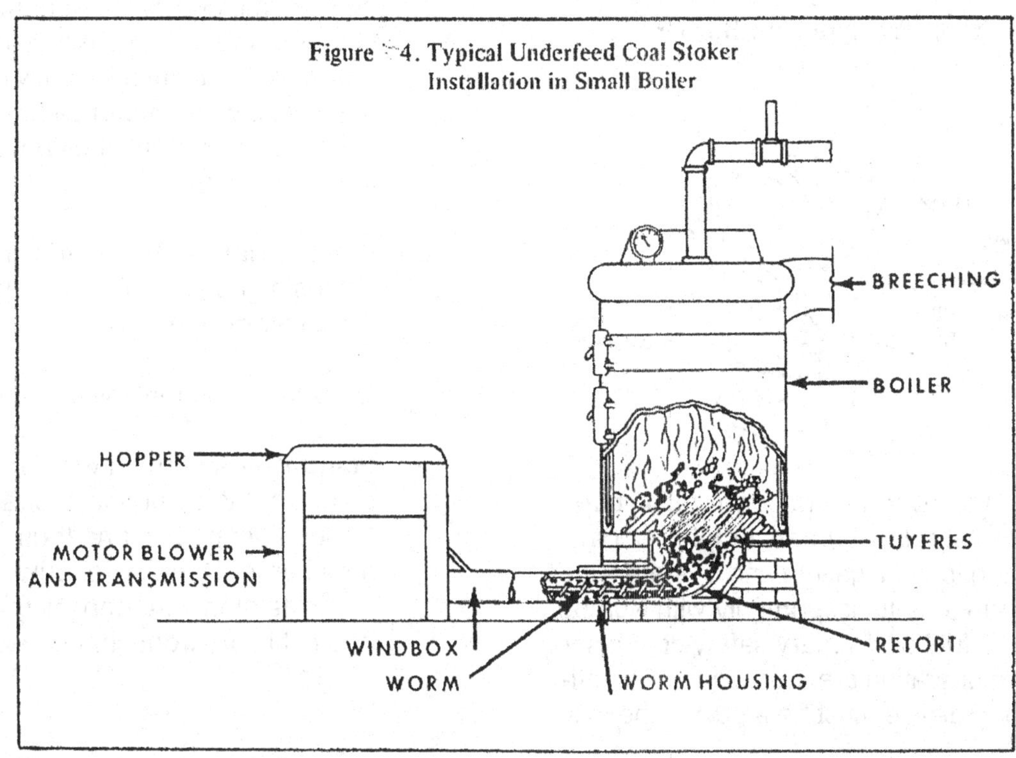

siderably in excess of this are sometimes used.

The form and parts of low-pressure air-atomizing burners (see Figure 5), are similar to high-pressure atomizing burners except for addition of a small air pump, and a different way of delivering air and oil to the nozzle or orifice.

b **Vertical rotary burners** - The atomizing-type burner, sometimes known as a radiant or suspended-flame burner, atomizes oil by throwing it from the circumference of a rapidly rotating motor-driven cup. The burner is installed so that the driving parts are protected from the heat of the flame by a hearth of refractory material at about the grate elevation. Oil is fed by pump or gravity, while the draft is mechanical or a combination of natural and mechanical.

c **Horizontal rotary burners** These were originally designed for commercial and industrial use but are available in sizes suitable for domestic use. In this burner, oil is atomized by being thrown in a

Figure 5. Cut-Away of Typical High-Pressure Gun-Burner

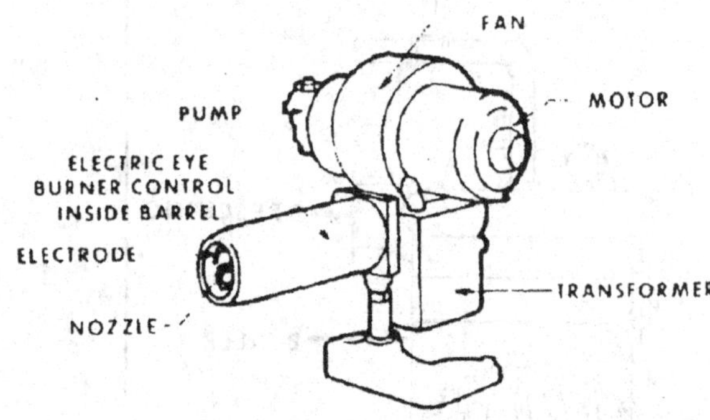

conical spray from a rapidly rotating cup. Horizontal rotary burners employ electric-gas or gas-pilot ignition and operate with a wide range of fuels, primarily with Numbers 1 and 2 fuel oil. Primary safety controls for burner operation are. necessary. An anti-flooding device must be a part of the system so that, if ignition in the burner should fail, the oil will not continue to flow. Likewise, a stack control is necessary to shut off the burner if the stack temperatures become excessive. A reset button on the older stack control units releases if excessive (predetermined) temperatures are exceeded and thus cuts off all power to the burner. This button must be reset before starting can be attempted. The newer models now use electric eye-type control on the burner itself.

2 **Ignition** — On the basis of the method employed to ignite fuels, burners are divided into five groups as follows:

a **Electric** — A high-voltage electric spark is made in the path of an oil and air mixture and this causes ignition. This electric spark may be continuous or may be in operation only long enough to ignite the oil. Electric ignition is almost universally used. Electrodes are located near the nozzles (see Figure 5) but not in the path of the oil spray.

b **Gas pilot** — A small gas pilot light that burns continuously is frequently used. Gas pilots usually have expanding gas valves that automatically increase flame size when motor circuit starts. After a fixed interval, the flame reverts to normal size.

c. **Electric gas** — An electric spark ignites a gas jet, which in turn ignites the oil air mixture.

d **Oil pilot** — A small oil flame is used.

e **Manual** — A burning wick or torch is placed in the combustion space through peepholes and thus ignites the charge. Operator should stand to one side of the fire door to guard against injury from chance explosion.

VI. Refractory

The refractory lining or material should be an insulating fireproof brick-like substance. Never use ordinary firebrick. The insulating brick should be set on end so as to build a 2 inch-thick wall in the pot. Size and shape of the refractory pot vary from furnace to furnace (see Figure 6 for various shapes). The shape can be either round or square, whichever is more convenient to build. It is important to use a special cement having properties similar to that of the insulating refractory-type brick.

VII. Heating Systems

A Steam Heating Systems - Steam heating systems are classified according to the pipe arrangement, accessories used, method of returning the con-densate to the boiler, method of expelling air from the system, or the type of control employed. The successful operation of a steam heating system consists of generating steam in sufficient quantity to equalize building heat loss at maximum efficiency, expelling entrapped air, and returning all condensate to the boiler rapidly. Steam cannot enter a space filled with air or water at pressure equal to the steam pressure. It is important, therefore, to eliminate air and to remove water from the distribution system. All hot pipe lines exposed to contact by residents must be properly insulated or guarded.

Steam heating systems are classified according to the method of returning the condensate to the boiler.

1 Gravity One-pipe Air-vent System — The gravity one-pipe air-vent system is one of the earliest types used. The condensate is returned to the boiler by gravity. This system is generally found in one-building-type heating systems. The steam is supplied by the boiler and carried through a single system or pipe to radiators as shown in Figure 7. Return of the condensate is dependent on hydrostatic head. Therefore, the end of the steam main, where it attaches to the boiler, must be full of water (termed a wet return) for a distance above the boiler line to create a pressure drop balance between the boiler and the steam main.

Radiators are equipped with an inlet valve and with an air valve (see Figure 8). The air valve permits venting of air from the radiator and its displacement by steam. Condensate is drained from the radiator through the same pipe that supplies steam.

2 Two-pipe Steam Vapor System with Return Trap — The two-pipe vapor system with boiler return trap and air eliminator is an improvement of the one-pipe system. The return connection of the radiator has a thermostatic trap that permits flow of condensate and air only from the radiator and prevents steam from leaving the radiator. Since the return main is at atmospheric pressure or less, a boiler return trap is installed to equalize condensate return pressure with boiler pressure.

B Hot Water Heating Systems — All hot water heating systems are similar in design and operating principle.

1 One-pipe Gravity System —The one-pipe gravity hot water heating system is the most elementary of the gravity systems and is shown in Figure 9. Water is heated at the lowest point in the system. It rises through a single main because of a difference in density between hot and cold water. The supply rise or radiator branch takes off from the top of the main to supply water to the radiators. After the water gives up heat in the radiator it goes back to the same main through return piping from the radiator. This cooler return water mixes with water in the supply main and causes the water to cool a little. As a result, the next radiator on the system has a lower emission rate and must be larger.

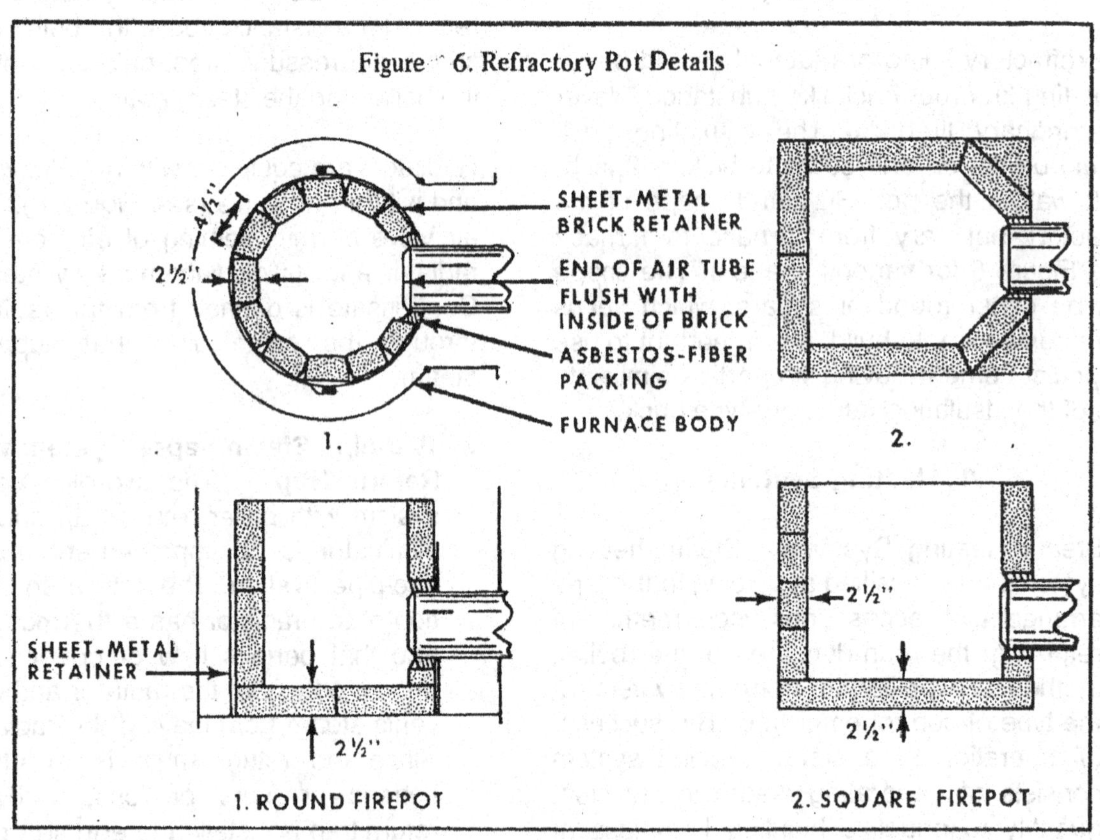

Figure 6. Refractory Pot Details

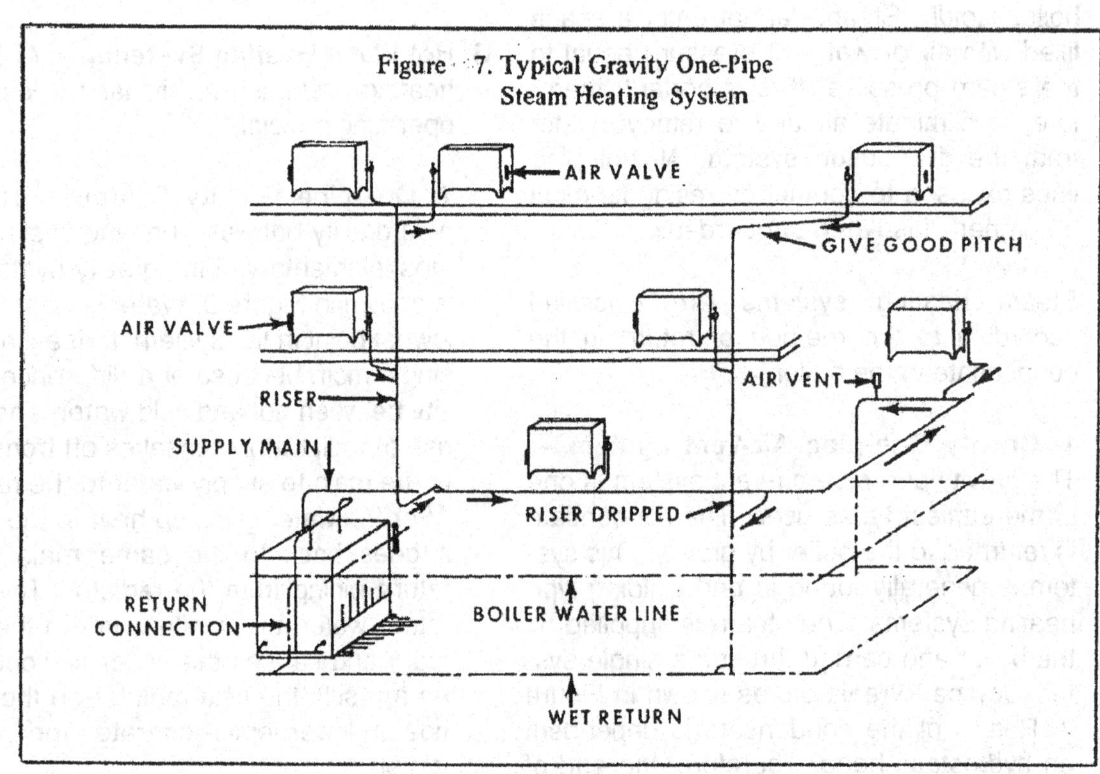

Figure 7. Typical Gravity One-Pipe Steam Heating System

Figure 8. Safety Air Valve

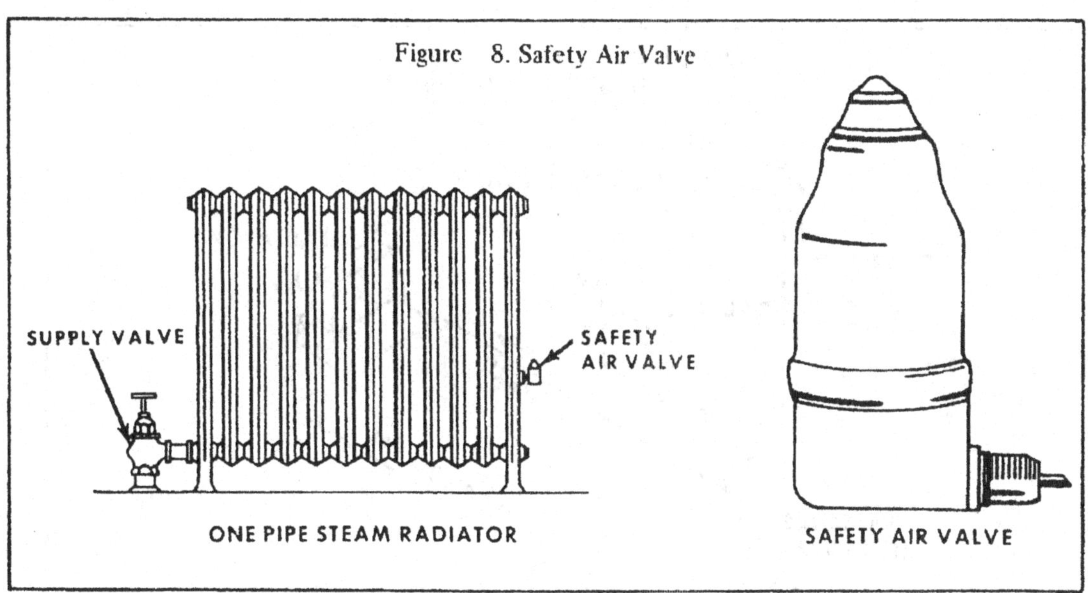

Note in Figure 9 that the high points of the hot water system are vented and the low points are drained. In this case, the radiators are the high points and the heater is the low point.

2 **One-pipe Forced-feed System** — If a pump or circulator is introduced in the main near the heater of the one-pipe system, we have a forced system that can be used for much larger

applications than the gravity type. This system can operate at higher water temperatures than the gravity system. The faster moving higher temperature water "Hakes a more responsive system with a smaller temperature drop through each radiator. Higher operating temperatures and lower temperature drops permit the use of smaller radiators for the same heating load.

3 **Two-pipe Gravity Systems** — One-pipe gravity systems may become a two-pipe system if the return radiator branch connects to a second main that returns water to the heater (see Figure 10). Water temperature is practically the same in all the radiators.

4 **Two-pipe Forced-circulation System** — This system is similar to a one-pipe forced-circulation system except that the same piping arrangement is found in the two-pipe gravity flow system.

5 **Expansion Tanks** — When water is heated it tends to expand. Therefore, in a hot water system an expansion tank is necessary. The expansion tank, either of open or closed type, must be of sufficient size to permit a change in water volume within the heating system. If the expansion tank is of the open type it must be placed at least 3 feet above the highest point of the system. It will require a vent and an overflow. The open tank is usually in an attic, where it needs protection from freezing.

The enclosed expansion tank is found in modern installations. An air cushion in the tank compresses and expands according to the change of volume and pressure in the system. Closed tanks are usually at the low point in the system and close to the heater. They can, however, be placed at almost any location within the heating system.

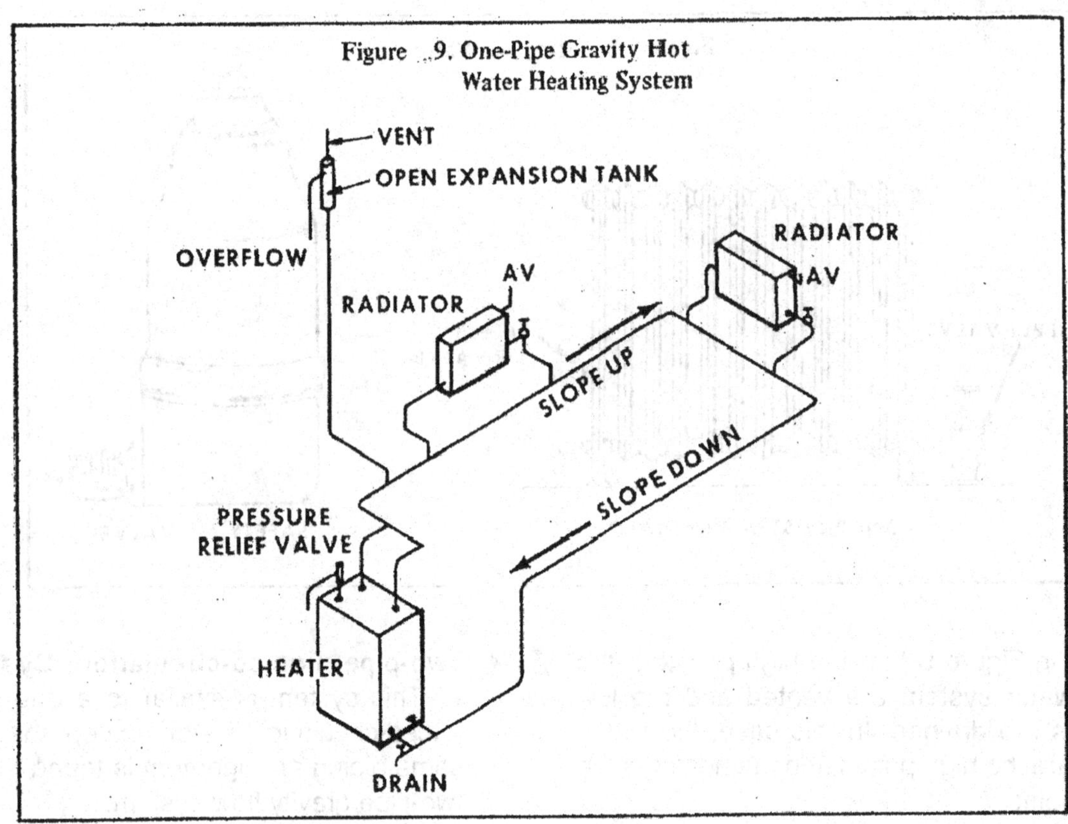

Figure ..9. One-Pipe Gravity Hot Water Heating System

Figure 10. Two-Pipe Gravity Hot-Water System

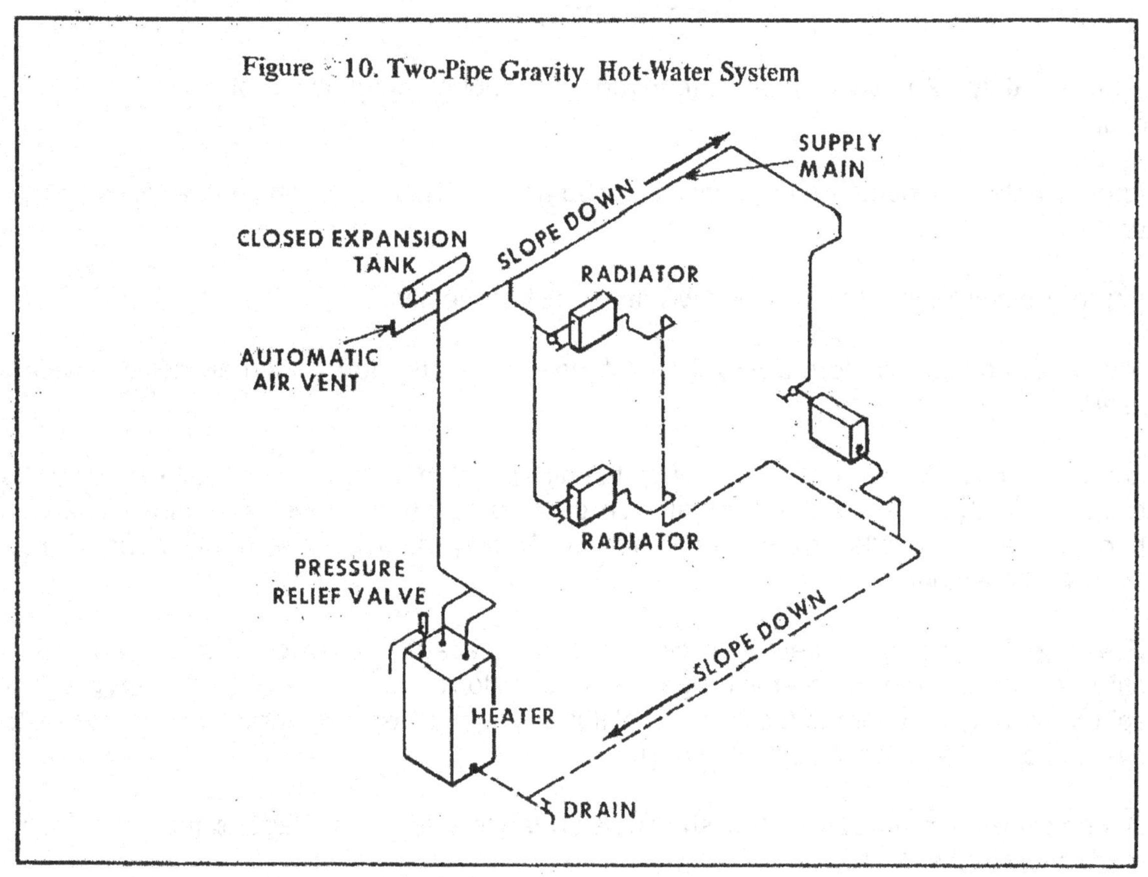

Figure 11. Hot Air Furnace

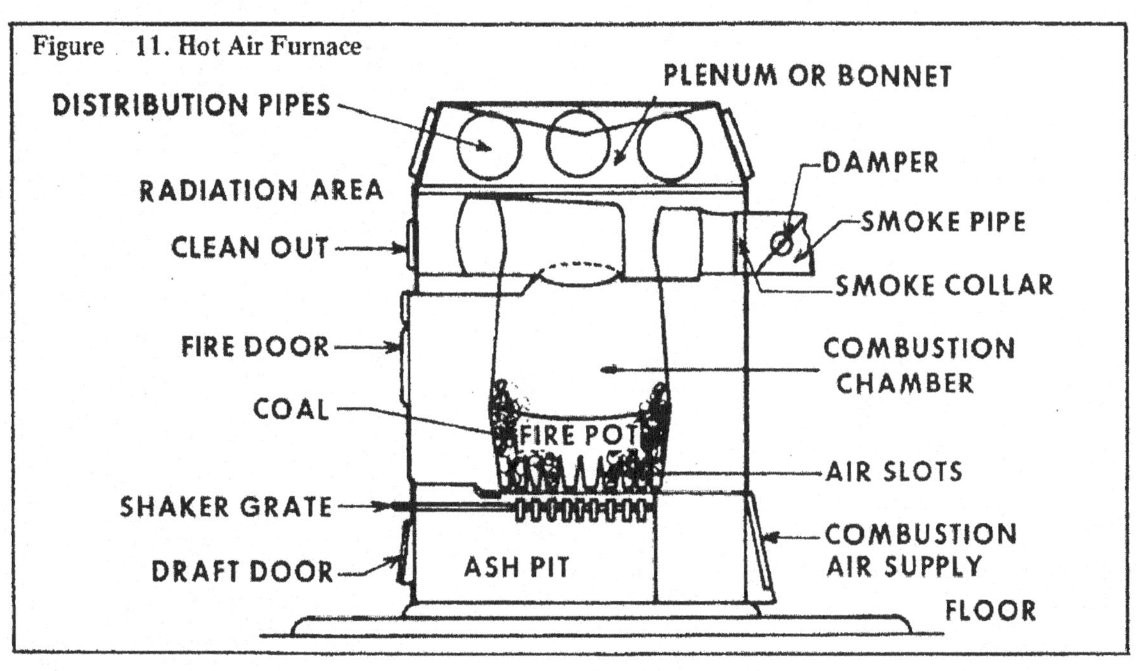

16

COAL NOTES

1. Approximately 12 pounds of air is required for complete combustion of 1 pound of hard coal.

2. Approximately 5 pounds of hard coal is consumed per hour for each square foot of grate area.

3. Approximately 12 inches of fire bed will heat most efficiently.

4. Anthracite coal burns more slowly than soft coal, is cleaner to handle-hence more widely used.

5. Large-size coal does not compact-hence the air spaces are too great and allows gases to escape into the flue unburned. Small size coal compacts too much and inhibits airflow through the coal to allow for good combustion. Mixing of coal size is recommended, i.e., stove and chestnut.

6. Fires burn best when the weather is clear and cold, because of reduced atmospheric pressure on the air in the flue—hence greater draft velocity. During periods of heavy atmosphere or rainy weather the temperature of flue gases must exceed normal temperatures to overcome the heavier atmospheric weight.

7. During extreme cold weather, coal should be added to a fire once in approximately 8 hours; moderate weather-12 hours.

C Hot Air Heating Systems

1 **Gravity-Warm-Air Heating Systems** — These operate because of the difference in specific gravity of warm air and cold air. Warm air is lighter than cold air and rises if cold air is available to replace it (see Figure 11).

a **Operation** — Satisfactory operation of a gravity-warm-air heating system depends on three factors. They are: (1) size of warm air and cold ducts, (2) heat loss of the building, (3) heat available from the furnace.

b **Heat distribution**—The most common source of trouble in these systems is insufficient pipe area usually in the return or cold air duct. The total cross-section area of the cold duct or ducts must be at least equal to the total cross-section area of all warm ducts.

c **Pipeless furnaces**—The pipeless hot-air furnace is the simplest type of hot-air furnace and is suitable for small homes where all rooms can be grouped about a single large register (see Figure 3). Other pipeless gravity furnaces are often installed at floor level. These are really oversized jacketed space heaters. The most common difficulty experienced with this type of furnace is supplying a return air opening of sufficient size on the floor.

2 **Forced-Warm-Air Heating** Systems — The mechanical warm-air furnace is the most modern type of warm-air equipment (see Figure 12). It is the safest type because it operates at low temperatures. The principle of a forced-warm-air heating system is very similar to that of the gravity system, except that a fan or blower is added to increase air movement. Because of the assistance of the fan or blower, the pitch of the ducts or leaders can be disregarded and it is therefore practical to deliver heated air in the most convenient places.

a **Operation** — In a forced-air system, operation of the fan or blower must be controlled by air temperature in a bonnet or by a blower control furnacestat. The blower control starts the fan or blower when the temperature reaches a certain point and turns the fan or blower off when the temperature drops to a predetermined point.

b **Heat distribution** — Dampers in the various warm-air ducts control distribution

Figure 12. Cross-Sectional View of Building Showing Forced-Warm-Air Heating System

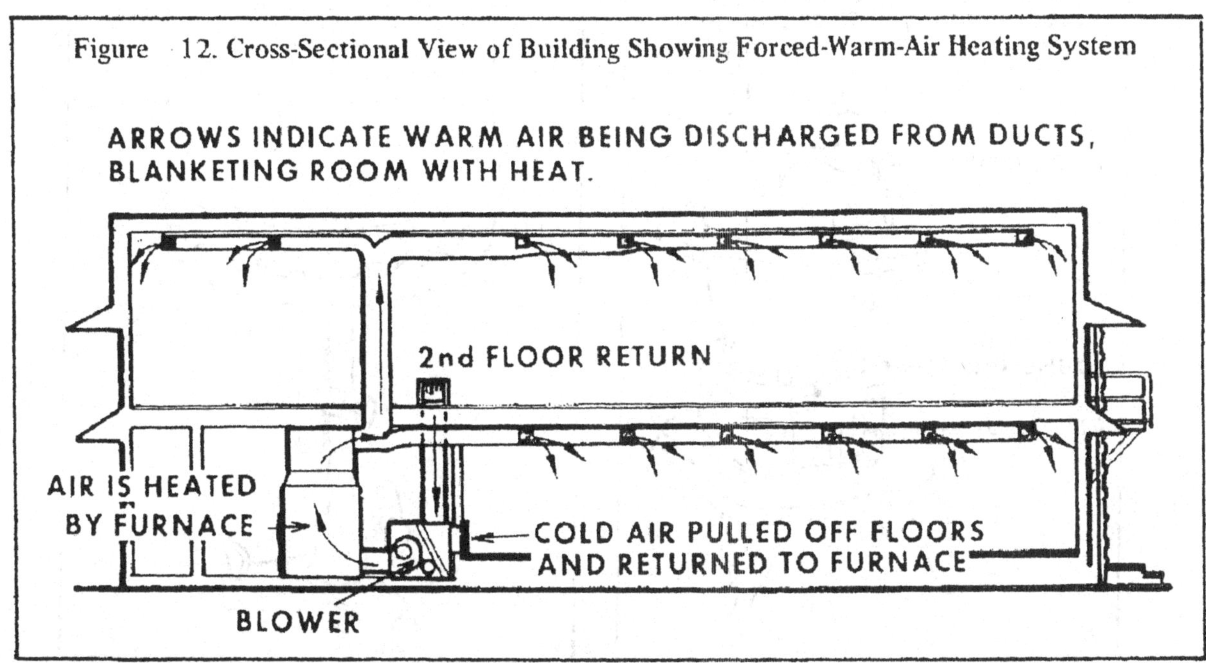

of warm air either at the branch takeoff or at the warm-air outlet.

Humidifiers are often mounted in the supply bonnet in order to regulate the humidity within the residence.

D Space Heaters — Space unit heaters are the least desirable from the viewpoint of fire safety and housing inspection. All space unit heaters must be vented to the flue.

1 Coal-Fired Space Heaters (Cannon stove) — This is illustrated in Figure 13 and is made entirely of cast iron. In operation, coal on the grates receives primary air for combustion through the grates from the ash-door draft intake. Combustible gases driven from the coal by heat burn in the barrel of the stove, where they received additional or secondary air through the feed door. Side and top of the stove absorb the heat of combustion and radiate it to the surrounding space.

2 Oil-Fired Space Heaters — Oil-fired space heaters have atmospheric vaporizing-type burners. The burners require a light grade of fuel oil that vaporizes easily and is comparatively low in temperature. In addition, the oil must be such that it leaves only a small amount of carbon residue and ash within the heater. Oil-fired space heaters are basically of two types:

a Perforated-sleeve burner — The perforated-sleeve burner (see Figure 14) consists essentially of a metal base formed of two or more angular fuel-vaporizing bowl burners (see Figure 15) and is widely used in space heaters and some water heaters.

The burner consists essentially of a bowl, 8 to 13 inches in diameter, with perforations in the side that admit air for combustion. The upper part of the bowl has a flame ring or collar. When several space heaters are installed in a building, an oil supply from an

Figure 13. Cannon Stove

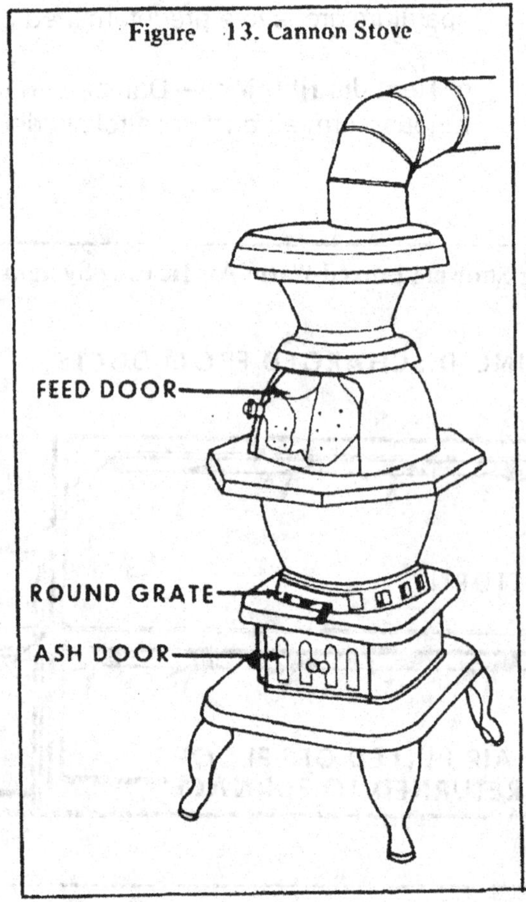

Figure 14. Perforated-Sleeve Burner

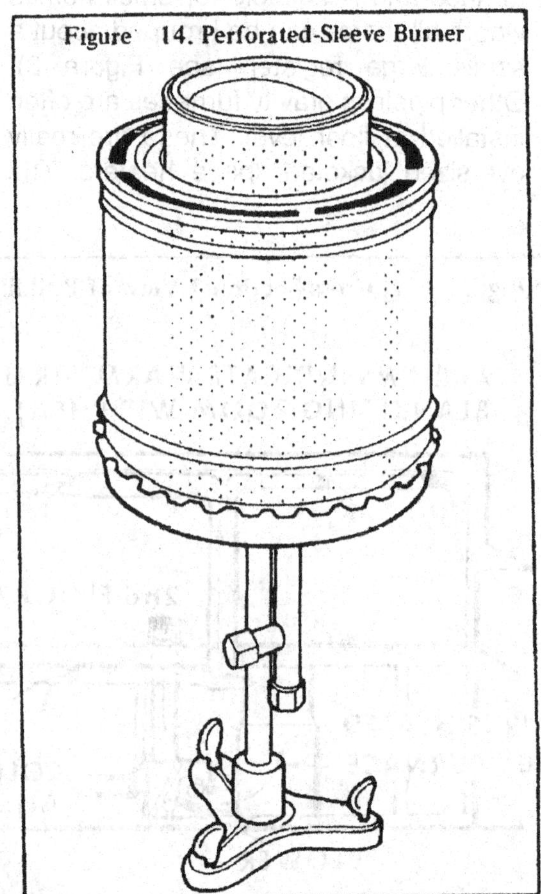

outside tank to all heaters is often desirable. Figure 16 shows the condition of a burner flame with different rates of fuel flow and indicates the ideal flame height.

Figure 15. Natural-Draft Pot Burner

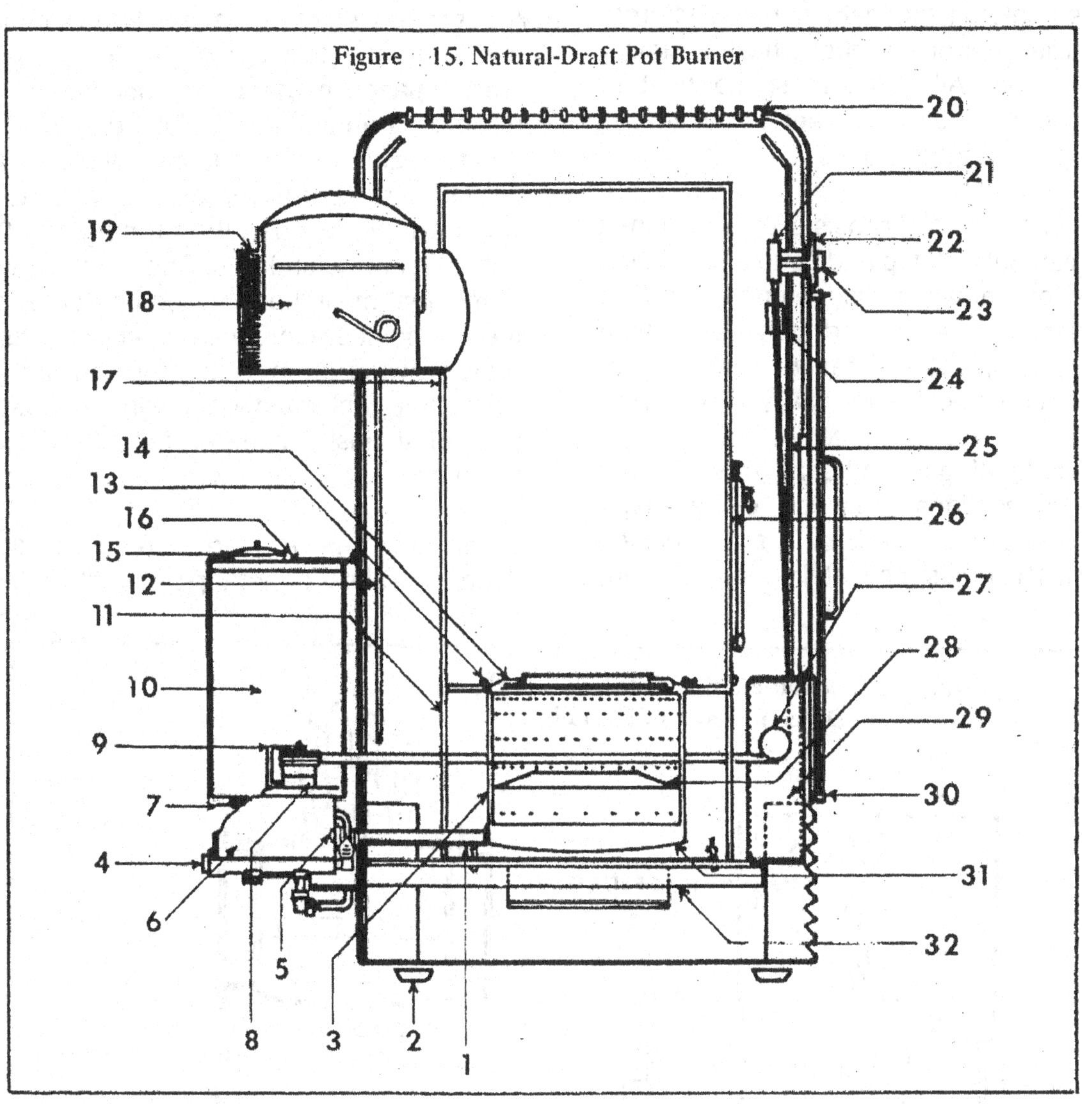

1 Burner-pot pipe.
2 Leg Leveler.
3 Pilot-ring clip.
4 Strainer unit.
5 Burner-pot drain plug.
6 Constant-level valve.
7 Tank valve
8 Control drum (to fit 6).
9 Control pulley bracket
10 Fuel tank.
11 Lower heat unit.
12 Heat shield (rear).
13 Burner-ring clamp.
14 Burner-top ring.
15 Fuel tank cap.
16 Tank fuel gauge.
17 Heat unit.
18 Cold draft regulator.
19 Flue connections, 6-inch diameter.
20 Top grille.
21 Dial control drum.
22 Escutcheon plate.
23 Dial control knob.
24 Pulley assembly (short).
25 Heat shield (front).
26 Heat-unit door.
27 Pulley assembly (long).
28 Pilot ring.
29 Humidifier.
30 Trim bar.
31 Burner pot.
32 Heat-unit support.

3 Gas-Fired Space Heaters—There are three types of gas-fired space heaters: natural, manufactured, and liquified petroleum gas. Space heaters using natural, manufactured, or liquified petroleum gases have a similar construction. All gas-fired space heaters must be vented to prevent a dangerous buildup of poisonous gases.

Each unit console consists of an enamel steel cabinet with top and bottom circulating grilles or openings, gas burners, heating element, gas pilot, and gas valve (see Figure 17). The heating element or combustion chamber is usually cast iron.

CAUTION: All gas-fired space heaters and their connections must be of the type approved by the American Gas Association (AGA). They must be installed in accordance with the recommendations of that organization or the local code.

a Venting — Use of proper venting materials and correct installation of venting for gas-fired space heaters is necessary to minimize harmful effects of condensation and to ensure that combustion products are carried off. (Approximately 12 gallons of water are produced in the burning of 1,000 cubic feet of natural gas. The inner surface of the vent must therefore be heated above the dewpoint of the combustion products to prevent water from forming in the flue.) A horizontal vent must be given an upward pitch of at least 1 inch per foot of horizontal distance.

When the smoke pipe extends through floors or walls the metal pipe must be insu-

Figure 16. Condition of Burner Flame with Different Rates of Fuel Flow

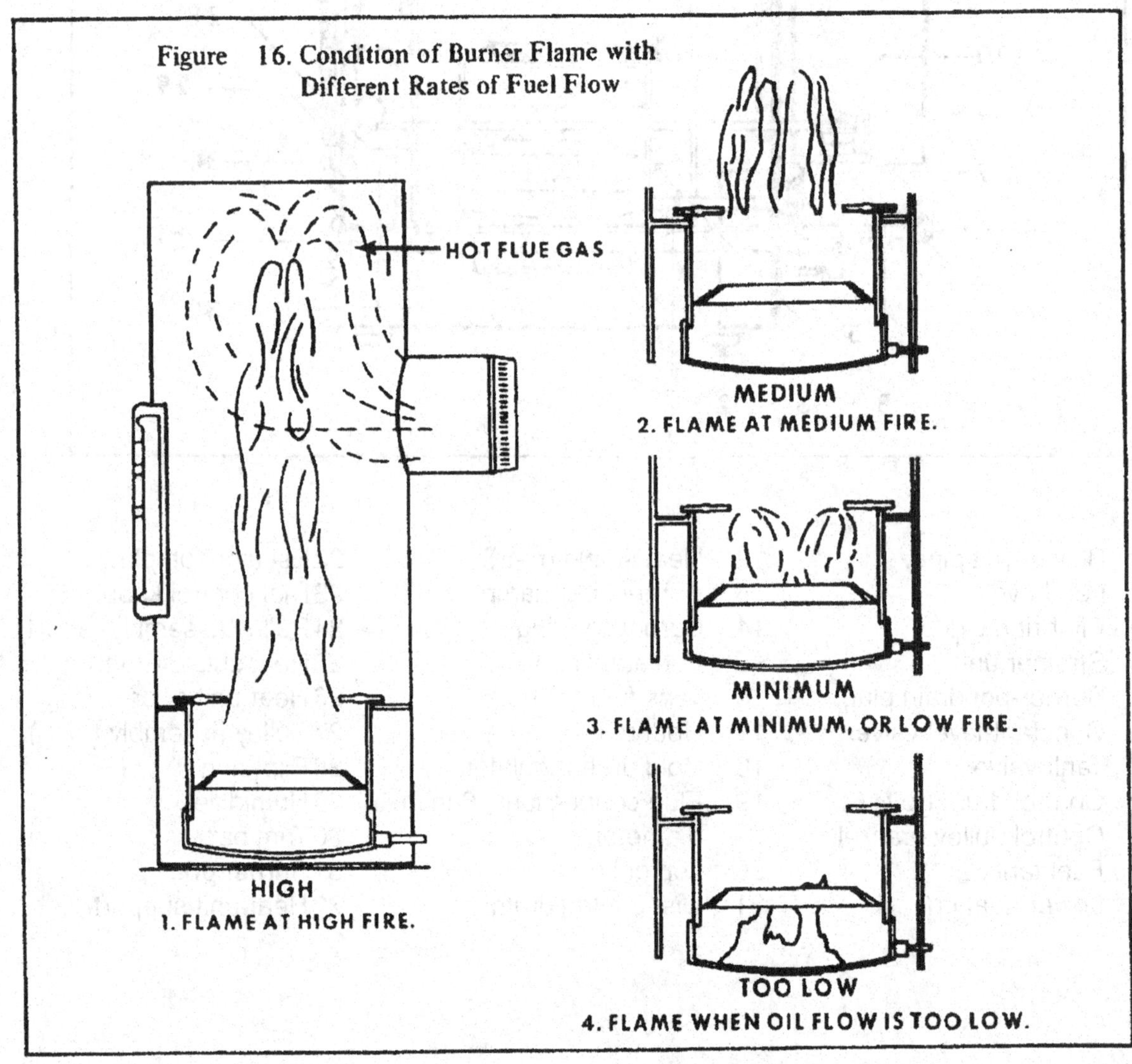

lated from the floor or wall system by an air space (see Figure 18). Avoid sharp bends. A 90° vent elbow has a resistance to flow equivalent to a straight section of pipe having a length of 10 times the elbow diameter. Be sure vent is of a rigid construction and resistant to corrosion by flue gas products. Several types of venting material are available such as B-vent and several other ceramic-type materials. A chimney lined with fire-brick type of terra cotta must be relined with an acceptable vent material if it is to be used for venting gas-fired appliances.

Use the same size vent pipe throughout its length. Never make a vent smaller than heater outlet except when two or more vents converge from separate heaters. To determine the size of vents beyond the point of convergence, add one-half the area of each vent to the area of the largest heater's vent.

Figure 17. Typical Gas-Fired Space Heater

Figure 18. Wall and Ceiling Clearance Reduction

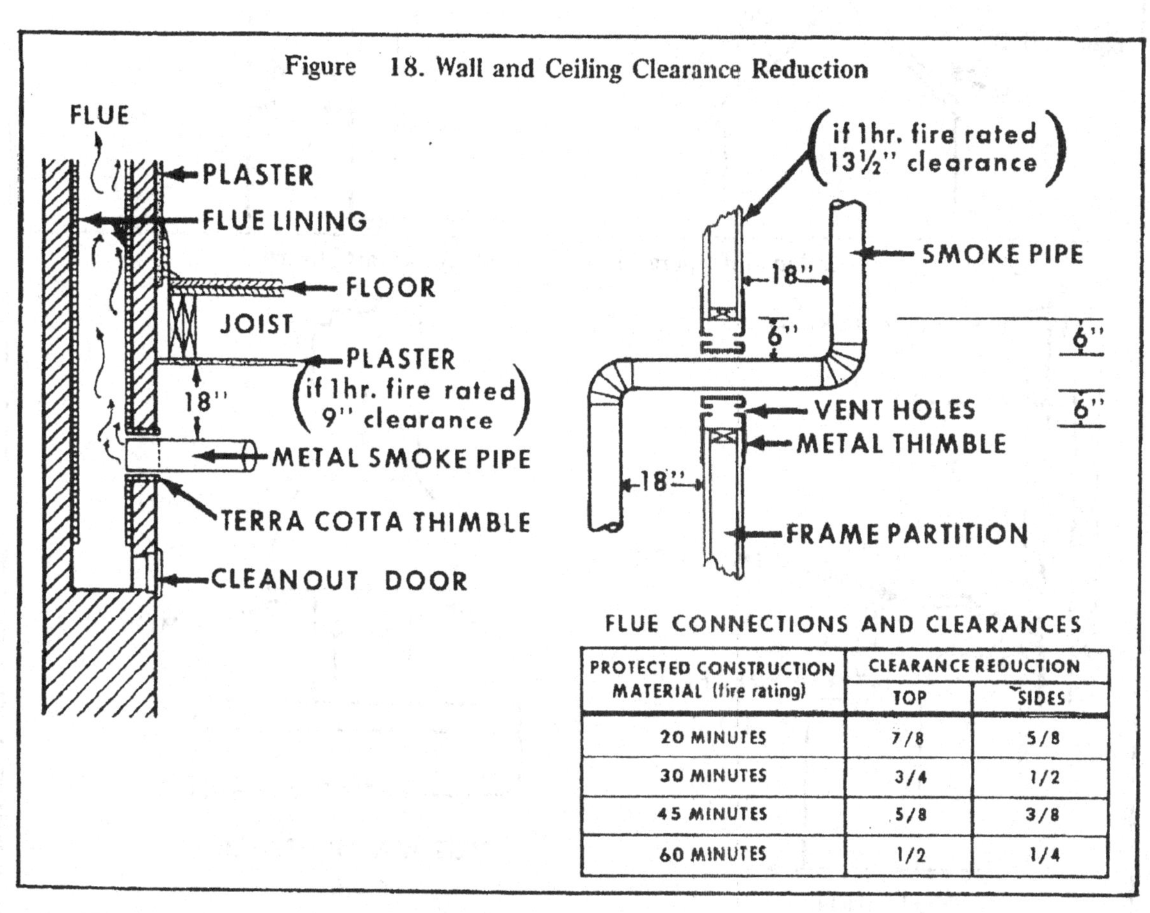

FLUE CONNECTIONS AND CLEARANCES

PROTECTED CONSTRUCTION MATERIAL (fire rating)	CLEARANCE REDUCTION	
	TOP	SIDES
20 MINUTES	7/8	5/8
30 MINUTES	3/4	1/2
45 MINUTES	5/8	3/8
60 MINUTES	1/2	1/4

Install vents with male ends of inner liner down to ensure condensate is kept within pipes on a cold start. The vertical length of each vent or stack should be at least 2 feet greater than the length between horizontal connection and stack.

Run vent at least 3 feet above any projection of the building within 20 feet to place it above a possible pressure zone due to wind currents (see Figure 19). End it with a weather cap designed to prevent entrance of rain and snow.

Gas-fired space heaters as well as gas furnaces and hot water heaters must be equipped with a backdraft diverter (see Figure ,20) designed to protect heaters against downdrafts and excessive updrafts. Use only draft diverters of the type approved by the AGA.

The combustion chamber or firebox must be insulated from the floor, usually with an air-space of 15 to 18 inches, or the firebox is sometimes insulated within the unit and thus allows for lesser clearance for combustibles.

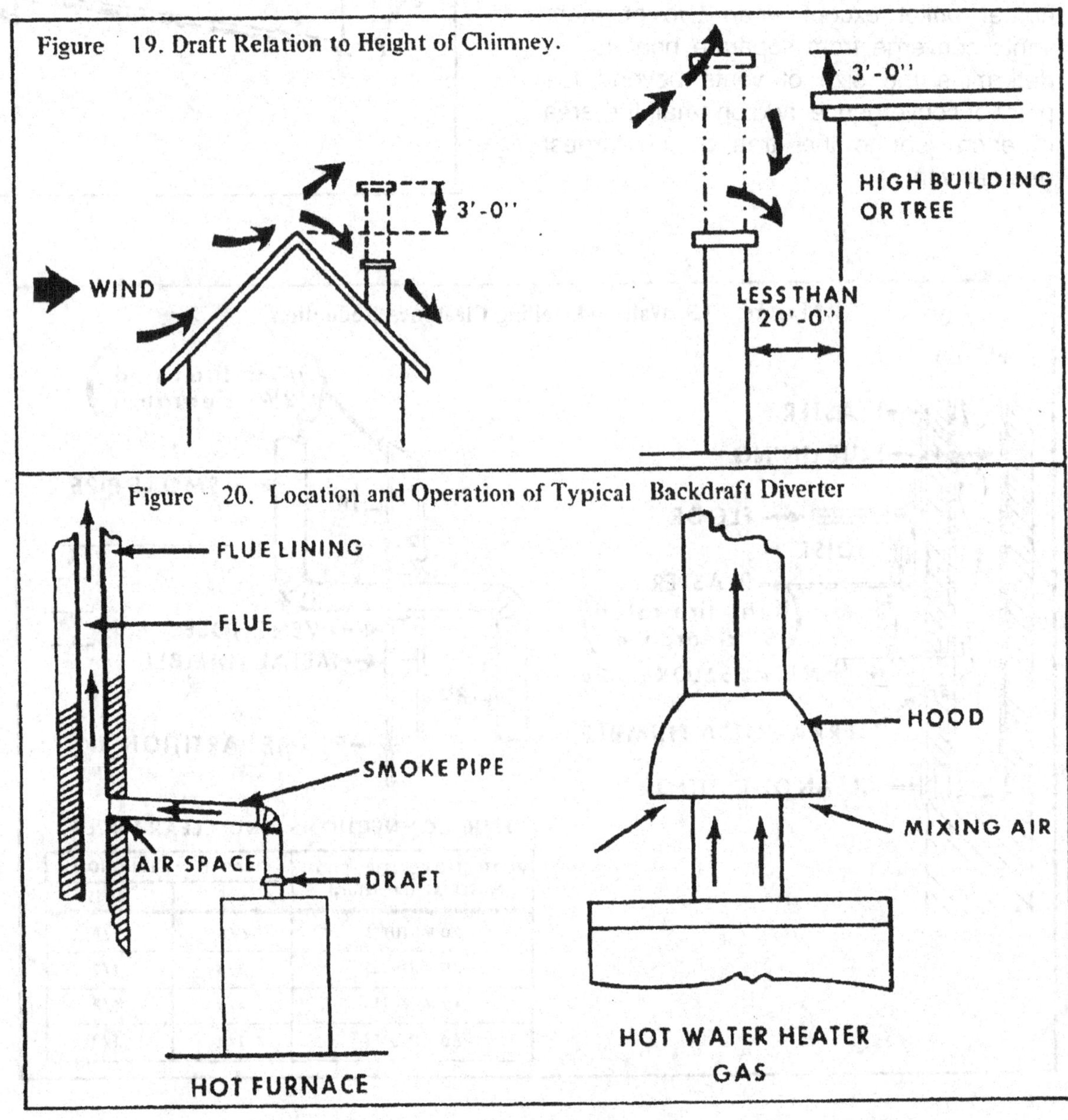

Figure 19. Draft Relation to Height of Chimney.

Figure 20. Location and Operation of Typical Backdraft Diverter

Where coal space heaters are located, a floor protection should be provided. This would be a metal-covered asbestos board or a similar durable insulation material. One reason for the floor protection would be to allow cooling off of hot coals and ashes if they drop out while ashes are being removed from the ash chamber. Walls and ceilings of a non-combustible construction exposed to furnace radiation should be installed, and the following clearances are recommended: Space heaters — A top or ceiling clearance of 36 inches, a wall clearance of 18 inches, and a smoke pipe clearance of 18 inches, (see Figure 18).

VIII. Domestic Hot Water Jack Stoves (Coal Stoves)

Domestic hot water jack stoves (coal stoves) equipped with water jackets to supply hot water for domestic use are to be treated as coal-fired furnaces or boilers previously discussed. Note that flue connections should not exceed two to the same flue unless the draft and size are sufficient to accommodate both exhausting requirements. One flue with one smoke pipe is the rule; however, housing inspectors may find a jack stove and main furnace connected to the same flue. Where these conditions are encountered and no complaint about malfunctioning of this system is found, it can be assumed that the system is operating satisfactorily. Where more than two units, other than gas, are attached to a single flue, the building agency should be notified, since this can be considered an improper installation. Gas, oil, and electric hot water heating units for domestic hot water should be treated the same as previously discussed for central heating units.

IX. Hazardous Installations

A **Generalities** — The housing inspector should be on the alert for unvented open burning flame heaters, such as manually operated gas logs. Coil-type wall-mounted hot-water heaters that do not have safety relief valves are not permitted. Kerosene (portable) units for cooking or heating should be prohibited. Generally, open-flame portable units are not allowed under fire safety regulations.

In oil heating units, other than integral tank units, the oil filling and vent must be located on the exterior of the building. Filling of oil within buildings is prohibited.

Electric wiring to heating units must be installed as indicated in the electrical section. Cutoff switches should be close to the entry but outside of the boiler room. The inspector should be able to appraise the heating installation and determine its adequacy. Any installation that indicates haphazard location, workmanship, or operation, whether it be building, zoning, plumbing, electrical, or housing, will dictate further inspection.

B **Chimneys (see Figure 21 and 22)** - Chimneys, as all inspectors know, are an integral part of the building. The chimney is a point of building safety and should be understood by the housing inspector. The chimney, if of masonry, must be tight and sound; flues should be terra cotta lined, and where no linings are installed, the brick should be tight to permit proper draft and elimination of combustion gases.

Chimneys that act as flues for gas-fired equipment must be lined with either B-vent or terra cotta.

To the inspector, on exterior inspection, "banana peel" on the portion of the chimney above the roof will indicate trouble and a need for rebuilding. Exterior deterioration of the chimney will, if let go too long, gradually permit erosion from within the flues and eventually block the flue opening.

Rusted flashing at the roof level will also contribute to the chimney's deterioration. Effervescence on the inside wall of the chimney below the roof and on the outside of the chimney, if exposed, will show salt accumulations — a tell-tale sign of water penetration and flue gas escape and a sign of chimney deterioration. In the spring and fall, during rain seasons, if terra cotta chimneys leak, the joint will be indicated by dark areas permitting actual counting of the number of flues inside the masonry chimney. When this condition occurs, it usually requires 2 or 3 months to dry out. Upon drying out, the mortar joints are discolored (brown), and so after a few years of this type of deterioration the joints can be distinguished wet or dry. The above-listed conditions usually develop during coal operation and become more pronounced usually 2 to 5 years after conversion to oil or gas.

An unlined chimney can be checked for deterioration below the roof line by checking the residue deposited at the base of the chimney, usually accessible through a clea-nout (door or plug) or breaching. Red gran-ular or fine powder showing through coal soot or oil soot will generally indicate, if in quantity (a handful), that deterioration is excessive and repairs are needed.

Gas units attached to unlined chimneys will be devoid of soot, but will usually show similar tell-tale brick powder and deterioration as previously mentioned. Manufactured gas has a greater tendency to dehydrate and decompose brick in chimney flues than natural gas. For gas installations in older homes, utility companies usually specify chimney requirements before installation, and so older chimneys may require the installation of terra cotta liners, lead-lined copper liners, or transite pipe. Oil burner operation using a low air ratio and high oil consumption is usually indicated by black carbon deposits around the top of the chimney. Prolonged operation in this burner setting results in long carbon water deposits down the chimney for 4 to 6 feet or more and should indicate to the inspector a possibility of poor burner maintenance. This will accent his need to be more thorough on the ensuing inspection. This type of condition can result from other related causes, such as improper chimney height or exterior obstructions such as trees or buildings that will cause downdrafts or insufficient draft or contribute to a faulty heating operation.
Rust spots and soot-mold usually occur on galvanized smoke pipe deterioration.

C Fireplace — Careful attention should be given to the construction of the fireplace. Improperly built fireplaces are a serious safety and fire hazard (see Figure 22). The most common causes of fireplace fires are thin walls, combustible materials such as studding or trim against sides and back of the fireplace, wood mantels, and unsafe hearths.

Fireplace walls should be not less than 8 inches thick, and if built of stone or hollow masonry units, not less than 12 inches thick. The faces of all walls exposed to fire should be lined with firebrick or other suitable fire-resistive material. When the lining consists of 4 inches of firebrick, such lining thickness may be included in the required minimum thickness of the wall.

The fireplace hearth should be constructed of brick, stone, tile, or similar incombustible material and should be supported on a fireproof slab or on a brick arch. The hearth should extend at least 20 inches beyond the chimney breast and not less than 12 inches beyond each side of the fireplace opening

Figure 21. Chimney Plan

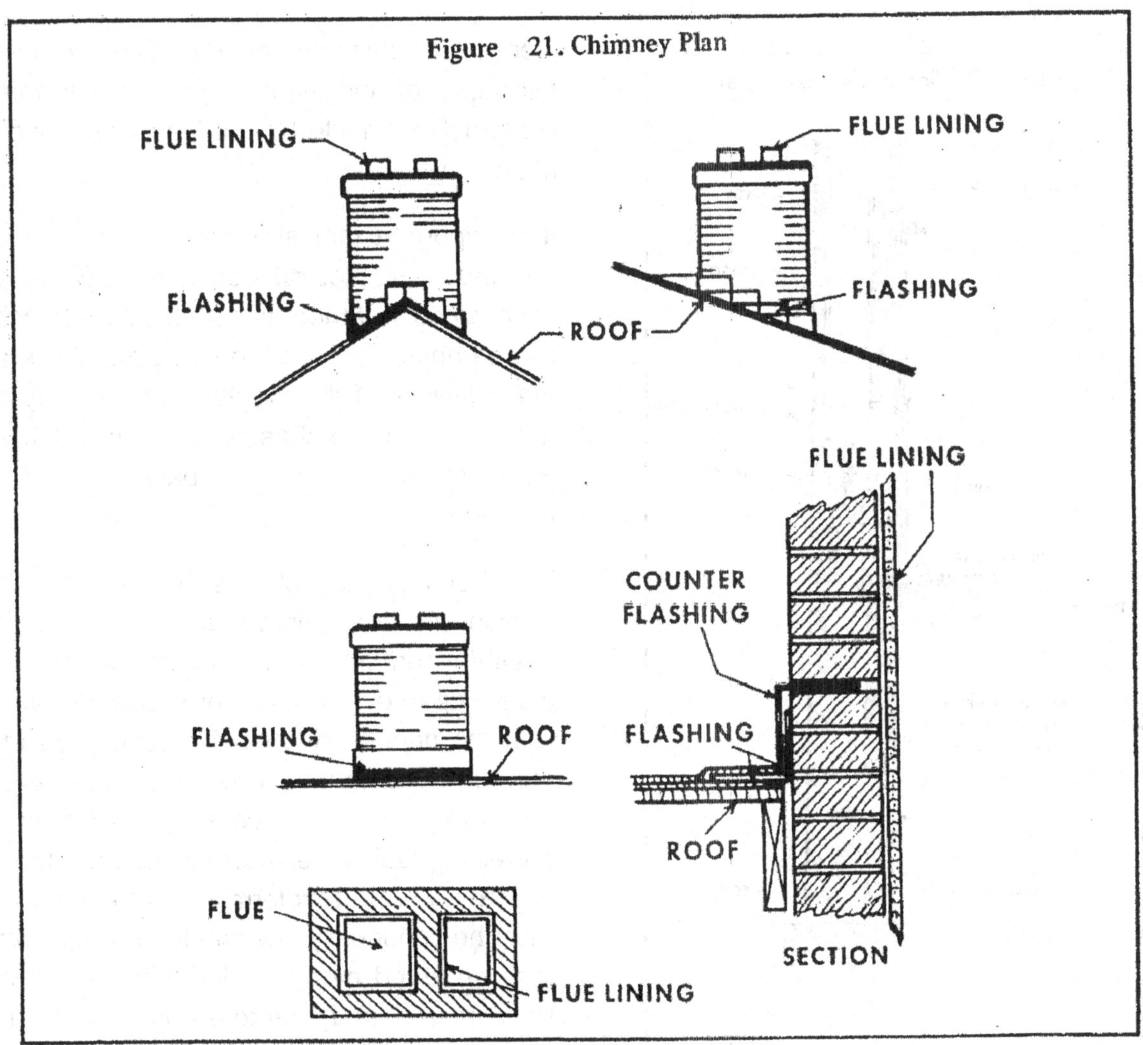

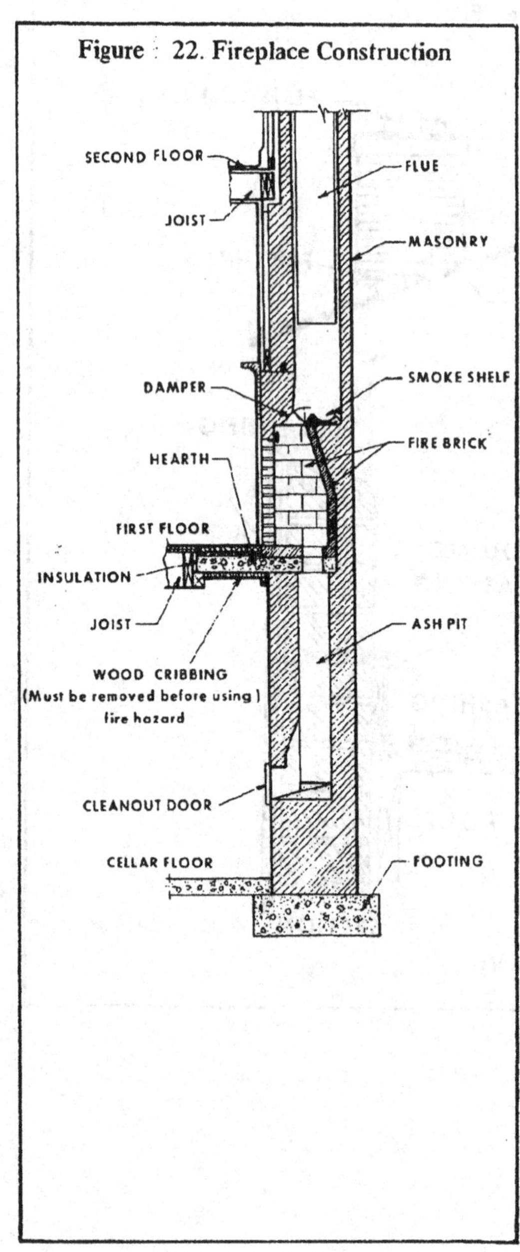

Figure 22. Fireplace Construction

along the chimney breast. The combined thickness of the hearth and its supporting construction should be not less than 6 inches at any point.

It is important that all wooden beams, joists, and studs are set off from the fireplace and chimney so that there is not less than 2 inches of clearance between the wood members and the sidewalls of the fireplace or chimney and not less than 4 inches of clearance between wood members and the back wall of the fireplace.

The housing inspector is a very important person in maintaining sound, safe, and healthful community growth. This should be a challenge to every inspector to provide himself with the necessary tools for better and more efficient housing inspection. He must develop the extra senses so necessary in spotting and correcting faults. He must know when to refer and to whom the referral is to be made; he must be continually seeking knowledge, which may be found by consulting with technicians, tradesmen, and professionals. No finer satisfaction can be realized than to know and feel that the security, safety, and comfort of each and every family within your community has a better and more healthful life because of that extra bit of knowledge you have imparted. "An inspector who stops learning today is uneducated tomorrow."
